JOINING IN

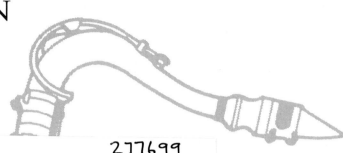

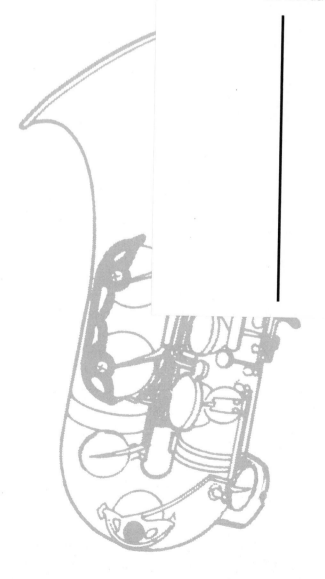

Massed cellos at Birmingham Symphony Hall where nearly 3,000 young musicians aimed to create the world's largest orchestra, organised by Music for Youth, the national music charity. (photo: David Jones)

ANTHONY EVERITT

JOINING IN

AN INVESTIGATION INTO PARTICIPATORY MUSIC

CALOUSTE GULBENKIAN FOUNDATION, LONDON

For Roddy

Published by the Calouste Gulbenkian Foundation
98 Portland Place
London W1N 4ET
Tel: 0171 636 5313

ISBN 0 903319 76 4

British Library Cataloguing-in-Publication Data
A catalogue record for this book is available from the British Library

Designed by Chris Hyde
Printed by Expression Printers Ltd, London N5 1JT
Distributed by Turnaround Publisher Services Ltd, Unit 3, Olympia Trading Estate, Coburg Road, Wood Green, London N22 6TZ. Tel: 0181 829 3000

CONTENTS

FOREWORD

Few would dispute that they have been profoundly moved by music, at ceremony, concert or rave, or had their personal histories touched, to quote Noël Coward, by 'the potency of cheap music'. Which of us has not, after checking that the house is empty, practised *bel canto* in the bath, strummed an imaginary guitar before the mirror or energetically conducted a rousing film score on the radio? This report is for everyone who wanted to know about participating in music but was afraid to ask.

The research in this book reveals that there is an astounding number and variety in music-making, from members of steel pan bands to choirs, bhangra groups, brass bands, jazz bands, pop groups, folk groups, operatic companies, string quartets and much more. There is some wonderful music being made and we can learn from each other's examples. What's more, there are plenty of opportunities for us all to overcome our tentativeness and join in.

This book's purpose also has an element of missionary zeal. The latest in scientific research is beginning to prove that music is good for us. It helps us to communicate and learn more easily, it makes us respect each other in group situations and allows us to express our identities and a sense of belonging even in a potentially disconnected society. In short, its inclusion in our daily lives is essential to our well-being as individuals and social creatures. Let's have more of it.

Some years ago the Sports Council broadcast the idea that sport was good for us all – not just the hearty souls or the keen spectators. The idea caught on and influenced national and local policies for provision. Now access to good leisure centres and sports halls is commonplace. We can take up new sports, hire equipment, join classes, watch our team, improve our game or simply do it for fun. Anyone can take part. The analogy between sport and music would become strained if pursued too far, but the notions of easy access and lack of elitism are important ones and they should influence the policy-makers. The time is particularly ripe given the potentially radical changes to the funding situation as a result of the National Lottery. There is much work to be done and this book is only a start.

When I first presented Anthony Everitt with the brief, none of us knew what his research would reveal or where it might lead. As he went about tirelessly over the ensuing months, reading, interviewing and travelling, we became more and more surprised at the size of the task and the implications the research might have for policy-makers and individual participants alike. I am indebted to him for his energy, insight, creative thinking and great good humour. I am also grateful to our distinguished Steering Group, whose fascinating discussions should have been recorded, and especially to its Chair, Jo Shapcott, who managed the debates with intelligence and wit and also did a lot of encouraging work behind the scenes. I am sure that readers will enjoy this book for its own sake. I very much hope it will inspire us all to change the culture of participation in music in Britain over the next few years.

Siân Ede
Assistant Director (Arts)
Calouste Gulbenkian Foundation
September 1997

PREFACE

Joining In is the story of a journey through a country I have often visited as a tourist, but with whose true character I was unfamiliar. Like all travel writing, it is a mix of facts and impressions. It makes no claims to comprehensiveness, but I hope the book (the first, I think, to attempt a synoptic view of this particular field) will be useful to other travellers as well to the natives. That is its purpose.

I owe a great deal to my guides, especially Siân Ede at the Calouste Gulbenkian Foundation (UK branch) who commissioned this report, the poet Jo Shapcott and the distinguished Steering Group which she chaired. I am also grateful to those I met on my travels, the musicians and the composers, the managers and the officials, who uncomplainingly gave me so much of their time and attention – more than a hundred of them in all. I have not been able to make use of everything they told me because I have tried to tell my story through selective examples rather than overburden the reader with comprehensive listings of common practice. They did their best to steer me away from the elephant traps I kept stumbling into and gave me good directions through difficult terrain; some of them were kind enough to read sections of the draft. They deserve most of the credit for whatever is good in this volume, but I alone am responsible for any mistakes.

Anthony Everitt
Wivenhoe
September 1997

Selective glossary of acronyms

ABO	Association of British Orchestras
ACE	Arts Council of England
ACGB	Arts Council of Great Britain
ACNI	Arts Council of Northern Ireland
ACW/CCC	Arts Council of Wales/Cyngor Celfyddydau Cymru
ADOOR	Association for the Development of Open Opportunity in Recreation
ALP	Adult Learning Project
APC	Association of Professional Composers
BABS	British Association of Barbershop Singers
BASBWE	British Association of Symphonic Bands and Wind Ensembles
BASCA	British Association of Songwriters, Composers and Authors
BBC	British Broadcasting Corporation
BBHT	Brass Band Heritage Trust
BBMA	British Bluegrass Music Association
BFBB	British Federation of Brass Bands
BFMF	British Federation of Music Festivals
BFYC	British Federation of Youth Choirs
BMIC	British Music Information Centre
CBSO	City of Birmingham Symphony Orchestra
CBTO	City of Birmingham Touring Opera
CEMA	Council for the Encouragement of Music and the Arts
CGGB	Composers' Guild of Great Britain
CIPFA	Chartered Institute for Public Finance and Accountancy
CME	Community Music East
CMH	Council for Music in Hospitals
CML	Community Music London
CMW	Community Music Wales
COMA	Contemporary Music-making for Amateurs
DfEE	Department for Education and Employment
DNH	Department of National Heritage (since this book went to press the name has changed to the Department of Culture, Media and Sport)
EFDS	English Folk Dance Society
EFDSS	English Folk Dance and Song Society
ELLSO	East London Late Starters Orchestra
EMA (EMAB)	East Midlands Arts (Board)
EMS	Enterprise Music Scotland
ENO	English National Opera
FEFC	Further Education Funding Council
FSS	Folk Song Society
HMI	Her Majesty's Inspectorate
INSET	In-service training (for teachers)
ISM	Incorporated Society of Musicians
LAB	London Arts Board

LCM	London College of Music (at Thames Valley University)
LEA	Local Education Authority
LIPA	Liverpool Institute of Performing Arts
LMN	Live Music Now
LPO	London Philharmonic Orchestra
LSO	London Symphony Orchestra
MU	Musicians' Union
NAC	National Association of Choirs
NCA	National Campaign for the Arts
NCET	National Council for Educational Technology
NEYN	National Early Years Network
NFDSW	National Folk Dance Society of Wales
NFER	National Federation for Educational Research
NFMS	National Federation of Music Societies
NIACE	National Institute for Adult and Continuing Education
NODA	National Operatic and Dramatic Association
NYBBGB	National Youth Brass Band of Great Britain
NYBBW	National Youth Brass Band of Wales
NYCW	National Youth Choir of Wales
OFSTED	Office for Standards in Education
OMTF	Opera and Music Theatre Forum
PRS	Performing Right Society
RAA	Regional Arts Association
RAB	Regional Arts Board
RAM	Royal Academy of Music
RCM	Royal College of Music
RNEW	Royal National Eisteddfod of Wales
ROH	Royal Opera House
RPO	Royal Philharmonic Orchestra
RSA	Royal Society of Arts
RSCDS	Royal Scottish Country Dance Society
RSPBA	Royal Scottish Pipe Band Association
SAC	Scottish Arts Council
SAMPAD	South Asian Music Performance and Dance
SBC	South Bank Centre
SCAA	Schools Curriculum and Assessment Authority (now the Qualifications and Curriculum Authority)
SCO	Scottish Chamber Orchestra
SHAPE	Not an acronym
SOAS	School of Oriental and African Studies
SPNM	Society for the Promotion of New Music
STIW	Society for the Traditional Instruments of Wales
SWICA	South Wales Intercultural Community Arts
TAPS	Traditional Arts Projects
TMSAC	Traditional Music and Song Association of Scotland
VAN	Voluntary Arts Network
WAMF	Welsh Amateur Music Federation
WOMAD	World of Music and Dance
YAN	Youth Arts Network

INTRODUCTION

If I had to live my life over again, I would have made a rule to read some poetry and to listen to some music at least once every week. For perhaps parts of my brain now atrophied would thus have been kept active through use. The loss of these tastes is a loss of happiness and may possibly be injurious to the intellect and more probably to the moral character by enfeebling the emotional parts of our nature.

CHARLES DARWIN, *AUTOBIOGRAPHY*

At the outset of this project to survey participation in music, my aim was quite straightforward. It was to produce a report; it would be comprehensive and objective and would close with a list of crafted recommendations. It would, in the language of arts bureaucracy, 'identify examples of good practice' and 'address the relevant issues'.

I plunged into a cascade of interviews and soon realised that this approach would not do; something rather more informal and discursive was required, for two reasons. The British Isles resound to a multitude of musics, most of them amateur. Millions of people sing or play instruments for love and not for money. They play the *tabla* and the church organ. In a restless ferment, they form rock or pop groups. They come together in youth orchestras or brass bands. They revive and bring up to date the folk musics of past centuries. They use the latest technologies to manipulate and customise the music of others. They stage operas and musical comedies in village halls up and down the country. Community musicians work with those who, for educational or economic reasons, have not had the opportunity to express themselves creatively or who, from disability or other forms of exclusion, find themselves disbarred from access to cultural engagement. In Wales a network of *eisteddfodau* keeps alive the long traditions of a proud culture. In Scotland a new spirit of national consciousness feeds on the vigour of Gaelic music. Professional music organisations, among them the country's orchestras and opera companies, have developed education and community outreach wings.

An unrecorded number of local musicians help to service and facilitate this mass of musical activity, moving easily between professional and amateur roles. These are the music teachers, the church organists, the choir leaders, the jazz musicians, the music critics in local newspapers.

This is a largely uncharted world. Maps have been produced of one territory or another, but no one has yet designed a Mercator's projection which embraces the full complexity of British music-making. A central purpose of this book is to give some account of what is actually going on. That this has not been done before (so far as I am aware) is a consequence no doubt of a long-standing lack of serious attention or value accorded to the field.

But opinion is now decisively shifting. The professional music world and the arts funding system, which for many years (and with some striking exceptions) turned a blind eye on amateur music-making and focused their approval on a professional virtuosity which they saw as constituting true excellence, are coming to accept the diversity of British culture and to recognise that the high achievements of the European classical tradition are only a part, albeit a crucial one, of a larger scene.

This survey is aimed in part at them, the opinion-formers and decision-makers, and describes a domain of music-making with which they may not yet be altogether familiar or comfortable. I hope too that it will be of interest to general readers, especially those who sing or play in their leisure hours.

The second reason why *Joining In* will not read altogether as a conventional report is that I discovered during my enquiries a kaleidoscope not simply of music, but of conflicting ideas *about* music. These ideas are expressed with passion. Genres jostle competitively with one another and even within them there are different points of view. Unless these matters are carefully examined and debated, within a historical perspective, it will be hard to achieve a consensus about the importance of the participatory principle.

The nature of participation in music is the first question to address and forms the theme of the following chapter. It takes us directly to the heart of the matter, for there has long been discord between the claims of participation and of performance. There are those who argue that a piece of music must be performed to the highest possible standards of excellence. This is held to imply the need for a class of well-trained, dedicated players able to take instructions from the great composers of past and present. If the rest of us want a sing-song or a knees-up, that is fine, but fun and social bonding should not be confused with art. Conversely, for others the specialisation of music and its isolation from ordinary life – the cult of professionalism in the concert hall – is an innovation of the last couple of centuries: history, they say, confirmed by the richness of today's participatory musics, teaches us that music is a social art and should be returned to the people at large.

A related claim is made which, at first glance, seems much more unexceptional. This is that some music is better than others. While it begs the question of what is meant by 'good', many would go along with the view that it is possible to discriminate (say) between two sonatas in ways which would gain at least the rough-and-ready consent of thoughtful listeners. Likewise, some performances are thought to be better than others. Even if people differ in their judgments, discussion of any kind would be pointless if there were not the *possibility* of agreement. But this is not to say that there is a hierarchy of musical genres, ordered according to merit. One of my aims is to illustrate the extent of Britain's musical diversity and to show that there is wonderful music-making of every kind to be enjoyed. Instead of a contrast between extremes, music in Britain is a multicoloured continuum where every genre has its place.

It is essential to be clear from the outset what is meant by participation in music and why it is right to give it a high value. Participation is usually understood to mean hands-on involvement in a process. But an engagement with art as a listener, reader or spectator is also an *active* act. The distinction between 'making' and 'using' has always been an artificial one, but it has never been more so than today when a combination of social and technological change has blurred the boundaries between the two.

The concept of musical participation cannot be readily understood outside the contemporary social and cultural context. Social change on a massive scale has transformed most aspects of life today and it would be surprising if it had left our attitudes to music untouched. A number of factors need to be taken into account – in particular, the decline of old ideas of community, the rise of individualism and the emergence of relative value systems. I argue that consumption of goods and services is increasingly an active, rather than a passive, process. The day of the couch potato is passing. While it may be true that mass culture has homogenised taste, it is also creating novel opportunities for individuals to define themselves and to customise their lifestyles.

For all that, the live event is as popular as ever, if for reasons somewhat different from those that applied in the past. It is less a way of asserting or celebrating one's sense of social and physical place than of exploring today's diverse menu of possibilities. As much as ever, people still want to associate to make art – perhaps partly in reaction to the solitary pleasures afforded by the electronic technologies.

The participatory arts have a special contribution to make to the ongoing debate about civil society. When people come together in voluntary associations (whether to make music or, for that matter, to play chess or to protect birds), they are contributing to a stable and inventive society where state structures guard, but are not allowed to overshadow, the freedoms and creativity of individuals.

The value of creativity has received remarkable support from a completely different quarter. Scientific research into music and the brain and psychological studies of the value of music in education have made great advances in recent years. They demonstrate that music-making is interlinked with a range of mental activities and can foster personal and intellectual development. Charles Darwin's assertion of the intellectual and emotional importance of listening to music, which I quote at the opening of this chapter, turns out to be well-grounded in fact – and indeed is equally true of playing and singing it.

After discussing these issues, I move on to give an extended description of the musical scene in Britain today. It can only be a sketch because no comprehensive audit exists. Nobody knows, for example, how much financial support is given by local authorities to community music, or how many community musicians there are, or exactly how much in-service training is on offer to music teachers.

What is certain, however, is that a huge number of amateur music-makers exist, with a wide range of activity. The network of music societies and clubs is mostly interested in classical music of one kind or another. But the situation is beginning to change in favour of a more catholic taste. Many of the numerous choral societies which flourished in the last part of the nineteenth and the first half of the twentieth centuries are still going strong, but have ageing memberships (interestingly, this is not a problem faced by the more family-oriented brass band movement). Amateur groups have tended to take a rather conventional approach to the music they play or present, in part at least because the funding system has paid them so little attention and also because of the technical difficulty of much contemporary composition. However, for some time they have been showing a growing interest in commissioning new work and some music societies are beginning to involve themselves in community activity.[1] While brass bands are regular commissioners, choirs are rather less so than in the past.

1 'Community' is a word with many meanings which I discuss in a later chapter. Self-evidently, amateurs live and work in the community. It is enough to say for the time being that what I mean by the phrase 'community activity' is music-making with the specific aim of opening access to all sections of the community, especially those who may find themselves excluded from the arts and from opportunities for creative expression.

Other forms of non-professional music-making are burgeoning, but often in financially difficult circumstances. There has been what one might call a revived revival of folk music, building on the work of early twentieth-century pioneers, but this time round less concerned with preserving and recording the past than with adapting tradition for new times and new publics. Among today's musicians there is less of an obsession with purity but a greater interest in allowing folk to meet, or 'fuse', with other forms, especially rock and pop and non-European musics. Some of them are fully professional performers, an unwelcome development for those who believe folk's strength lies in its rootedness among the people and their informal social gatherings. For them, from being a way of living it risks becoming an art.

In some parts of the UK, the folk resurgence raises political issues around notions of cultural identity – in the North-East, for example, but even more powerfully in Scotland, where Gaelic music has been 'rescued' from an Anglicised ruling class and now speaks, or plays and sings, for nationalist aspirations.

With the general decline of music-making in the home in the last 70 years or so, school provides the first introduction for many children to singing and playing instruments. Music teaching in schools has undergone a transformation. A long process of rethinking by educationists, highly critical of much classroom practice, has led to a new music curriculum which emphasises the importance of composing and music-making as well as appreciation and understanding. This is a remarkable advance and, if effectively implemented, could in the course of time revolutionise not only schooling but also the quality of musical life in society at large. In many respects the principles of the curriculum are analogous to the thinking that underlies community music workshop practice. However, many music teachers, accustomed to another way of doing things, feel themselves to be ill-trained and ill-equipped to deal with the new imperatives. There are also, quite simply, too few of them to do justice to the demands of the new curriculum. In addition, a good number of schools in the public sector apparently remain unconvinced of the contribution music can make to personal and intellectual development.

The term 'community music' has socio-political overtones. Emerging from the ferment of the 1960s, it is as much concerned with personal and social development among those disadvantaged by poverty, and with the failure of the educational system, as it is with music in itself. It is part of the larger community arts movement, but has taken longer to establish itself than some of the other art-forms. Despite lack of recognition and low levels of public funding, it has substantial achievements to its credit, but coverage across the country is patchy and community musicians are so poorly resourced that they often find themselves chained to a treadmill of one-off projects which, although worthwhile in themselves, raise long-term expectations that prove difficult to satisfy.

The efforts of musicians, composers and educationists to develop theories which can underpin efforts to reintegrate music into the broader streams of cultural and social life and reflect the startling findings of psychological and neurological research have had important results. They have established a new set of common values: inclusiveness, a commitment to diversity and participation, a concern for individual creativity among 'ordinary' people and an understanding of the relevance of social change to music and *vice versa*.

The inclusiveness has created a framework in which non-European musicians, whether as British citizens or visitors from abroad, can make a contribution to the musical scene and receive due acknowledgment for doing so. At the same time, indigenous musicians have responded with enthusiasm to the culturally diverse nature of contemporary society. Some have brought together musics from many cultures, making use of the reservoirs of talent in the settled British communities of African, Afro-Caribbean and Asian origin. The accessibility of these musics has been one of the factors which challenge the long-standing dominance and prestige of the Western tradition. The popularity of world music is stimulating a greater public awareness of the validity of other cultures across the globe and, in the last 10 years or so a growing interculturalism has led to the development of hybrid or 'fusion' music, where different cultural conventions mingle.

The arrival of recorded music, both as a technology and as an industry, has had a profound impact, both for listeners and for players. Where previously the enjoyment of music had in the nature of things been a social act, it is now commonly a private and individual one. For millions of people today, their front rooms have become arts centres which many prefer to use in place of the sometimes daunting and uncomfortable experience of concert-going. The notion of the live performance has been subverted in another way; the recording of a Beethoven symphony or a David Bowie album does not capture a single real-life event (as it implicitly purports to do), for it usually consists of a collage of bits and pieces of recordings selected and stuck together to create a 'perfect' rendering.

The new technologies, controlled by multinational corporations, have enabled the emergence of rock and pop as a hugely powerful cultural and artistic force. What we have seen over the last half-century is the triumph of a newly invented mass 'folk' tradition in the sense of a music that is very close to people's lives and where participation is in many ways as important as performance. A rave or a rock concert is not simply a presentation which audiences attend, but a communal event (like a secular church service) in which everyone has an active part. In addition, it is a form which many thousands of its admirers can and do play as well as listen to. Rock and pop are generationally defined and closely associated with a distinct youth culture; but this is less of a limiting factor than it used to be, for 40 years on those who grew up with the rock and pop 'revolution', although now ageing, have seldom abandoned their early tastes.

The power to record and manipulate sound has not only helped to create new forms of music with mass appeal; it has also opened new avenues for composers who can now, if they wish, abandon instruments and the notes they make for the raw noises of the natural world and the sounds which computer software can invent. This has had the effect of making the business of composition available in principle to everybody who is interested and it is likely to make a huge contribution to the delivery of the new music curriculum. It also facilitates hybridisation and transfers the responsibility for musical virtuosity from the professional instrumentalist to a machine.

The final chapters of *Joining In* offer an analysis of problems that need to be addressed and a list of suggested solutions which could help to ensure that the present richness of activity continues to develop and flourish in the future.

While there is by no means universal agreement, there is a growing consensus about the value of amateur music-making and community-based practice. Further than that, it is possible to distinguish, even if tentatively, an integrated philosophy of music-making that embraces the complete, rich variety of practice. Old labels have in consequence lost much of their force and, except when making specialist points, I shall abandon conventional categories such as 'amateur' and 'community' music in favour of the wider scope of 'participation' and 'participatory'.

However, the new philosophy is not comprehensively applied or fully understood. Sometimes there is a reluctance to co-operate across sectors and a lack of interest in other musicians' work. If I am right to say that there are more things that unite music-lovers than divide them, there are many ways in which different interest groups could win practical benefits by acknowledging their mutual interdependence.

The first major problem I try to address picks up on the theme of artistic standards. There is a failure of critical debate in that it is not always clear what community musicians wish to achieve when launching projects nor whether they can show they achieved it once they are over. This is not altogether surprising when one considers the difficult conditions in which many of them work. They are often isolated and have comparatively little opportunity to see and judge each others' work, or learn from it. Pay and conditions are so poor that there is a high turnover of musicians working in the field. One particular approach – workshop practice, as it is called – has become something of an orthodoxy and there is a good case for participatory musicians to make use of a more extensive range of means, suiting cases to circumstances rather than routinely applying a dominant methodology.

But, most importantly, we need to confront a difficulty inherent in an artistic process which is not just concerned with turning out 'excellent' product but with encouraging critical understanding and the stimulation of individual creativity. Evaluation of any human activity is tough at the best of times, but even more so when what is being evaluated is internal rather than external, subjective rather than objective, and when one of its key purposes is self-evaluation. I try to set out a more decentralised model of evaluation demanding greater trust by all the parties involved – the funding bodies, managers, project leaders and, above all, those actually taking part in projects. Just as we need to move away from a hierarchy of musics, so we should avoid supposing that there is a superior class of functionaries equipped to pass judgment on practitioners who, in some cases or at some levels, are the only ones capable of giving a value to what they are doing.

These questions are relevant not only to professional musicians who work in the community or in education, but also to amateur music-makers who are interested in community and outreach work themselves or explicitly see their activities as fitting into a social context or a culture of personal development. Even where music is no more than an enjoyable leisure pursuit, is the notion of self-improvement completely beside the point?

A second, much less theoretical, challenge relates to training. Amateur musicians in every genre from rock to folk would benefit from musical and organisational training. In higher education there are limited opportunities to learn musics other than the Western classical tradition. The conservatoires are beginning to widen the scope of their courses to take account of the community and educational work in which more and more professional musicians are engaged. Music teachers in schools have only patchy access to effective INSET training to help them handle the music curriculum. Although money and facilities are required to address these deficiencies, a great deal could be done through increased planning and collaboration. There is much excellent training practice in different corners of the musical world and, rather than re-inventing the wheel, we would be wiser to identify these resources and enable them to be shared. So, to cite just one example from many, the initiative of the Birmingham Conservatoire in working with a local community music group, Sound It Out, on the development of a community music module is warmly to be welcomed.

A third reason why participatory musics are disparate, fragmented and under-resourced is the lack of appropriate well-funded institutions which can offer space, equipment, instruments and (most important of all) meeting places where amateurs and professionals can exchange ideas and practice.

Finally, the situation has been aggravated by the way in which the state funds music. Certain kinds of music receive the lion's share of the available money, even if its recipients feel it to be woefully insufficient. Meanwhile, others have been largely ignored and at best have to survive on leavings from the feast. On the face of it the commercial music industry thrives, but focuses its attention on a conservative view of what will be profitable. In the meantime, there is a large hinterland of music-makers – professional, amateur and pro-am – who seem to gain little benefit from either subsidy or commerce, but who attract substantial followings.

But things change. It is interesting to see that in the last few years the public funding agencies have become more willing to widen their policies. The latest dramatic step in this process was taken last year when the Arts Councils announced new Lottery schemes which prioritise amateur, youth and community-based arts practice. There are, however, a number of contradictions in the present arrangements that may lead to difficulties and I suggest ways by which they can be resolved. Above all, I argue that an arts funding system which is moving from a policy of bringing art to the citizen to one which recognises the citizen as artist will have to become less judgmental and interventionist and more open, responsive – and humble.

The arrival of the National Lottery has been timely. Vast financial resources have suddenly become available at the very moment when people of good will are coming to set a true value on the cultural contribution made by the many millions who participate in music-making of every kind. They increasingly see the overriding need to heal the schism between the amateur and the professional, and between the social and aesthetic uses of an art-form that penetrates every corner of our mental and emotional lives. Music is too important to be left to musicians: it belongs to all of us.

photo: mac, The Centre for Birmingham

1 THE CASE FOR PARTICIPATION

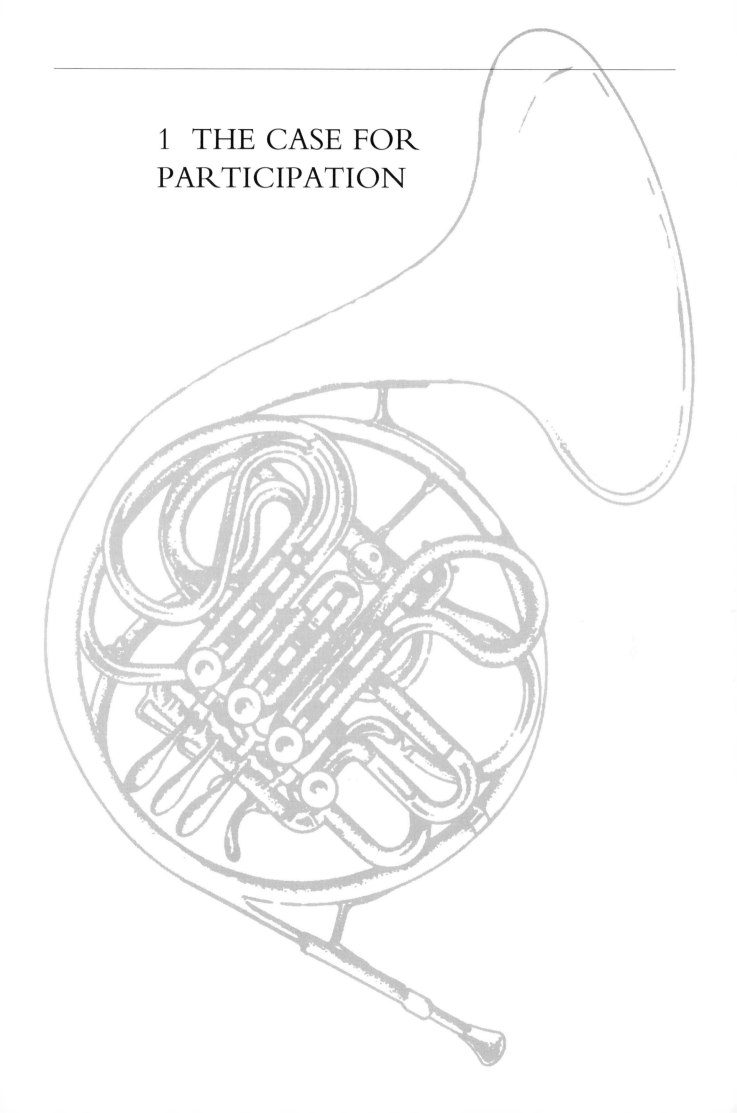

*Everyone is potentially creative. An overemphasis on rationality alone, technocratic reasoning,
restrictive organisational or community structures and an over-reliance on traditional approaches can
restrict or destroy this potential. This is why it is important that the prestige attached to the arts
should not lead to the neglect of countless, modest imaginative undertakings that inject a vital
substance into the social fabric. All people need to communicate their experiences, their hopes and
fears, as they have always done.*
                                      OUR CREATIVE DIVERSITY, 1996[1]

Of all the world, few inherit themselves.
                     LAURA RIDING

What do we mean by participation?

Participation in music and the arts is widespread, almost universal, yet generally
undervalued. It is assumed – in a loose, vague way – either to be worthwhile, or
(worse) worthy. In comparison with professional practice, it is a Cinderella, a
second-class activity for those who must be, by implication, second-class citizens. It keeps
the kids off the streets. It is a sort of fatigue duty for the ranks.

The cause of cultural participation is not helped by those who promote its virtues. A
typical note is struck in a recent consultative document on new National Lottery
programmes, published by the Arts Council of England.

> 'Take participation. The assumption here is that participating in the arts is good for
> individuals and good for society. ... We expect children to be taught to paint or sing,
> and as parents we praise their work and their initiative when they bring home a pot or
> when they take part in a school concert. For what, if we don't encourage the same in
> adults? It is patronising to suggest that anyone prefers doing things badly [but] it is
> primarily about taking part ... The quality of the product or the artistic event, though
> it may indeed be high, is secondary to the right to have a go.'[2]

The text gives itself away when it refers to children's creative activity. Which of us cannot
remember the determined benevolence of adults when confronted with juvenile work,
whether botched or brilliant? The point is to praise, not to value. Is 'having a go' enough
to justify the importance the author gives to cultural participation? Is the unexamined
assumption that it is good for us all that there is to say on the subject?

It would hardly be worth devoting a book to participation in music if that were the case.
Fortunately, it is not. My aim in this chapter is to seek out the reasons for supposing that
creative involvement is of value. They turn out to be both specific and wide-ranging.

1 *Our Creative
Diversity, Report of the
World Commission on
Culture and Development*
(Paris, UNESCO
Publishing, 1996) p.79.

2 *New Lottery
Programmes* (London,
Arts Council of
England, June 1996)
p.25.

3 *Shorter Oxford
Dictionary* (Oxford
University Press, 1964).

The first step in this search is to be clear what participation entails. The dictionary
definition speaks of 'sharing' or 'partaking'.[3] Broadly speaking, in the field of music, we
can identify three distinct levels of engagement. The first is a comparatively inert joining
in – singalongs, moving and clapping to gospel music and chants at football matches are
examples. The second involves a certain degree of reflection. One thinks of Victorian
families singing and playing music to each other during their long television-less evenings
or, to come up to date, the activity of choral societies and brass bands. Choices are made
about 'when', 'how good', 'what kind', 'who with' and so forth, but such choices are
probably based on instinct and taste rather than analysis. The third overlaps with the
second level, but is no longer simply a question of music-making but of discussing matters
of taste, quality and style and of becoming knowledgeable about the material to be played

or sung, its history and context. We are talking here not just of practice, for the sake of it or the fun of it, but of the conscious development of critical understanding.

So participation in music can be, at its most intensive, a serious business of learning, and learning *about*, an art-form and, in the process, of extending and developing one's knowledge and creativity.

However, before we look further into the practicalities, we must assess the nature and significance of participation itself. It has long been one of the key objects of cultural policy: according to the United Nations Declaration of Cultural Rights, Covenant 15, it is a fundamental human right and encompasses all those activities which open culture to as many people as possible. In a democratic society, culture should belong to everybody, not just to a social elite or a circle of specialists, and the division between those who make it and those who use it should be eliminated.

Participation is a means of asserting and enjoying one's membership of an identifiable community. We usually do this through cultural means – that is:

> 'through the use of coded, expressive modes of behaviour or communication, including language, dress, traditional kinship patterns, institutions, religion and the arts ... our cultural identity is what makes us feel we belong, in a deep and permanent way, to a group, a community.'[4]

In this sense, membership of a choral society, dancing with one's coevals at a party or singing in a local production of a Gilbert and Sullivan operetta are not only examples of artistic enterprise, but can be a way of showing one's loyalty to one's village, neighbourhood or town.

In fact, most music by far is used in social contexts from which it gains much of its force and meaning. It is heard at private ceremonies such as funerals as well as at official occasions such as coronations or the State Opening of Parliament. It is an important dimension of socialised leisure. National anthems are not the only mechanism for deploying music as political rhetoric. The churches long ago made sure the Devil did not have all the best tunes. The history of twentieth-century popular music is evidence (apart from anything else) of its capacity to assert class discriminations – whether it is Coward's camp celebration of middle-class tastes and values, the breakthrough of the lower middle classes in the songs of the Beatles or the traditional working-class vigour of *Doing the Lambeth Walk* and (following the discovery of Torremolinos) *Viva España*. In many cases, people make music alone or with others and do not define themselves as semi-detached audiences with nothing to do except listen. Rhythm and melody are a familiar method of resolving emotional conflicts and encouraging social bonding; a song sung together enables those taking part to feel that they are engaging in a common experience and, for the time being at least, the outcome is goodwill and solidarity. This is the enduring secret of Scout Jamborees.

If we turn from social to personal responses, memory adds accretions of significance to favourite tunes. During and after the war, the BBC understood very well that certain tunes were a life-saving line thrown across the airwaves to men in the armed forces who had been torn from their homes and loved ones. This was the function of the BBC's *Two Way Family Favourites*. *Desert Island Discs* is an even longer-running radio programme which allows celebrities to tell their autobiographies in musical terms; a melody can be as evocative as a photograph, perhaps more so, in summoning up the past as a living experience. Long-dead events are preserved in melodic amber.

4 *In from the Margins, A contribution to the debate on Culture and Development in Europe,* (Strasbourg, Council of Europe, 1996).

It may be countered that none of this has anything to do with music itself, for in such cases it is rather like the bell Pavlov's dogs learnt to identify with the arrival of their food. The bell can make any sound it likes without affecting this process. But this hardly matters, for the fact remains that for many people music is used as a storage depot of emotion, for their feelings of individual or community identity. To push it to one side is to refuse to accept how human beings behave. It is on this primary perception that the case for promoting participation largely rests.

Changing values

At this point we encounter a difficulty. The dizzying progress of social change in this century means that we are obliged to discard at least some of our old ideas of community and to adopt a new and different notion of participation. By this I mean that the relatively stable, geographically-defined communities of our grandparents' day bulk less large in people's minds and emotions than they did. Also, advances in communications technology and retail production and marketing have created ways of engaging creatively with one's environment and customising it to one's needs.

The single most important social trend since the Second World War has been a growing individualisation and a corresponding weakening of social structures, controls and values. It has been echoed by the logic of market liberalism (succinctly expressed by Mrs Thatcher when she was quoted as claiming: 'There is no such thing as society'). Relations between the generations have been changing. Generational hierarchies have been challenged and youth culture has become an essential component of popular culture, its dynamics governed by adaptability to continually shifting social and technological contexts (which young people learn as readily from the mass media as from the formal education system). Sexual behaviour has been transformed as part of a general liberalisation of moral attitudes and the traditional nuclear family has become less common. More people live alone, marry or cohabit later in life, live in one-parent households, divorce or are voluntarily childless couples.

This general move towards individualisation is ubiquitous and it is hard to imagine it going into reverse. It is embodied in the growing range of consumer products, the customisation of various goods and the increased personal use of the car for all kinds of specialised leisure activities. In mass entertainment and communications, equipment is becoming independent of fixed infrastructures (for instance, the Walkman, the mobile telephone and the portable computer). Popular culture is packaged so that it can be accessed whenever it is wanted and for more or less any length of time. Consumer electronics increasingly feature interactivity – a technical development expected to expand in future years. Not unnaturally, lifestyles are becoming more and more diverse. As a recent European survey points out: 'People's timetables are now an *à la carte* menu rather than the old, familial and collective *table d'hôte*.'[5]

The growth of the leisure industries has reflected the new individualism. In the 1960s and 1970s sociologists announced that a post-industrial age of leisure was approaching. The number of hours worked was declining, as was the work ethic, defined as 'a system of values in which work is defined as intrinsically virtuous ... and which requires that other spheres of life be subordinated to its demands'.[6] Things did not quite turn out as expected, with escalating unemployment and, for many of those lucky enough to have jobs, *increased* working hours. However, public policies for sport and recreation, parks, countryside, tourism, heritage, arts and entertainment were

5 *Ibid*, p.130.

6 Roberts, Kenneth, *Contemporary Society and the Growth of Leisure*, (London, Longman, 1978).

established alongside a burgeoning commercial leisure sector, much of it international in its scope.

These developments, combined with rising affluence, job mobility and greater opportunities for travel, have had a major impact on people's lives. When at home, we are well equipped to amuse ourselves and our living rooms, stocked with television, VCR and stereo equipment, have become electronic arts centres. While reading remains popular, habits are changing, with younger age groups depending less on the written word. Emerging world musics and rock and pop are as fashionable as ever, underpinning a boom in radio listening, music videos and attendance at live music events. While cinema attendances have fluctuated in recent decades, going to the movies remains the most popular form of cultural activity outside the home. User-friendly museums and galleries are enjoying a renaissance. Holidays form a large part of people's expenditure across most social classes, although the poorest members of the population still cannot afford extended breaks.

The picture I am drawing is of a society of individuals who define their lifestyles and demonstrate their values by choosing from a wide range of cultural goods and services and, in the arts, a kaleidoscope of images and sounds. The speculations of post-modernism are relevant in this context. They propose a moral relativism to accompany the discrediting of old certainties and all-embracing rational explanations ('grand narratives'). As the Council of Europe report on culture and development remarks, this goes hand in hand with a new (but often playful) prominence for the arts:

> 'Post-modernist commentators have pointed to an increasing interest in culture in general (design and aesthetics, heritage culture) and urban culture in particular (prestigious architecture, local vernacular styles, cosmopolitan diversity, urban sociability). A remarkable example of this was the dominance of rock and pop in youth culture from the 1960s to the 1980s, not simply as art, but as a way of life. All of this, it is plausibly argued, marks a move away from the Modernist past, with its emphasis on universalising rationality, standardised functionality and instrumentalism; its notion of a planned society; its fixed aesthetic, ethnic and national hierarchies and its neglect of everyday life, tradition, morality and the particular. Instead, post-modern culture has embraced simulation, spectacle, pastiche and stylistic bricolage. The result has been a wider acceptance of, and aesthetic interest in, popular entertainments, advertising, electronic and commercial culture, ethnic cultural expressions and vernacular cultural forms. This has been taken to the point where the kitsch and the banal have become the (sometimes ironic and playful) object of aesthetic display. Hierarchies of value, in sum, have become fluid and contested.'[7]

In this context, it is as well to note the changing nature of contemporary retail consumption. A traditional view has been that this is a wasteful and passive process: consumers are the dupes of manufacturers and the mechanisms of advertising and marketing, and they accept without question the values which are implicit in the packaging and sale of products. In recent years researchers have shown that this is not actually how people behave in the marketplace. Countless retail outlets, selling clothing or furniture or food or interior design, reflect varying lifestyles in what they sell. People understand the messages they are receiving when they buy goods or services, but do not necessarily accept them. Rather, they put their 'symbolic creativity' to the service of their own wishes and in so doing signal their membership of subcultures to which they may belong or their view of society and established values. Thus the old, autocratic seasonal hierarchies of the fashion industry have been subverted by the uses to which young consumers have made of the second-hand clothes market and the way in which they alter and customise.

7 *In from the Margins,*
op cit, p.135.

What is true of fashion can be applied to other forms of consumption. So, for example, the recording industry has brought within most people's reach a library of classical and pop music of every period, enabling them to assert a personal eclecticism which conflicts with the commercial imperative of the fashion of the moment. Satellite television and video have made available the same opportunities in the case of feature films and television programmes. Audiences for mass culture are not uniformly uncritical, but rather interact with what they see and hear – judging, assessing and reworking products to suit the construction of their own lives. Consumers are now in a position, by selecting from a wide range of products, to devise their own cultures and to determine (in E M Forster's phrase) their particular 'angle to the universe'.

As the communications technologies converge (broadcasting, narrowcasting, telephony, sound and video recording and publication), the potential for interaction and customisation is growing. The Internet, which enables millions of individual owners of computers to communicate with one another (free for the first time in history from state surveillance or intervention), is the latest refinement of a completely new, non-social form of participation.

The Japanese invention of the *karaoke* bar, where customers sing to recorded music, is not only a remarkable innovation in itself, but can stand as an image of the new world I have been sketching. Individuals gather together as groups of like-minded people rather than as members of socially representative communities. They consume popular music not by listening to it or by creating it, but by collaborating with and modifying it.

George Odam draws an interesting comparison between disco dancing and country dancing which illustrates the impact of the social changes I have been describing:

> 'The collective nature of modern disco dancing is interesting since it is undoubtedly collective, but the action for any one participant is entirely individual. In such dancing we enact the problems we find of living in an increasingly dense world population as members of a society which becomes increasingly individualistic as it gets more crowded.'[8]

What conclusions can we draw from this analysis? The first thing is to be clear why we should argue for the importance of engagement in *live* activity. Many people still live in and are loyal to geographical communities – for example, the Highlands of Scotland or the Welsh valleys; 98% of those living in the Rhondda Valley were born there. Nevertheless, it would seem that for most of us this is changing. When we 'share' or 'partake' with others, it is often to meet those of our own age or tastes or type rather than to place ourselves in a microcosm which mirrors a larger stable and ordered society and defines our place in it. We will see later in this book that this will entail a redefinition of terms such as 'community arts' and 'community music' and their replacement by the more flexible notion of 'participation'. Something momentous has been lost from the way our society works and, unless we believe it is possible to retrieve it (a forlorn hope, surely), we must come to terms with the situation as it is.

Today's market democracies are moderated by the imperatives of civil society and, in this respect, participation has a new, highly valuable role to play. According to Salvador Giner:

> 'Civil society is an historically evolved sphere of individual rights, freedoms and voluntary associations whose politically undisturbed competition with each other in the pursuit of their respective private concerns, interests, preferences and intentions is guaranteed by a public institution, called the state. Any mature civil society

8 Odam, George, *The Sounding Symbol* (Cheltenham, Stanley Thornes [Publishers] Ltd, 1995) p.86.

exhibits at least five prominent dimensions: individualism, privacy, the market, pluralism and class.'[9]

Unfortunately experience tends to show that the state may guarantee, but can also threaten, the liberties of its members. Montesquieu considered social cohesion depended on intermediary associations in civil society which guarded the individual from the potential for states to exhibit despotic tendencies. Nowadays the risk is perhaps that individuals will withdraw from collective organisation, especially the popular involvement that is a prerequisite of democratic politics.

Citizens who participate in intermediary associations are helping to create a network of groups that can offer a counterbalance to the overweening authority of public institutions. Often distributors of mutual benefits to their members and sometimes designed to act as pressure groups, they are essential components of civil society precisely because they are independent. They are not state-inspired and are formed by individuals who share a common concern and come together to express it. Some of them have charitable objectives, but their primary purpose is not to serve the public interest directly, but a multiplicity of private concerns. These so-called 'Third Sector' organisations range across the full scope of human activity, but cultural and sports groups are among the most popular and widespread.

So if participation was once understood to be a means by which communities of all kinds (old and new) and their members asserted their shared identity, it is now better seen as a mechanism which enables individuals not merely to pursue shared interests but also to protect their future freedom to do so. As well as a personal benefit, it brings an undoubted political advantage.

The social uses of music

That, then, is the case for participation in general. What is there to be said about participation in *music*? Two main points need to be made. The first is that the extraordinary proliferation of music-making of every kind, which I will be charting in future chapters, promises to transform our ideas about the value of music as an art. Further, it promises to challenge the predominance of Western classical music and of the view of the professional musician and composer as members of a priestly caste, whose talents are held to transcend the clumsy creativities of ordinary people. Having argued above that people do indeed use music for social reasons, I want now to show that non-European cultures have philosophies of, or grounded attitudes to, music which are socially – rather than aesthetically – based and that there is a good deal we can learn from them.

9 Giner, Salvador, *Civil Society and its Future*, keynote address, European Round Table of the CIRCLE Network, Budapest, March 1994. Cited in *Trial, Trust and Tribulation*, ed. Anthony Everitt, CIRCLE Publication no. 8, Helsinki, Arts Council of Finland, 1996.

Secondly, science is beginning to justify the high (if somewhat mysterious) importance traditionally given to music. Indeed, music may pre-date verbal language and its practice seems to echo back to the prehistoric past of *homo sapiens* and is implicated in the deep workings of the brain and mental processes. Educational psychologists are able to show how music conveys its meanings and how music-making is an essential ingredient of self-development. Once poorly substantiated claims can now be shown to rest on a solid foundation of observation.

One of the enduring features of modernism has been its dissociation of art from the communal practices of everyday life. This is not the place for a cultural history of the West, so it is enough to say here that we stand at the culmination of a long process of aesthetic development whose beginnings can be detected in the Renaissance, but which matured after the French and Industrial Revolutions. They initiated a breakdown of social hierarchy as well as of secular scepticism, individualism and the specialisation of the means of production. Artists began to see themselves as estranged from ordinary values and by means of superhuman talent offered quasi-magical access to unexplored realms of transcendent feeling.

Post-Baroque music, like the other performing arts, began to be appreciated for its own sake and withdrew from the church, the marketplace and the banqueting chamber into specially designed, extra-social spaces, the concert hall and the darkened theatre. As Christopher Small points out:

> 'The music of this tradition is essentially without function ... There is no feeling that a particular music belongs exclusively to a certain time, season or setting: masses, coronation anthems and requiems are commonly presented indiscriminately for our appreciation in concert halls without any feeling of inappropriateness. The development of records and radio have enhanced this tendency, making all music available at all times and in all places (one wonders whether a culture which was as much concerned, as many are, with the fitness of a particular music to a specific time or place would have developed recording techniques at all). The listener's experience of music is essentially private: the structure and seating arrangement of a concert hall or opera house does not facilitate communal interaction any more than does that of the conventional classroom.'[10]

The evolution of an efficient means of notating pitch and rhythm (largely complete by the early Renaissance) liberated musicians in two far-reaching ways. One was to enable them to create 'music' away from any music-making source – direct from brain to paper – and have it, like a pre-cooked frozen meal, reconstituted at any convenient time or place by players and singers suitably trained to decode the signs. The second enabled the 'composer' (for it was now possible to define the act of composition quite separately from the act of playing or singing) to plan and organise sonorities on paper in increasingly complex patterns of harmony and orchestration. By the nineteenth century, the isolation of the composer had become not just a matter of convenience, but a crucial factor in defining the status of a creator of music. And as composers produced ever more sophisticated and challenging written-out scores, players were obliged to address these challenges with more intensive and effective training. Others came to spectate, appreciating not just the subtleties of compositional refinement but the virtuosity of performers who had taken their skills well beyond the attainment of most 'amateur' players.

Thus, the musical centre of gravity in Europe shifted from a largely improvisational, multi-skilled and multi-purpose activity to one based exclusively on a notion of literacy and intellectual endeavour, relying not on sounds but on signs written on paper. (Even today we unconsciously speak of 'music' when referring to the printed notation found in books and loose-leaf sheets in music shops.) Those who cannot read 'music' may well feel stigmatised, in the same way as those who cannot read language text. Music became a profession, with all the inherent hierarchies of status and skill that professions encourage, and fostered a mixture of respect, awe and mystification among those not inducted into its arcane ways.

10 Small, Christopher, *Music-Society-Education* (London, John Calder, 1977) p.28.

While all this was going on, the everyday, traditional music-making of ordinary people did not disappear – except from view. It continued on its way unabated, but became less and less visible to commentators, critics and historians. It was heard, but not seen.

Although, as the nineteenth century proceeded, composers found a rich source of musical ideas in folk music, it attracted little serious attention in and for itself for many years unless transformed into high art.

It is perhaps no accident that the splendid isolationism of 'official' music went hand in hand with a lack of interest in that of other cultures. More than that, Europeans came to think that post-Renaissance music was inherently superior, being based on the Western tonal system which was understood to be derived from nature and represented the truth of harmonics in their most remarkable form. A distinguished musical commentator wrote in the 1920s that tonal harmony was the musical analogue of perspective, another European invention. More recently, the conductor and composer Leonard Bernstein argued that there 'existed a phonology of music which evolves from the universal known as the harmonic series. And ... there is an equally universal musical syntax.'

It is true that the harmonic series is a universal based on invariant acoustic phenomena, as philosophers in ancient Greece realised when they found that pitch intervals conformed to mathematical principles. But this is not to claim, as some have, that the harmonic series is the unconscious foundation of Western harmony and the tonal system. Assertions of this kind seem designed to justify the global spread of European and American musics, something which has undeniably happened, but is perhaps more readily accounted for as the unsurprising concomitant of nineteenth-century imperialism.

Jeremy Montagu wrote to Anthony Storr:

'What puzzles me, about the influence of Pythagoras etc. is how small a part of the world's population produces music which is recognisably related to the harmonic series. We do in Europe today in our art music (a lot of folk music doesn't), and so they do in India, and that's about it. Even the African areas which use the musical bow (and therefore use harmonics in their music) use different intervals when singing. Even the ancient Greeks used some very odd intervals indeed in their music.'[11]

The view of Western superiority was important if the project to set music apart in an elevated sphere of its own was to be maintained. Despite its pretension to universality, it is no more than two or three centuries old and bears little relation to other musical genres which Europeans played and enjoyed throughout its history and, of course, still do.

The paradox of empire is that although one of its purposes is to export one's own culture to provinces and colonies, the traffic is not all one-way. Towards the end of the last century the sounds of other cultures made themselves heard in Europe. Composers began to rethink their positions. The gamelan arrived as early as 1889, at the Paris World Exhibition, and made a considerable impression on Debussy who heard in it 'the eternal rhythm of the sea, the wind among the leaves and in the thousand sounds of nature which they understand without consulting any arbitrary thesis'.[12]

Post-war immigration into Britain has reinforced the impression that, for all the grandeur and beauty of the classical tradition, its successes have been purchased at a high price. Christopher Small remarks:

'We may be reluctant to think of our musical life, with its great symphony orchestras, its Bach, its Beethoven, its mighty concert halls and opera houses, as in any way impoverished, and yet we must admit that we have nothing to compare with the rhythmic sophistication of Indian, or what we are inclined to dismiss as "primitive" African music, that our ears are deaf to the subtleties of pitch inflection of Indian raga or Byzantine church music, that the cultivation of *bel canto* as the ideal of the singing

11 Cited in Storr, Anthony, *Music and the Mind* (London, HarperCollins, 1993) p.62.

12 Cited in Lockspeiser, Edward, *Debussy: His Life and Mind*, vol 1 (London, Cassell, 1962) p.115.

voice has shut us off from all but a very small part of the human voice's sound
possibilities or expressive potential, such as are part of the everyday resources of a
Balkan folk singer or an Eskimo, and that the smooth mellifluous sound of the
romantic symphony drowns out the fascinating buzzes and distortions cultivated alike
by African and medieval European musicians.'[13]

Small was writing in the 1970s and, although there are still those who take the
Eurocentric view he is attacking, the phenomenal popularity of world musics is evidence
that in recent years British musical taste has become much more multiculturally catholic
than it used to be.

Just as important as the sheer otherness of other musics is the way they lock into their
cultures like the matching teeth of a zip. In Bali, a territory with a great music tradition, it
is odd to find that the inhabitants have no word for music. The closest they can get to its
meaning is a concern to 'do things as well as possible'. It mingles inextricably with village
rituals, innumerable temple festivals, night-long music-dramas featuring shadow puppets
or live actors, all kinds of ceremonial both public and private.

Among the many cultures of Africa, as in Bali, music is interfused with the patterns of
daily life. While it is often presented as entertainment with expert and professional
performers, their relation to their audiences is quite different from that in the West. In
contrast to the silent detachment to which we are used when attending a performance of
orchestral music, where a cough is an anarchistic act, there are usually opportunities for
participation; dancing, clapping and choral singing. People react loudly and actively to
what they are hearing, for a performance is (among other things) a means of social
interaction. There are work songs, cradle songs, songs which form part of royal rituals or
initiation ceremonies, even songs which are a medium for the exchange of gossip or news.
Others address religious or philosophical themes, and various trades or occupations have
their own forms of musical expression.

To explain the power of music we are no longer forced to rely exclusively on its formal
structural properties and its character (that is, whether it is active or passive, heavy or
light, happy or sad). We can add all the various meanings that flow from its many
different purposes and uses. One of the difficulties with classical music, set apart as it is in
its transcendental ghetto, is that theorists are able to offer only a partial account and have
to 'talk up' the impact of musical events in ways that are reminiscent rather of religious
faith than of rational discourse.

Nevertheless, one has to accept evidence from music-lovers that it is possible to be
profoundly moved by a Mozart symphony for what the sounds in themselves seem to
convey without the apparent intervention of memory or communal togetherness. This is
not to contradict what I have just said about social context, but to suggest that what may
be happening in the brain complements or runs alongside what is happening in the world.

The discoveries of science

Scientific investigations into the workings of the brain show how deeply rooted music is
in our genetic and neural make-up. Through a tragic irony, it was the brain damage
suffered by the composer Maurice Ravel in a car accident that first led researchers to
suppose that different parts or systems of the brain might be charged with different
functions and (so to speak) to re-invent phrenology, this time on a scientific basis. The
brain has developed in stages throughout evolution; the oldest layer is the brain stem

13 Small, Christopher,
op cit, p.1.

which emerges from the top of the spine and originally evolved from reptiles. It manages our basic functions. The brain stem is surrounded by the limbic system which is the seat of emotions. Above this lies the cerebral cortex which handles higher cognitive and motor functions of a specifically human kind – consciousness, morality, speech. It appears that the rhythms and formal behavioural patterns we associate with music can be traced back to the reptilian stem. As Paul Robertson puts it, 'one substratum of musical language works at this primitive, structured, unconscious and unemotional level'.[14]

The cerebral cortex is divided into two parts, the left and right hemispheres. The left concerns itself with rational analysis, sequential logic and verbal language. It is where we think. The right hemisphere is the seat of the emotions and of spatial awareness; it allows us to endow our perceptions with meaning. Also, it is here that music is registered and enjoyed.

In a telling study, Professor Justine Sergeant of McGill University in Toronto brain-scanned 10 musicians while they engaging in a series of keyboard and sight-reading tests. The brain areas responsible for skilled movement of the fingers showed up during the scan. But the scan also demonstrated the existence of a neural network concerned exclusively with the appreciation of musical sounds. This was stimulated when the musicians were listening to or playing music (in this case, Bach's Partita BWV 767), but not when they were listening to or playing scales.[15]

It would seem that we are programmed to appreciate harmonious sounds and to respond negatively to discord. A recent experiment at Harvard tested the hypothesis of an innate bias favouring consonance over dissonance: a sample of 32 infants was presented with two short unfamiliar melodies in a consonant and a dissonant version. They looked significantly longer at the music source and showed less motor activity when hearing the former than the latter. The researchers interpreted their findings as tending to show that 'the human infant may possess a biological preparedness that makes consonance perceptually more attractive than dissonance'.[16]

Some psychologists, noting that we can hear sound when in the womb and that it is, in fact, the foetus's prime sensory stimulus, have argued that very young babies display a sophisticated ability to recognise musical structures, which may be related to their sensitive response to the tone of voices, especially that of their mother. At this very early stage, intonations of voice and music appear to resemble each other. No wonder that it is beginning to be recognised that musical experience in childhood has long-lasting effects; it is now recognised that the right temporal lobe of the brain apparently contains a complete record of all the music heard between the ages of about eight and 11 years.

Paul Robertson reports on the work of Mireille Besson of the Cognitive Neuroscience Laboratory at Marseille, who has been measuring the electrical activity of the brain when it hears a wrong note. The brain is a creature of habit and primes itself to anticipate events; when meeting a discrepancy, it reacts sharply. Besson shows that these reactions are shared equally by trained musicians and non-musicians:

> 'The real significance of these studies seems to be that we are all wired to be "musical", in the sense that all of us implicitly understand the clichés of familiar tonal melodies. Professional training does not create or increase our musicality ... Music then relies on inherent neurological responses that we all have.'[17]

Another extraordinary chain of research points to a link between music and abstract thought, echoing the Platonic view that all mathematical truths find expression in the

14 Robertson, Paul, *Music and the Mind* (London, Channel 4 Television, 1996) p.17.

15 See Wrathall, C, 'Mind over grey matter', in *BBC Music Magazine*, November 1992.

16 Zentner, Marcel R, and Kagan, Jerome, Department of Psychology, Harvard University, 'Perception of music by infants', correspondence in *Nature*, 383, 5 September 1996.

17 Robertson, Paul, *op cit*, pp.9,10.

phenomenal world. Looking for an algorithm to describe how neurones trigger connections in the brain, a researcher produced a visual computer print-out of neurones firing; these patterns were then converted into sound and, to the general surprise, sounded distinctly like tonal music. This suggested a further experiment to see if listening to music improved performance in solving abstract reasoning tasks. The results were positive. Paul Robertson again:

> 'The ability to recognise patterns requires both memory and access to many subconscious neurological brain pathways and biological systems. Our ability to recognise patterns and imagine them modified by action is the essence of spatial imagination and the key to human ascendancy. Music calls on all these functions.'

In short, 'science is telling us that to be human is to be intrinsically musical'.[18]

The worlds of medicine and educational psychology have long argued that there is a powerful link between music and other forms of human behaviour or experience. Music has been used as an aid to healing and the reduction of anxiety and pain. It is closely associated with movement and forms of collective action. Movement learning is fundamentally important to humans and the development of sophisticated thought processes appears to emerge only through the mediation of movement. Movement learning is an ingredient of the early years of schooling in most if not all cultures; as children develop, movement is a useful reinforcement of the learning process. The interrelationship between the ear and bodily function is close and underpins the claims for the unique part which music education can play in schools.

Dr Frank R Wilson of the University of California writes:

> 'A strong case can be made for the inclusion of music in any general curriculum because of some special features of the human brain and the muscular system to which it is bonded. Like all moving creatures, we have a central nervous system that regulates the body in its interactions with the outside world. Because we are primates – that is, mammals who walk upright – our upper limbs are not used to support our body weight against gravity ... we find an enormous elaboration in the brain of a motor control system that seems dedicated to permitting extraordinary refinement of movement of our upper limbs. We also have the gift of exceptional control of the muscles of the face and oral cavity, and the brain mechanisms for controlling the muscles just as precisely as we control those of the upper limbs. What makes us special in the biological sense, in other words, is the unique control we have of our upper limbs and vocal apparatus, and the linkage of these capabilities to a strong urge to communicate to ourselves and to others around us.'[19]

These physiological and neural accounts, which have emerged in the last couple of decades, tend to confirm the well-established findings of educationists. As long ago as the 1960s, a ground-breaking study of musical education in Hungary demonstrated that the academic record of children attending music primary schools was much better than that of those attending ordinary primary schools.[20] Children trained in singing differed from untrained children of the same age in their physical development and breathing and mental and physical co-ordination (that is, in activity of the cerebral cortex). They showed an increased capacity to memorise, to develop their reasoning capacity and emotional range and to engage in active social participation. If, as seems reasonable, we extrapolate from these findings and apply them to the population at large, we can say with reasonable confidence that making music is a way of exercising the complete personality.

18 *Ibid*, p.19.

19 Wilson, F R, 'Music as basic schooling for the brain', cited in Odam, George, *op cit,* p.17.

20 Frigyes, Sándor, *Musical Education in Hungary* (Budapest, Corvina Press, 1996) p.145ff.

These findings have been broadly confirmed by an important recent study.[21] A survey of 1,200 children in Switzerland found that those who were given extra music lessons performed better than those who were not. According to one of the researchers, Maria Spychiger at the University of Fribourg, music can have a positive influence on the emotions and on co-operative behaviour. 'When children play or sing together, they have to listen to one another. Competing behaviour is not compatible with making music.' No differences were found in the intelligence of children in the two groups, but the children given extra music lessons were better at languages and no worse at mathematics, although they had received fewer lessons in those subjects. They showed improvements in their ability to retell in writing or pictures a story that had been read to them and also learnt to read more easily. There was much less social tension in the classes that had been taught more music.

All this scientific research has yielded enough information about the psychology and the neurology of musical response to provide useful guidance for policy-makers. It is surely time for the relevant government departments and the arts funding system to open systematic channels of communication with the scientific community. Also, scientists would be well advised to seek ways of expressing research in non-technical terms for the benefit of all those concerned in the development of participatory musics, both in education and in the music world. Interestingly, following the success of Paul Robertson's television series *Music and the Mind*, first shown on Channel 4 in 1996, the Music Research Institute has been formed with just such an objective in mind: its aims are to serve as a focal point for research and to disseminate information on the subject.

In summary, then, participation in music is rather more than simply the 'right to have a go'. Some quite specific claims can be made. It is a means by which a social animal is able not simply to socialise at leisure, but to embody its sense of shared community in public ceremony. Furthermore, the institutional infrastructure which enables music-making to take place – the clubs, societies and associations – makes a significant contribution to the contemporary polity and is a valuable support for the maintenance of a thriving and balanced civil society. This is of particular importance in an age of increasing individualisation where the stable, geographical communities of the past are giving way to provisional, multi-level and changeable groupings.

Individualisation has been accompanied by technological advance and old forms of participation are now competing with new. Active engagement with the imagery and sounds of electronic communications no longer calls for the living presence of other people. Collectivity can be virtual. This state of affairs offers dazzling and universal opportunities for cultural involvement and creative expression. But there is a downside. The widespread popularity of music-making in the traditional manner among all sectors of the population suggests that many feel the need to balance the potentially solipsistic power of the new media with real sharing by real people in real space.

Cultural participation of any kind is acknowledged as a basic human right. But participation in music stands in a class of its own: it should not be ranked alongside (say) horse-racing or bingo; scientific and educational research has made it clear that it speaks to human beings' profoundest impulses; more than words, it is the very language of the brain, the seat of intellect, emotion and the control of physical behaviour. It is the aesthetic analogue of the electrochemical firings of millions of neurones inside our skulls.

21 See Edwards, Rob, *New Scientist*, 18 May 1996.

photo: Matthew Bentley-Walls

2 THE MUSIC-MAKERS

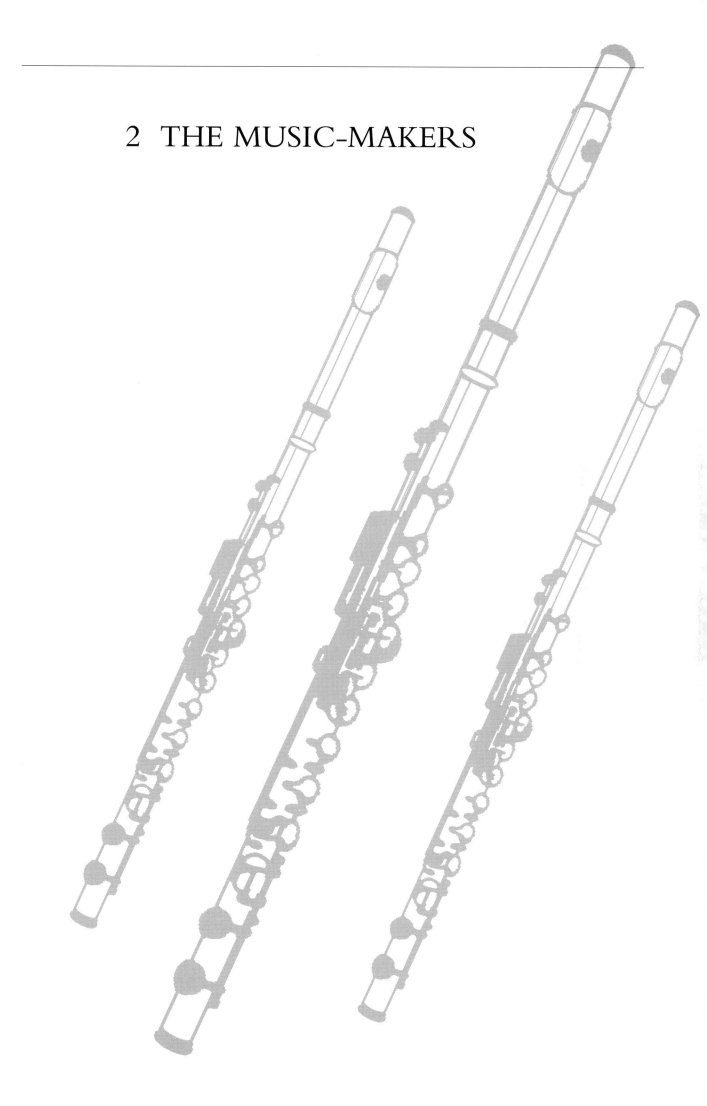

The English may not like music – but they absolutely love the noise it makes.
                    SIR THOMAS BEECHAM

The hills are alive with the sound of music
With the songs they have sung
For a thousand years.
                    OSCAR HAMMERSTEIN, *THE SOUND OF MUSIC*

A land without music? Hardly. Whatever truth there may once have been in the old slur, the reverse is the case today. The United Kingdom is shaking with sound. The broadcasting and recording industries are continuing their long expansion. The last 50 years have seen a growth in orchestral music, maintained by a subsidy regime which, although ungenerous by some European comparisons, has superintended a rise in both audiences and standards. Opera continues to boom.

But professional music is only the tip of an iceberg. What lies below the waves is even more extensive, if largely uncharted. Done for love rather than money, for sheer delight, amateur music-making of all kinds is hugely popular and in recent years some genres have taken on a new lease of life. Community music, ill-regarded and poorly funded, has developed its own distinctive modes of practice (influenced by, and interacting with, developments in music education theory). The recently introduced music curriculum in schools has – at least in principle – broadened the scope of educational opportunity for all.

This is a considerable success story, but much of what has been achieved has been pushed along against the odds. The funding system is unfairly skewed in favour of professional classical music and against amateur and community-based work. Failures in teacher training are threatening the future of music in schools. There is evidence that community-based practice is hampered by lack of continuity in its work and limp evaluation. Music development has grown like Topsy and many observers believe there is trouble ahead if policy-makers do not abandon their thoroughly British tendency to muddle through in favour of a comprehensive and integrated strategy.

This strategy should have at its heart an acknowledgment of the meaning that making and listening to music have in most people's lives. It should be citizen-based rather than artist-based, not only for democratic reasons but also because the creative impulse stretches far beyond the narrow scope of professional practice.

In this chapter, I will be diving below the surface of the water to survey the full extent of the iceberg. I will be looking at general trends and national movements. But participatory music-making is by its nature local and specific. It is what our friends and neighbours do, not the metropolitan talents whom we hear so much of in the media. We tend to call them, a little patronisingly, ordinary people; but they are doing extraordinary things.

Statistics and facts do not do full justice to that extraordinariness. So I will begin by telling the story of what has happened, and is still happening, in one particular place. I have chosen the Pottery Towns because the history of music-making there has been recorded in two separate texts – the first an account of the emergence of choral singing in the nineteenth century and the second a survey of amateur practice at the beginning of the 1990s. It is a stirring tale.

Music in the Pottery Towns – then and now

The Pottery towns in the middle of the nineteenth century were a classic case of industrial desolation.[1] They formed a working-class conurbation, where there were few

1 This section is indebted to R Nettel's fascinating *Music in the Five Towns 1840-1914, A Study of the Social Influence of Music in an Industrial District,* (London, Oxford University Press, 1944).

representatives of the middle or upper classes and few public buildings apart from churches, nor many other facilities. There was little in the way of musical tradition, as there was in a city such as Birmingham with its choral festivals. The most important cultural force was Methodism and this led to a strong desire to improve the quality of congregational singing. This in turn called for tuition and a method of reading music 'which could be understood by a community containing, only too often, a large proportion of members either semi- or wholly illiterate'.[2] The development in the middle of the century of the Tonic Sol-fa system of music notation made it possible for two local amateurs, Burslem's Town Clerk and a pottery manufacturer, to organise singing classes, junior and adult choirs and competitions. Choral singing became extremely popular and the Burslem Tonic Sol-fa Choir began to win national prizes by the early 1860s. Twenty years later, 'the power to sing at sight had become so common as to excite no remark.'[3] When the jubilee of Tonic Sol-fa was celebrated in 1891, the Potteries sent a contingent of 1,000 singers to a festival in London to mark the occasion.

These artistic achievements had a considerable social impact:

> 'A cultural change in the social life of the district began to take place, with people at last being able to enjoy music such as they had very rare opportunities of hearing previously, and secondly, it was discovered by others that voices from this district had a distinctive natural beauty that came as a pleasant surprise to those who heard them up and down the country, in places where the potters soon went to engage in musical competitions ... Even more important than the appreciation of music critics was the social change that had in a few years taken place in an obviously backward district.'[4]

Arnold Bennett, whose *Clayhanger* novels are a fictional chronicle of the Pottery towns, noticed what was going on and wrote of choirs 'which sang at dinners, free-and-easies, concerts, and Martinmas tea-meetings. They sang for the glory, and when there was no demand for their services, they sang to themselves for the sake of singing.'[5]

By the 1880s a powerful personality had emerged, James Garner, who further developed choral singing and whose choir, the Hanley Glee and Madrigal Society, acquired a national reputation. When he died in 1905, 15,000 attended his funeral. He was evidently an inspired, if strict, teacher. Describing this early version of 'workshop practice', he said:

> 'In dealing with masses of trained and untrained voices I have found it of the utmost importance to check inattention from the outset. I do everything to make my choralists earnest. When I face them I let them know that if the music is unfamiliar to them it is not so to me; that I know what is wanted. Such preparation, I find, has a reflex action. Singers become anxious to reach my standard, however high it may be.'[6]

Choral singing at this time reflected Nonconformist popular taste and was little influenced by educated opinion or metropolitan musical fashion. It was a respectable alternative to theatre and music hall. Choirs tended to progress artistically in three stages; unaccompanied part-songs, cantatas and, finally, oratorios. Cut off from rural life, men like Garner enjoyed the Elizabethan composers and religious or moral ballads, but had little or no time for folk music.

In the 1890s a new figure arrived on the scene – Charles Swinnerton Heap, a composer, organist, pianist and festival organiser, who had studied at Leipzig and Cambridge and was active in Birmingham and the Midlands. A concert hall was built in Hanley and Swinnerton Heap was charged with the establishment of a regular festival along the lines of the Three Choirs Festival at Worcester, Hereford and Gloucester. Nine local choral

2   Nettel, R, *op cit*, p.9.

3   *Ibid*, p9.

4   *Ibid*, pp.9,10.

5   Cited in *ibid*, p.10.

6   *Ibid*, p.17.

societies were brought together to form the North Staffordshire Festival Choir. It was a decisive move away from the competitive festival, dependent on the existing repertoire, towards major musical events featuring new compositions.

In 1896 Elgar conducted at Hanley the first performance of his oratorio, *King Olaf*. The Pottery towns were now on the map. Other premieres followed (among them, Coleridge-Taylor's *The Death of Minnehaha*). Great artists made their way to Hanley – Madame Patti, Clara Butt, Paderewski and Hans Richter with the Hallé Orchestra and many others. Swinnerton Heap died in 1900 and with him the triennial festivals, but the link with contemporary composers, including Havergal Brian, Delius and, in particular, Elgar, remained.

Elgar brought the North Staffordshire District Choir to London for the English premiere of *The Dream of Gerontius* and was a frequent visitor to the Potteries for performances of his choral works. His last appearance was in 1932. After the Great War much was altered and, although the choirs continued, the great days of national celebrity were over. The failure of the Potteries to create a professional orchestra was a limiting factor, but musical and popular cultural taste had shifted too, and few composers continued to write oratorios.

But in its time the choral movement in the Potteries was a remarkable example of the coming together of social and artistic imperatives. It originated in deprivation and was the autonomous cultural expression of a community's sense of a new identity. As it grew in authority and reputation it made a direct contribution to the development of contemporary music. Its historian, R Nettel, summed up its contribution:

> 'Our nineteenth century choirs arose out of a natural urge for some means of expression denied to men in the lives they were leading, and not because people of superior learning fired the workers with enthusiasm for a new art-form. The madrigal was a product of Tudor society, folk songs were a product of rural society, sea-songs of the comradeship of the fo'c'sle, and the modern choral society of the gregarious existence of the victims of nineteenth century industrialism.'[7]

A hundred years have passed since the musical heyday of the Potteries. What is the situation today? To what extent have old traditions survived in one form or another, and to what extent have new ones been founded? In the Policy Studies Institute's survey of amateur arts and crafts in the United Kingdom published in 1991, the results of a review of provision in Stoke-on-Trent and Newcastle-under-Lyme are described at some length. It gives an account of how matters stood at the beginning of the present decade.[8]

Throughout the twentieth century industrialisation has continued to be the dominant feature, for both good and ill, of life in the Potteries, which still suffer from being roughly equidistant between the great urban centres of Manchester and Birmingham and have never been able to rival their economic and cultural influence. They were hard hit by the post-war decline of Britain's manufacturing industries. The closure of the Shelton Bar steelworks, angrily mourned in a famous documentary drama devised by Peter Cheeseman for the local Victoria Theatre, was a major blow. Although the 1986 National Garden Festival, on the site of the steelworks, attracted more than two million visitors and helped to stimulate new developments in retailing and other services, Stoke was not accorded assisted area status and, in consequence, the process of reclaiming derelict industrial areas has taken longer to accomplish than in many other parts of the country.

Unsurprisingly, perhaps, the area has never been noted for its enthusiasm for the arts and,

7 *Ibid*, p.110.

8 Hutchinson, Robert, and Feist, Andrew, *Amateur Arts in the UK* (London, Policy Studies Institute, 1991) pp.200-210.

apart from a new museum and a purpose-built home for the regional theatre company, the New Vic, there has not been the level of capital development seen in cities such as Birmingham or Nottingham.

Nevertheless, musical life in Stoke and its environs is lively and substantial. Although many performing and music groups were founded after 1970, organisations such as the North Staffs Operatic Society and the North Staffordshire Symphony Orchestra, which were founded in 1892 and 1904 respectively, maintain a link with the past and the world of Elgar and Swinnerton Heap. The operatic society 'completely runs the theatre' when it puts on productions at the Queen's Theatre, Burslem. Although audiences had declined from an average of 15,000 to 20,000 per show on the 1970s, the Society's performances still attracted between 10,000 and 12,000 fifteen years later. The orchestra's aims are 'to give local amateur instrumentalists the opportunity to perform orchestral music to the highest possible standards'.

At the time of the survey there were four amateur orchestras in all, and a wind band. Eight choirs carried on the great tradition initiated by James Garner. It is estimated that in Stoke and Newcastle choral and orchestral performances attracted about 30,000 attendances a year and about 60,000 watched 60-odd operatic and light operatic performances. Three brass bands are also recorded and four folk music and dance groups. There were eight festivals and carnivals.

Two institutions exist today which make significant cultural interventions and whose support would have made all the difference to the Victorian pioneers had they been on the scene in the nineteenth century. The Staffordshire County Music Department is a vigorous part of the local education authority and, before the full impact of the government's education reforms was felt, 10,000 Staffordshire children were learning to play a musical instrument (then a free service within school hours). Outside hours, about 3,000 schoolchildren were regularly involved in bands, choirs and orchestras. The University of Keele has its own Keele Philharmonic Society, whose aim is to 'provide the best amateur music available ... we do use professionals when the requirements and standards of the works performed demand it.'

The University also adds to the local stock of young people and the Potteries boast a considerable amount of popular musical activity – jazz, rock and so forth. The report identified 20 rock bands, 13 rhythm and blues bands, 20 indie/pop bands, 14 jazz bands, 19 punk and thrash, two soul, one reggae, two dance and four folk bands in Stoke and Newcastle. Ensembles of this kind come and go and musical fashions change, but some local enquiries leave me with the impression that, although the balance of genres has changed in favour of rhythm and blues and indie, the overall level of activity has not substantially changed. The Potteries have even made a marginal contribution to the national pop scene, for one member of Take That and another from Guns and Roses have Stoke associations.

It is hard to be anything but impressed by this portrait of busy creativity. Both for variety and quantity, the present compares very well with the past, even if today's Elgars and Beechams no longer beat their way to the Potteries. The forefathers of today's local musicians built well, but their successors have added their own extensions to the original edifice and designed rooms and spaces of their own. This brief musical history of the Five Towns suggests that participatory music in this country is as bustling and variegated as it has ever been.

Participatory music today

Now it will be hard to make much sense of the world of participatory music unless we re-examine the value we place on the terms 'amateur' and 'professional'. On the face of it, both of them are neutrally descriptive, whereas in truth they are value-loaded. An easy way of demonstrating this is to add '-ism' to each of them. 'Amateurism' evokes dabbling, the cultivation of a pastime, shambolic goings-on in village halls. 'Professionalism' signifies membership of a trained and exclusive elite of dedicated specialists who (as my dictionary says) have raised their 'trade to the dignity of a learned profession'.

There is no doubt that the distinction is real. It is perhaps no accident that the terms were first recorded in the middle of the eighteenth century when the impact of industrialisation led to a growth of work specialisation and the invention of the concept of unpaid leisure as an antithesis to paid labour. They are also associated with a continual rise in the status of art and those who produce it; the Romantic idea of the genius with unique insight into the nature of things underpins the economics of professionalism. The genius had an equivalent in the interpretative arts of the musician, dancer or actor; this was the prodigy, often discovered in childhood, who might not be as creatively inventive as the composer or playwright, but whose technical virtuosity was so extraordinary as to seem almost magical.

Although artists have made a living from their work throughout recorded history, these were novel attitudes. Until about 300 years ago, the difference between full-time and part-time creative practice was one of circumstance and economic or social class rather than of seriousness of intention or talent. The boundaries between art as art for its own sake and art as craft either did not exist or, where they did, were blurred and ambiguous.

But, at the same time and paradoxically, the distinction is also unreal. Throughout the twentieth century composers worked with amateurs and drew much from folk music traditions. In the last 20 years or so, the establishment of non-European communities has introduced musics for which professionalism and amateurism are irrelevant and misleading concepts. The resurgence of traditional musics has brought back to the fore a kind of music-making where participation is as important as technical virtuosity, where there is little distinction between composer and player and where meaning emerges from social context and use. Specialisation has also been challenged in the field of mass popular music, where the separated skills of composer, lyricist and player in Tin Pan Alley music have given way to a combining of talents in much of the best rock and pop music. The development of community music and new thinking in formal education have encouraged classical musicians and composers to work in more open and collaborative ways. All over the country there is an active class of local musician who straddles amateur and professional music-making.

At this point it may be useful to examine the relationship between community and amateur arts. This is more easily said than done. A few years ago an attempt at a definition was made by the National Enquiry into Arts and Community:

> 'Amateur arts is primarily the practice of the arts for its own sake. Community-oriented arts is arts with additional social purposes. These include personal development and social cohesion; expressing or re-interpreting cultural, religious or ethnic affiliations; articulating feelings about social issues or local problems; and stimulating or contributing to local action, democracy and change.'[9]

9 Cited in *A Creative Future: the way forward for the arts, crafts and media in England* (London, Arts Council of Great Britain, 1991) p.84.

This formulation does not survive close scrutiny. Much amateur work (one thinks of brass bands in mining, or ex-mining, villages) is evidently concerned with the expression of individual creativity and social involvement. Likewise many amateurs who are taking part in the remarkable revival of traditional Gaelic musics are doing so at least in part because it enables them to express their feelings about social development and democratic change. The best that can be said is that most, but not all, amateur activity emerges spontaneously from local communities or groups of enthusiasts and that most, but not all, community arts are the result of external intervention by professional artists. In other words amateur music is usually demand-led, and community music supply-led.

So while it is still legitimate to speak of amateurs and professionals (whether conventional performers or community musicians), they increasingly occupy a broad interactive spectrum of practice. It is important not to see this development as some kind of revolutionary innovation. The habit of collaboration never died out completely. The emergence of choral singing in the Victorian age is just one instance of the contribution which amateurs made to modern English classical music and, at the same time, illustrates the part music can play in the recovery of community life. The story of the great choirs of the Pottery towns exemplifies a wider trend in the North of England and Wales among an urban proletariat uprooted from their rural origins.

According to the Policy Studies Institute[10] there are more than 5,400 amateur music-making groups in membership of nine umbrella organisations, with a total individual membership of 258,000. There are 240 youth choirs and orchestras with a membership of more than 28,000. There are more than 1,700 folk or traditional music and dance clubs or societies with a membership of 57,000. There are more than 260 music-promoting societies with a membership of 36,000. It was estimated in 1991 that 11% of the population took part in disco dancing; 5% played a musical instrument; 4% were involved in ballroom dancing; 2% engaged in choral singing, 2% in pop music and 1% in orchestral music.[11] The National Music Council reports that at least 600,000 people actively participate in amateur and voluntary music-making.[12]

Ensembles, music societies and choirs are largely self-financing and depend on support from their local communities. The arts funding system helps with money towards new commissions. Local authorities and educational establishments have been able to make their own venues available at subsidised rates, although government pressure to maximise commercial revenues means that this avenue of support is increasingly being closed off. The provision of music materials from libraries is a significant hidden subvention. The value of music supplied by one local authority music library to 12 choral societies for Christmas concerts alone was calculated recently as over £20,000 (for purchase or hire of printed choral and orchestral music materials had they not been available from library sources).[13]

Umbrella bodies play a leading part in the governance of some, but not all, sectors of amateur music-making. Pop, rock and Country and Western are barely covered, except in Northern Ireland where pop and rock bands are represented by the Federation of Music Collectives, a North-South venture based in Dublin. Perhaps in these genres the amateur/professional divide is felt to have less relevance than elsewhere. Some bodies pre-date the Second World War – the National Federation of Music Societies (NFMS), the National Association of Choirs, the National Operatic and Dramatic Association and the British Federation of Music Festivals. The British Federation of Brass Bands (BFBB), with a UK remit but an English bias in its membership, and the Welsh Amateur Music Federation (WAMF) were formed in the 1960s. In Northern Ireland the Association of Irish Musical Societies and the Northern Ireland Bands Association represent the interests of amateur musical and operatic societies and various types of band (flute, silver, pipe, accordion, concert). In the past 20 years a range of new bodies have sprung up such as the

10 Op cit, passim.

11 Research Surveys of Great Britain Ltd, RSGB Omnibus Arts Survey: Report on a Survey on Arts and Cultural Activities in GB (London, Arts Council of Great Britain, 1991).

12 The Value of Music, National Music Council report into the value of the UK music industry (London, University of Westminster, 1996) p.2 (summary version).

13 Cited in a letter to the author from Roger Taylor, President, International Association of Music Libraries, Archives and Documentation Centres, 2 January 1997.

British Bluegrass Music Association and the British Association of Barbershop Singers. They bear witness to increased specialisation and a growing interest in the internationalisation of musical forms. The British Association of Symphonic Bands and Wind Ensembles (BASBWE) is tangible evidence of the growth of peripatetic music teaching since the war together with the increased popularity of certain woodwind instruments. Even inside the amateur world, we find the usual funding imbalances: of the principal music bodies, only NFMS, WAMF and BASBWE receive regular subsidy from central sources (although BFBB and the Brass Band Heritage Trust received small Arts Council of England (ACE) grants in 1997 for the first time).

Umbrella organisations offer a varying range of services, such as publications, insurance, training, libraries and the promotion of national events. Three of them also distribute grants; NFMS, which has branches in Scotland, Wales, Northern Ireland and the English regions, WAMF, and the British Federation of Youth Choirs (BFYC). In addition, Enterprise Music Scotland, set up in 1992 from a Scottish Arts Council initiative, supports, co-ordinates and develops 'voluntary music promoters' through grants and other means. The question arises (to be discussed in a later chapter) whether this role could be usefully expanded with the arrival of the new National Lottery scheme in England, *Arts4Everyone*, and its counterparts in Scotland, *New Directions*, in Wales, *Arts for All*, and in Northern Ireland, *Access to the Arts*.

In 1991 an umbrella association for amateur umbrella organisations, the Voluntary Arts Network (VAN), was founded under the presidency of a former Minister for the Arts, Sir Richard Luce. Its origins lay in a letter to *The Times* in 1984 by Sir Ian Hunter, advocating the establishment of a separate Arts Council for the amateur arts. Taking the hint, the Carnegie UK Trust convened a conference to discuss the amateur arts scene in Britain; a further conference in York led to VAN's creation. Its responsibilities cover all art-forms and it works with about 220 specialist umbrella bodies of which 54 are concerned with music.

The largest and, arguably, the most influential of the music umbrella bodies is NFMS, which represents the interests of some 1,700 organisations, including choirs, orchestras and music-promoting clubs. Together they present or promote 7,500 concerts each year to an aggregate audience of one and a half million.

Music has been something of an exception among the amateur art-forms, most of which stand in an uneasy relationship with professional practice.

> 'Voluntary promoters (music clubs, choirs, singers, orchestras and instrumentalists) provide a lot of employment for professionals; this is particularly valuable for young career musicians ... Amateur musicians also commission and perform works by professional composers: without their contribution, it is unlikely that much large-scale choral music would be written, much less heard. Amateur musicians also make up a significant proportion of audiences for professionals, and are important consumers for the music industry.'[14]

In fact, NFMS was founded in 1935 because of a concern to further the interests of professional musicians (in 1994 its members spent some £5,700,000 on professional engagements). Although the Musicians' Union is anxious about the threat posed by amateur performing groups undercutting professionals, it is widely accepted that the amateur sector is an informal training ground for aspirants to a musical career. Ruth Finnegan claims that 'professional music feeds directly on local amateur activities and would be impossible to sustain without them.'[15]

14 Cited in Hutchinson, Robert, and Feist, Andrew, *op cit*, p.106.

15 Finnegan, Ruth, *The Hidden Musicians, Music-making in an English Town* (Cambridge, Cambridge University Press, 1989).

Music societies, choirs, brass bands and festivals

Amateur classical musicians have a somewhat conservative image and are supposed to have little interest in playing contemporary works. This reputation is only partly deserved. The story of the nineteenth-century Potteries choirs with their enthusiasm for premiering oratorios by composers such as Elgar demonstrates a long-standing commitment to the new. Today arts funding bodies encourage music societies to develop commissioning policies. It is interesting to note that more than 50% of commissions funded by the Arts Council of Wales/Cyngor Celfyddydau Cymru (ACW/CCC) have been placed by, or written to involve, amateur music groups. The NFMS and the brass band movement have been commissioning new compositions for a number of years.

A remarkable new organisation has joined them in this work. Its origins lie in the East London Late Starters Orchestra (ELLSO) in Tower Hamlets, an amateur orchestra with a difference. Founded in 1982, it emerged from holiday music courses for London schoolchildren managed by Simon Foxley to which parents were also invited. This led to an adult education class which, in its turn, led to ELLSO. Membership is open to everyone who wants to learn to play a stringed instrument, regardless of background, education or income. Professional tuition is laid on (including an annual residential weekend) and the music played is scored at different ability levels for each instrument. Committed to overcoming the barriers to contemporary music and extending the repertoire for the amateur orchestra, ELLSO regularly commissions composers and encourages individuals and groups within ELLSO to write for it. It also works with professional orchestral players and ensembles.

An ambitious initiative emerged from the orchestra's 10th birthday celebrations, which, in essence, proposed to disseminate its philosophy of commissioning nation-wide. Called Contemporary Music-making for Amateurs (with the less than apt acronym, COMA), its founder director, Chris Shurety, set out to establish a UK-wide organisation whose central aim was to make up for a serious deficiency in much contemporary music – that it is too difficult for amateurs to play – by commissioning technically accessible music. Its 1994 annual report explains:

> 'Such works need to be suited to the forces generally available to amateur ensembles. This is not to say we are looking for "easy" music. Rather, we are aiming to generate a repertoire of artistically challenging music that is consistent with the composer's current artistic aspirations.'[16]

COMA was an almost instant success and has 10 regional branches in England and one each in Scotland, Wales and Ireland. A wide range of composers has become involved. A flavour of COMA's work can be suggested by two important events in 1996: Michael Finnissy conducted the COMA Ensemble in a performance of his piece, *Plain Harmony,* at the Huddersfield Contemporary Music Festival, and a key feature of the 1996 annual residential summer school was a major project based on John Cage's *Music Circus,* which involved participants composing much of their own material inside an overall structure devised by Stephen Montague. Daryl Runswick's reaction to working with COMA is typical of many composers who have had the same opportunity: 'As a contemporary composer you've never, ever, felt a buzz like the COMA summer course – 70 avid enthusiasts making music day and night, and not a note of Mozart or any other museum music to be heard.'[17]

The situation in Wales is generally more favourable to the amateur than that in England. As Emyr Jenkins, the Director of ACW/CCC, pointed out in 1994:

16 COMA, *Annual Report 1994*, London, p.5.

17 Runswick, Daryl, 'Composing for amateurs is composing for musicians', in *New Notes*, Society for the Promotion of New Music (SPNM) January 1997, p.1.

'Due to the historical background, ... the emphasis has been far greater on the amateur tradition and the status given to the amateur has been far higher than that given to the amateur in other parts of the United Kingdom.'[18]

WAMF serves over 350 affiliated societies throughout the principality, representing some 25,000 performers. These include brass bands, choirs, orchestras, amateur operatic societies and Welsh folk song and dance groups as well as community-based, multicultural and experimental projects.

It might be supposed that most of the United Kingdom's many amateur music clubs and societies make or listen to music for the joy of it and have few other motives for their activity. There is some truth in this, but the situation is changing, in large part thanks to the persuasion of NFMS. The Federation understands very well that it is not enough for its members to make or promote good music and sit on their laurels. It observes in its five-year development plan:

'Perhaps ... the nature of the people we are in today's complex society poses a threat [to the amateur tradition]? The tendency towards individualism; the sound-bite form of communication; low attention spans; the challenges to the traditional family unit; the changing nature of employment; careers; retirement – these are all challenges to what music societies do in the community and for the community.'[19]

There are two points being made here: firstly, music societies are not simply to be seen as groups of self-serving dilettantes but as community resources; and, secondly, to survive in today's changing world they need to be proactive. The NFMS is encouraging its members to take their music into the community and to prioritise the involvement of young people. Among the social trends influencing the traditional amateur sector, the most important is an ageing membership.

Research into young people's attitudes to the arts shows that a disappointingly small percentage are willing and active participants. According to NFMS:

'amateur music, as practised by music societies, is often perceived by those under 30 years of age to be a middle-class, middle-aged pastime ... Is it any wonder that young people find classical music unappealing when the concept of presentation has not changed fundamentally since the eighteenth century – even professional musicians still wear nineteenth century concert dress.'[20]

According to a study published by the National Foundation for Educational Research (NFER), slightly less than a third of young people (defined as those between the ages of 14 and 24) participate in an arts activity which they deemed creative and imaginative. A disproportionately large number come from professional backgrounds and/or are students in higher or further education; more females involve themselves in the arts than males and fewer members of ethnic minorities.[21]

Interestingly, of those young people able to offer a clear definition of the arts, a significant number see them in a somewhat narrow light:

'Many interviewees rated the "traditional" arts as not important to them, yet expressed an interest in cultural activities which they did not class as "the arts" or even "music", "drama", "literature" and so on (eg "I don't like the arts, but I like Bob Marley").'[22]

Actively engaged in, and sometimes even swamped by a ubiquitous 'common culture' they often cast a cold eye on the high arts, which they feel are not for them.

Last year, NFMS and one of its member societies, the Danesborough Chorus,

18 Jenkins, Emyr, *The Arts in a Time of Change*, National Eisteddfod of Wales, (Llandysul, Dyfed, Gomer Press, 1994) p.6.

19 NFMS – *Serving Music, Five Year Development Plan 1996-2000* (London, National Federation of Music Societies, 1996) p.9.

20 NFMS, *op cit*, p.6.

21 Harland, John, Hartley, Kate and Kinder, Kay, *Arts in their View: A study of youth participation in the arts* (Slough, Berkshire, National Foundation for Educational Research, 1995).

22 *Ibid*, p.114.

commissioned a small-scale, but suggestive, piece of research on the same theme.[23] Group discussions were held with sixth-form students, young chamber orchestra players, members of an amateur funk/blues band and an amateur brass band. The study found that family encouragement is important in developing musical interest; as a child grows up, music teachers and friends are key motivators (in the case of friends, 'not always because of shared musical interests – often it is being different from peers that counts').

A number of findings suggest the scale of the challenge confronting music societies. Very often young people will attend a concert only if they 'know one or more of the pieces being performed; know somebody who was performing; accompany family members or friends'.[24] Ticket prices can also be a factor, although usually a minor one. A major deterrent for those still at school is their lack of independence, whether financially or in terms of transport. There was widespread criticism of music teaching in schools where, it was felt, only certain forms of music are considered legitimate and of value. Few of those interviewed were familiar with choral music and fewer still were likely to attend choral events.

Some of the most forward-looking music societies are coming to acknowledge a wide-ranging cultural role and believe that they should go to considerable lengths to attract the interest of young people. Luton Music Club is an interesting case in point. Although the core of its programme is Western classical chamber and instrumental music, a few times a year they move into other fields, including traditional and world musics, jazz, early music and 'songs from the shows'. The club is tentatively engaging in educational initiatives. Chris Thomas, the secretary, writes:

> 'We are now arranging five or six workshops each season, on the afternoon of a normal concert and in a selected school ... We have also had children take part in an evening concert by the ensemble Gemini by preparing Maxwell Davies' *Kirkwall Shopping Songs* ... The important thing as far as we are concerned is to get the children to the evening concerts: many of them had never set foot in the theatre before let alone been to a live concert. We are not so altruistic that we are content to subsidise the schools budgets without some spin-off for ourselves – and of course, hopefully, the children. We are feeling our way at the moment and building on experience, but it is an exciting and very rewarding new development. It is important enough for us to have appointed one of our committee to be Schools Liaison Officer!'[25]

Luton's mix of idealism and calculation is enabling them to address the uphill task of recruiting new and younger members which faces many clubs and societies. According to recent research, 74% of members of societies belonging to NFMS are more than 40 years old.[26] Chris Thomas again:

> 'The older generations who do patronise us renew themselves: if they didn't, we would have all died off years ago! Having said all this, it is important to keep trying to improve the age ratio of one's audience. We can do this by broadening the range of music played and by schools liaisons ... but we should go further than that. Too many clubs present such a fuddy-duddy image through their publicity and concert presentation (although things are improving slowly, I may say) that it is no wonder younger people don't want to attend.'[27]

The Scottish branch of NFMS follows the same basic strategy as the headquarters body in London, but is less sure of the practicality of developing education and outreach. According to its five-year plan, the issue is under consideration. Its 1997 annual conference intends to examine 'traditional musics with the crossover between classical and traditional and [the] possibilities it presents to member societies'.[28] Some societies are

23 Kirkwood, Adrian, *Young People and their Approach to Musical Participation: A Study for the Danesborough Chorus and the National Federation of Music Societies*, funded by a 1995 BT Innovation Award, 1996 (unpublished).

24 *Ibid*, p.14.

25 Cited from a letter to the author from Chris Thomas, Secretary, Luton Music Club, 30 August 1996.

26 NFMS, *op cit*, p.6.

27 *Ibid*.

28 National Federation of Music Societies, Scotland: *Four Year Plan, 1997/8, 1998/9, 1999/2000, 2000/01* (unpublished) p.3.

engaging in community work; for example, the Strathaven Choral Society set up links with local schools and student composers. A presentation of Malcolm Arnold's *Tam o' Shanter* was taken to local schools where the society gave some workshops and schoolchildren joined the choir for its performance.

A glance at the 1996 BT Innovation Award winners for music societies demonstrates that the number of these projects is growing. Unsurprisingly, Strathaven appears on the list for its plans to involve pupils from six local primary schools in a project, *Lanarkshire Tapestry*, which aims to intermix local history, art, creative writing and musical composition; other awards went to the Studio Symphony Orchestra for a programme of concerts in deprived urban and rural areas of Northern Ireland, including two concerts in West Belfast on either side of the religious divide – one on the Shankill Road and the other on the Falls Road; and to the West Cumberland Choral Society for a proposal to encourage a wide age range of people in an isolated part of the country to become involved in the first performance of a new piece of music, a work by the Cumbrian composer, Roland Fudge, scored for chorus, children's chorus and instrumentation, and orchestra.

One might have thought that the enforced leisure brought about by rising unemployment in many strongly choral areas would have increased participation in music-making. But, by a strange paradox, the reverse has often been the case. Choral singing has been particularly badly affected by a lack of interest among school leavers and young adults; participation seems to pick up only among the mid-30 year-olds. This appears to have some connection with a decline in choral singing in schools. A Church of England report notes that in music teaching in schools, as in other subjects, 'the trend has been away from regimentation towards an individual approach and small group work.'[29] (It may be worth noting in passing that there is nothing new under the sun: as long ago as 1935, the musical establishment was worrying about the predicted demise of choral singing.)[30]

Wales offers a partial exception to the trend. In schools teaching in Welsh, the choral tradition is vigorous, if patchy. The Urdd Eisteddfod, for example, which involves thousands of young people in singing and other competitions, works closely with schools (especially Welsh-speaking schools). In 1996 there have been nearly 250 applications to join the National Youth Choir of Wales – more than double any previous entry. While adult male voice choirs are looking increasingly elderly, there has been a rise in the number of 'chamber choirs' (in part, because of unwanted reductions in membership, but also – and more significantly – out of financial considerations).

Music has long been an important aspect of organised religion and, despite a general decline of congregations, churches (especially of Nonconformist denominations) remain centres for participatory music-making. So far as the Church of England is concerned, a study in 1991 indicated that nearly two-thirds of churches have a choir and of that number more than 70% are in urban areas. One-fifth also have their own musical ensembles. The average church music budget is £350 a year. Cathedral choirs are on top form and standards are very high. In the parishes, the situation is more diverse. They are emerging from a transitional phase where the large traditional choir, representative of the parish as a whole, is often giving way to 'worship groups' where singing is accompanied by guitar, drum and some orchestral instruments and the musical style tends to be a variant on folk. One of the aims of this change was to attract young people to take part. There is no statistical information about the Roman Catholic Church, but liturgical reforms which place a strong emphasis on the participatory role of the congregation have led to a weakening in the importance of choirs. Much choral music is disappearing from the 'repertoire' because its texts were written in Latin which, since the reforms following

29 *In Tune with Heaven, The Report of the Archbishop's Commission on Church Music* (London, Church House Publishing and Hodder and Stoughton, 1992) p.133.

30 See Davies, Walford, Master of the King's Music, *News Chronicle Book of Part Songs* (London, 1935) introduction and preface.

Vatican II, is no longer used in church services. In the Free Churches the pattern of choral singing is stable and healthy, with an emphasis on congregational singing with support from instruments. It should be noted, of course, that in some revivalist congregations black gospel singing not only remains a powerful and essential component of worship, but is also an essential feature of the cultural life of the Afro-Caribbean community. Bucking the general rule, many black youngsters still follow the tradition of singing in choirs and later branch out into individual musical careers. Gospel music is attracting black audiences to mainstream venues, such as the Royal Albert Hall and the South Bank Centre.

Another significant factor has been the instrumental 'explosion' and many young people see choral singing as less glamorous and challenging than playing in an ensemble. No doubt this was one of the reasons for the Church of England's encouragement of its worship groups. According to a BFYC survey in 1991, 83.9% of children over 12 had no curriculum singing, with fewer than one in five schools having access to INSET (in-service training) courses in choral training. In primary schools, only one in four had any part-singing, with three-quarters of schools relying on non-specialist staff to teach music.[31]

The Church of England report adds:

> 'Not only do few children enter school with a wide repertoire of nursery and religious songs learnt at their parents' knees, but many primary schools lack a full-time specialist ... Many teenagers feel embarrassed when asked to sing ... Other than at football matches or on coach journeys, people sing less spontaneously than in previous generations. Even the great tradition of Welsh male-voice singing has declined, with fewer choirs and ageing membership.'[32]

In 1987, 26% of Welsh choral society members were under the age of 30,[33] but by 1996 this percentage had fallen to 18.5;[34] it should be added that the trend is most marked in single-sex choirs and that mixed choirs are more successful at maintaining a balance among the age groups. The greying of choirs has unhelpfully coincided with a decline in choral work with orchestras as a result of inadequate subsidies. The number of choral societies able to afford to employ a fully professional orchestra has decreased: a decade ago, for example, the City of Birmingham Symphony Orchestra would undertake some 20 choral society engagements each year, but now it plays for only two.[35] Choirs increasingly exploit the availability of good amateur and pick up (freelance) orchestras.

However, it doesn't do to be too gloomy. While choirs are having to cope with real difficulties, NFMS reports a positive indicator; its choral membership has risen from 700 societies 10 years ago to more than 1,000 today. While this may in part be due to the emergence of chamber choirs, to which I referred earlier, and to already established choirs enrolling for the first time, it is good evidence that, for all its difficulties, the choral tradition is more than holding its own. In Monmouth and Mold, for example, the choirs have recorded large increases in membership over the last 10 years; this has been due to the happy combination of the arrival of new conductors and concerted efforts to make the societies more 'user-friendly'. Under the auspices of the BT Innovation Awards, NFMS has sought to address the youth issue by publishing a guide, *How to Set up a Youth Choir*, which is full of practical tips and advice. The Sainsbury Youth Choir of the Year Award has also helped to give youth choirs a higher profile.

Brass bands appear to be the one major exception to the ageing membership syndrome. Like choirs, their tradition goes back to the Victorian era and they have had to cope with the challenges of the modern age. They have shown energy and flexibility. This, together with a strong family basis in the composition of bands, has meant that most bands have a

31 *Singing in Schools Survey* (Loughborough, British Federation of Youth choirs, 1991) *passim*.

32 *In Tune with Heaven, op cit*, p.135.

33 Eckstein, Jeremy, and Feist, Andrew, *Cultural Trends* 1991:12, Policy Studies Institute, London, p.35.

34 *Review of Activities*, Welsh Amateur Music Federation, Cardiff, autumn 1996, p.7.

35 NFMS Evidence to the House of Commons Select Committee for the National Heritage, November 1995, p.4. (It should be noted that these figures exclude youth choirs.)

wide age range of membership. There is an active youth band presence in the United Kingdom, with its own national championships and a National Youth Brass Band of Great Britain (NYBBGB), as well as National Youth Brass Bands in Scotland and Wales (NYBBW). A new charity, the Brass Band Heritage Trust, has been set up to advance the interests of youth brass bands and the brass band movement as a whole. It should also be recalled that the Salvation Army, with its extensive music programme and in-house music publications, places brass band music at the service of religion, as does the Boys' Brigade with its bugle bands in England and and pipe bands in Scotland..

As BFBB points out:

> 'somewhere near you can be pretty sure to find a brass band. Practising two or three nights a week, giving occasional concerts and "spots" at local events, taking part in regional and even national contests with other bands, involving teenagers and pensioners, fitters and financial analysts, all sharing the same enthusiasm and commitment to make music.'[36]

It is estimated that as many as 60,000 people take an active part in the movement. Competition is at the heart of brass band culture, with bands competing against each other for the best performances of 'test pieces'. Rather like football divisions they belong to different sections that indicate their playing quality (and ambitions) and have to qualify for promotion through the sections. National championships are held annually at the Royal Albert Hall and Wembley Conference Centres under the patronage of the music publisher, Boosey and Hawkes.

The BFBB, representing over 900 bands, is their national voice (there are also separate brass band associations in Wales, Scotland and England); there is a strong competitive element in the movement and there are some 80 or more bands linked to companies or corporate sponsors, of which 20 are, in effect, in a premier division. There are more than 1,200 so-called 'community' bands of whom about a third take part in competitions. Most of these are self-financing and little or no central or local government funding finds its way to them. If one recalls that there were more than 1,700 brass bands in 1938, it is clear that the movement has not lost its century-old momentum.

36 *Blowing (and Striking) a New Note*: a submission by the British Federation of Brass Bands and Brass Band Heritage Trust in response to the consultative Green Paper on publicly funded new music in England, May 1996, p.3.

37 *New Lottery Programmes: the brass band response*, a submission by the British Federation of Brass Bands in association with the Brass Band Heritage Trust to the Arts Council of England's consultative document, June 1996, p.8.

Just as choirs have suffered, so brass bands have benefited from the development of free instrumental teaching in schools. But with this service now being reorganised and reduced, BFBB acknowledges that 'the need for bands to be providers of tuition has once again arisen ... new initiatives urgently need developing including certification for "training the trainers".'[37]

Commissioning new music has been a feature of brass band practice since the 1930s, although this has not been without its critics in some quarters. Here there has been some funding, especially from Regional Arts Boards (RABs), although their Arts Council-inspired policies in favour of 'serious' music have sometimes militated against many bands' demand for high quality arrangements of popular standards and light music. The NYBBW has commissioned 15 new works in its 15-year history, all with help from ACW/CCC and WAMF. It is interesting to note that in 1996 the rigorous Society for the Promotion of New Music launched a series of brass band events featuring new commissions. In 1995 the Open Brass Band Championship commissioned Philip Wilby's *Symphony for Double Brass*: the composer has noted the practical value of new music in the context of competitions:

> 'Clearly the use of new music is both helpful and prestigious for the contest organiser; with unknown music every competitor starts from the same point. The eyes of the movement are inevitably drawn to a winning performance of a new work. There are

risks, of course, and the controversy which surrounds new scores is often a hard but vital cross to bear for composers and organisers alike.'[38]

For all that, there are in the brass band movement opponents to commissioning. Their hand is considerably strengthened by arts funding bodies' insistence on innovation. Bands do not see why music that is new, but not in the vanguard of contemporary practice, should often find itself excluded from subsidy. Not without reason, perhaps; what is aesthetically appropriate in the Purcell Room is not necessarily so in a Welsh town hall.

Brass bands are used to being self-sufficient and, although many have received support from the Arts Councils and English RABs, feel that their work is not always understood and valued (although the picture is changing rapidly, with nearly 160 Lottery awards worth £6.5 million having gone towards equipment purchase in the last couple of years). They raise money through the efforts of ladies' committees, business sponsors and special fund-raising events. 'Cultural Services officers of Local Authorities are usually considered unapproachable; the Regional Arts Board mechanisms for commissioning might as well be on another planet!'[39]

Many bands were associated with mining and heavy industry. The closure of mines and the crisis in manufacturing in the 1980s was a serious blow, for local communities were often no longer in a position to support their bands. In the old days, members of top bands were subsidised by colliery managements, which paid their wages but did not expect them to go down the pits. There has been an adjustment to new realities. Some bands died, but were soon revived. Local business now helps to fill the financial gap and the membership is not so exclusively working-class as it used to be. An increasing number of white-collar workers are joining up.

The movement faces new challenges. Although standards vary, it remains artistically vigorous. However, some observers argue that, as in the case of rugby football, the long-standing tradition of proud amateurism will have to give way to a more professional approach to management. Top section bands are run by paid administrators and it is an open secret that some of the best players are paid 'chair fees' in addition to expenses. A new generation of young players is emerging from specialist brass band university courses, but there is no career structure for them to enter. As the close-knit communities of the industrial past disappear, brass bands may be able to thrive and develop only if they adopt the techniques of the marketplace.

Competitive festivals have been an important feature of amateur music-making for more than 100 years. Although the principle of competition in the arts is more controversial than it used to be, they continue to thrive. The British Federation of Festivals for Music, Dance and Speech is the umbrella body for 325 festivals across the United Kingdom and in Ireland. The Federation also has overseas links in Bermuda, Hong Kong, Australia, Canada and Africa. The first records of competition festivals date from 1872, the same decade that saw the birth of organisations concerned with competitive sports (the Football Association was founded in 1873, Wimbledon in 1877 and Test Matches in 1878). The first known festival was the Workington Festival in Cumbria, which is still running to this day. As in the case of choral singing in the Pottery towns, composers such as Elgar, Holst and Bantock supported the festival movement and Vaughan Williams founded his own, the Leith Hill Musical Festival.

The Federation sees competition not as being important in itself but as a means to the attainment of high standards:

'The adjudicator needs to inspire greater appreciation of the work being performed and remarks made in public and on the written sheet for each performer, with an

38 *Ibid*, p.7.

39 *Ibid*, p.8.

evaluation of each performance, encourage the development of individual taste and judgment in the minds of the hearers. This is the real purpose of the Festival Movement, and the inspiration gained from the knowledge and help of skilled adjudicators raises standards in amateur work throughout the country.'[40]

The Federation also liaises with schools and partnerships have been set up where music and speech advisers use work performed at festivals as part of the music curriculum. Federation adjudicators have led teacher training days and workshop sessions at local festivals, bringing live performance, appraisal and listening to primary and junior school pupils. More and more festivals are showing an interest in South Asian musics and there has been a growth in facilities for disabled musicians.

There are of course many non-competitive festivals – more than 520, according to estimates. A remarkable organisation, Music for Youth, provides a framework for non-competitive festivals and concerts; in 1996 more than 41,000 young people applied to take part and the year culminated with a concert in Birmingham involving an 'orchestra' of 2,740 people under Sir Simon Rattle's baton. The number of festivals doubled in the 1980s and perhaps this represents a conscious reaction against home-centred cultural consumption. They rely heavily on voluntary support with amateurs and professionals working together in close harmony, and range from those organised entirely by local people to those which are administered by paid managements. Nearly 40% of festivals are run exclusively by volunteers and decide their programmes democratically after extensive consultation.

Irene McDonald, former Director of the King's Lynn Festival, told me:

'Festivals should be a flowering of what is happening in an area. At their best, they are the public appearance of a whole mass of activity that is already going on. If they don't reflect the aspirations and achievements of local people, the focus of the festival will have failed.'

Festivals are developing strategies to develop their audience profiles and are increasingly targeting groups in the community – young people, those from disadvantaged socio-economic classes and so forth – and often seek to widen their popular appeal through participative programmes of activity. So, for example, the Sidmouth International Folk Arts Festival involves more than 4,000 in workshops of various kinds.

As is the case with music societies, festival organisers are operating in a tough marketplace. Many volunteers would benefit from training in the setting of effective aims and objectives; good practice in management, fund-raising and marketing; and evaluation and monitoring skills.

A recent attempt to encourage music festivals was the establishment of National Music Day. Inspired by the hugely popular annual *Fête de la Musique* on Midsummer's Day in France, the then Minister for the Arts, Tim Renton, and the rock musician, Mick Jagger, launched a British equivalent in 1992. The concept was to persuade amateur and professional promoters to present musical events in a great simultaneous celebration during the last weekend in June. Specially staged large-scale concerts were mounted to provide a high media profile.

On paper the project has been a success; in 1996, National Music Day (supported by £140,000 worth of grants including £60,000 from the Department of National Heritage and £40,000 from ACE) listed 2,300 events which were attended by an estimated 3,700,000 people. Three million copies of the official guide were distributed. However, much of this activity was merely a re-labelling of performances which were going to take place in any event and, as the current Chief Executive of what is now called the National Music Festival has observed:

40 The British Federation of Festivals for Music, Dance and Speech, an undated promotional pamphlet.

> 'Whilst finding favour with a large number of event organisers, many of whom were novices, the concept failed to capture the imagination of the professional music industry, sponsors and the media. The perceived image of the " – Day" became generally Middle England, Middle of the Road and Middle Aged.'[41]

An attempt to create a link with the Euro 96 football competition failed to make much headway.

However, despite these difficulties, there was a Festival in 1997 (in August and pegged to the celebration of the 50th anniversary of Indian independence). It would appear that the organisers have not yet accomplished the feat of transforming a top-down governmental initiative into the genuinely grass-roots jamboree it was planned to be. But, if this can be achieved, there could be a not un-useful role for a yearly celebration of the value of music, and especially one that features participation by amateurs as well as professionals.

Non-European Minorities

It is quite wrong to think that people from non-European cultures made an appearance on these shores only after the Second World War. Ever since the British became world traders and set out on the long enterprise of building an empire, Africans, Asians and others came (often involuntarily) and settled here. In ports such as Bristol, Liverpool and London small communities established themselves.

However, it is only since the 1950s that large numbers have migrated to Britain. They were an uncovenanted legacy of empire and they brought many cultural gifts with them, although this has only recently begun to be appreciated. The earliest and most spectacular was the introduction of carnival from the Caribbean islands – a musical holiday of misrule. The Notting Hill Carnival in London emerged spontaneously in the 1960s from a context of ethnic discrimination and race riots as an expression of black consciousness and celebration. Internally, it survived managerial failure and divisions and, externally, official neglect and sometimes disapproval to become Europe's largest street festival. The bands, elaborate floats and colourful costumes are a remarkable expression of collective, (usually) non-professional artistry and attract massive multiracial audiences, which are, in fact, almost as much participants as spectators. The example of Notting Hill has spawned smaller carnivals in a number of provincial cities and helped popularise steel pan bands.

However, carnival aside, there is little evidence among black British citizens of analogues to indigenous amateur music-making. This is in good part a question of visibility rather than of absence. A number of musicians are interested in recovering lost traditional or folk musics, but they often operate more by word of mouth than through formal institutions and established promoters. An example of commitment to the practice of black indigenous music is the Carriacou big drum dance group in Huddersfield which has been performing music formats going back more than 400 years since the1950s. The main reason for this lies in the history of twentieth-century American and British popular and religious music. Jazz, pop and rock all owe a great deal to the music of Black Americans and new genres regularly emerge in the United States, the Caribbean or Britain – among them, reggae, rap, hip hop and jungle, whose impact sooner or later reaches beyond young black British people to the wider pop scene. So, in an important sense, black musical traditions and contemporary innovations are all around in mainstream popular culture.

One consequence is that much black music operates inside the commercial recording industry and, when it does not, aspires to do so. It is not surprising, therefore, that public sector funding

41 *National Music Festival 96, Interim Report as at 26 June 1996*, prepared by the Chief Executive, Keith R D Lownde FCA (unpublished report) p.1.

has been thin on the ground. The key challenge for young, up-and-coming musicians is to obtain commercial recognition or at least to get a first foot on the ladder. It is hard for them to attract the attention of an industry in which black people are seriously under-represented (although there are signs of embarrassed change in this respect). Young blacks also suspect discrimination in the broadcast media; where white bands get interviews on TV chat shows, black bands may simply be given a playing spot. Unsurprisingly black pirate radio stations are an important means by which young Afro-Caribbeans can communicate with one another and listen to the music they appreciate (garage, drum and bass and the like).

Although many millions of people listen to black music, indigenous newcomers often start their careers inside their own communities where the marketplace is, in the nature of things, small (the ethnic minority population in the United Kingdom is less than 3 million), and have a difficult time finding a commercially substantial audience. Keith Harris, lecturer, former recording company executive and chairman of the Arts Council-funded African and Caribbean Music Circuit, told me:

> 'Many kids take to their bedrooms and make music with digital technology, which they play to their friends. The fastest-rising street music is jungle, but none of the major record companies have taken it up.'

To a certain extent, the lack of a quick link into commerce has an advantage, in that it allows time for musicians to develop their work before it is assimilated. This is because the internationalism of black popular music makes local or national authenticity problematic. British black music is sometimes seen as derivative of the American scene and success can come on the other side of the Atlantic before it does in this country, even to the point where many listeners may mistakenly believe British musicians to be American.

However, more basic obstacles stand in the way of young black people (more often male than female). Economic deprivation, poor schooling and unemployment mean that their ambitions to enter the music business are seriously hampered by lack of training and basic equipment and facilities. Drum kits, steel pans and guitars are costly enough, but access to recording studios and rehearsal space are completely beyond most teenagers' pockets. A number of organisations up and down the country, which offer open-access recording studios targeted at community use, do their best to redress the situation, but they have to struggle against inadequate funding.

One example is Raw Material, a community project behind Kings Cross railway station in London, which introduces young black people to new music technologies. It has set itself social objectives to help alienated and unemployed youth in the locality, but its chief attraction to users lies in the fact that it offers potential entry into the commercial music business for ambitious youngsters. Founded in 1991 by Tim Brown, who once worked for the Inner London Education Authority at the Cockpit Theatre, it has no regular subsidy and has to devote much of its energies to fund-raising for specific projects. It provides access to well equipped studios and training courses. It works with, and offers services to, professional film-makers, community organisations and the like and enables participants to make a wide range of useful contacts.

Raw Material is realistic about the difficulties its trainees will face in entering the music profession and making it to stardom. It ensures that they have the skills not just to be recording artists, but to act as DJs, to stage events, run raves, become technicians and manage sound systems. Emphasis is placed on developing business expertise.

Local authorities and RABs in English conurbations support a range of music organisations of various kinds which, with varying degrees of success, seek to satisfy the needs of their black communities. Examples include The Drum in Birmingham; The Nia arts centre in Manchester; the Lewisham Music Academy, which, while not specifically a black project, offers training opportunities for young non-European musicians; and St Matthew's Church, the Brixton-based arts centre. St Matthew's is also the base for an innovative project, Digital Diaspora, which produces, promotes, markets and distributes black culture through the new technologies. It is piloting an Internet service dedicated to Afro-centric arts and promotes interactive live arts events involving digital technology. The African and Caribbean Music Circuit, founded by ACE, arranges regular tours.

A rich variety of South Asian communities live in this country.[42] Whether they are Bengali or Gujarati, Hindi or Muslim, music – often linked to dance and drama – is an important aspect of their social and religious lives. Economically more successful than many Afro-Caribbeans, they have a larger professional class of doctors, lawyers, teachers and businessmen. Conscious that their cultures are distinct from that of the West and committed to the extended family as a means of social development, South Asian communities tend to be economically self-sufficient and well organised.

What has become known as Indian classical music forms the basis of much cultural activity, although film music is also well-established; in recent years new hybrid genres such as bhangra have emerged. A growing number of musicians live and work in the United Kingdom, but links with the Indian subcontinent remain strong. Many leading artists tour this country or come over to offer training.

According to the recently published first edition of the Indian Subcontinent Asian Music Directory, about 60 clubs or voluntary associations present or support a range of musics.[43] The presence on this list of the Cleveland Society of Indian Doctors is an illustration of the organisational input of members of the professional classes. There are more than 10 agents, promoters or management companies. South Asian musics also benefit from the activities of organisations with a broad multicultural remit, such as the School of Oriental and African Studies (SOAS) at the University of London, the Commonwealth Institute, WOMAD, World Circuit Arts and the Asian Music Circuit (founded by ACE).

42 'South Asian' can be taken to refer, in geographical terms, to India, Pakistan, Bangladesh and Sri Lanka; however, many South Asian people living in the UK did not come directly from the subcontinent, but migrated from other parts of Asia or from Africa.

43 Muir, John, ed, *The Indian Subcontinent Asian Music Directory* (56 Longstone Road, Eastbourne, E Sussex, BN21 3JS, 1996).

44 Promotional leaflet, The Bhavan Centre (London, Institute of Indian Art and Culture, 1996).

A few higher education institutions offer educational opportunities in the field of South Asian musics, including Dartington Arts and International Summer School, Goldsmiths College at the University of London, the University of Kingston-upon-Thames, City of Leeds College of Music and the West London Institute of Higher Education. There is also a handful of independent schools or academies, of which the most influential is the Bhavan Centre in London.

One of an international network, it celebrates its 25th anniversary in 1998 (and the 60th of the foundation of the first centre in India). The Bhavan's mission is to preserve and study the cultural heritage of India; it 'tries to bridge the gap between the old and the new as well as between the immigrant and host communities'.[44] When it first opened, its main emphasis was on yoga training with a few music classes on the side. Now it runs three-year and five-year diploma classes in dance and music as well as introductory open classes. All the major music traditions are represented, together with the main dance styles including Bharatanatyam and Kathak. The Hindi, Gujarati, Tamil, Bengali and Sanskrit languages are taught. About 800 students are enrolled, of whom 10% are non-Indian.

Only a few go on to become professional musicians. Dr M Nandakumara, the Centre's Director, told me: 'Some become teachers or critics. But all of them will have come to understand Indian art and will make a good audience for the future.' The Bhavan attracts interest and commitment from family groups as well as individuals and a growing number of working-class South Asian people are becoming involved.

The Bhavan Centre is an extraordinary national resource, comparatively little known outside the communities it primarily serves, but it is less interested in the new innovatory and hybrid musics which many young Asians are developing than (in Dr Nandakumara's words) ensuring that 'modern generations, born here, do not lose a feeling for their roots'.

South Asian Music Performance and Dance (SAMPAD), a smaller, younger organisation based at *mac* (the Midlands Arts Centre) in Birmingham's Cannon Hill Park, would go along with the need to recover one's roots, but seeks actively to encourage new forms of music-making as well. It is a development agency for South Asian arts in Birmingham and the West Midlands and aims to increase opportunities for appreciation and participation at all levels, as well as 'creating greater cultural empathy locally, nationally and beyond'. Originally concentrating on music and dance, it has broadened its remit to cover the whole field of South Asian arts – including mime, storytelling, theatre, textiles, crafts and combined arts work. As well as engaging in community projects, it works in the formal education sector and helps schools to deliver the objectives of the national music curriculum.

In addition to celebrating the great traditions of the past, SAMPAD supports arts practice as it changes and develops among communities where new generations of young South Asians respond to the experiences of life in contemporary Britain. It is a philosophy which Naseem Khan, chair of ADITI (the National Development Agency for Asian Dance), articulated:

> 'The distinctive nature of South Asian arts should also be understood. They are informed by a vital but under-regarded groundswell of community-based work, including the popular bhangra and commercial arts. This does not feature on the approved cultural map.'[45]

It ought to do so, because music-making among young Asians is a strong and rising trend that deserves acknowledgment. It is usually commercially-oriented and blends Western and Asian traditions. Groups play at weddings and community occasions. Fusion bands such as Fun-de-mental are extremely popular and British bhangra has been exported to India.

Many other cultures from across the world, from Vietnam to Eritrea, are represented by small settled communities in different parts of the United Kingdom, but most notably in London. To varying degrees they maintain their sense of cultural identity through the promotion of arts events, and local authorities give *ad hoc* support from time to time.

Thus, there are substantial and long-established Chinese communities, some originating from Hong Kong, in London, Manchester and Liverpool, as well as families dispersed throughout the country, mainly working in the restaurant and food retail trades. Chinese New Year Festivals are familiar features in a number of British cities, but there is comparatively little general awareness of Chinese culture and limited interaction between the Chinese and the rest of British society. It was with this in mind that the Chinese Cultural Centre in London was established in 1986; it organises music and dance events, cultural exhibitions and an annual Chinese New Year Festival. One of its offshoots is the London Chinese orchestra, the first professional Chinese music ensemble in the United Kingdom which seeks not only to popularise Chinese music but to experiment with new styles and techniques. Since 1987 it has commissioned a number of new and arranged works and as well as presenting concerts, at a range of venues including the Purcell Room and the Queen Elizabeth Hall at the South Bank Centre, organises workshops and outreach activities.

45 *Summary of Speakers and Discussions, South Asian Performing Arts Conference*, promoted by SAMPAD and *mac* at the Midlands Arts Centre, Birmingham (unpublished report, 1994).

Jazz, rock and pop

Jazz is a participatory musical form *par excellence*, because improvisation lies at its heart. The term encompasses a very wide range of practice and jazz techniques have influenced a number of other genres, from folk to classical. They have extended the range of the trumpet, trombone and saxophone and composers or arrangers customarily write trumpet parts an octave higher that would have been the norm for the instrument in the 1920s. Originating from – and still dominated by – American black musicians, jazz has had many black players in Britain since the 1950s, although this was not always acknowledged by established jazz musicians and promoters and influential bodies such as the Arts Council and the BBC. Recent years have seen the emergence of a new wave of authentically black jazz (for example, the group Black Warriors). There are many jazz bands in schools and orchestral composers often make use of the jazz idiom. From being an oppositional and socially somewhat disreputable form it has become established and, in a certain sense, 'classical'.

Jazz is played throughout the country and no major city is without a lively jazz scene. British musicians have attained international reputations. Two specialist commercial radio stations, Jazz FM, for London listeners, and Jazz FM North West, have come into being in recent years. There has been a marked increase in jazz festivals in the United Kingdom from 10 in 1980 to 39 in 1992, ranging in scope from the Ealing Jazz Festival for local musicians living in the area to major international festivals in Brecon, Birmingham and Glasgow. The annual audience for live jazz events is about 3 million. Market research points to 8.6 million having an interest in jazz without attending events; 4.1 million watched jazz on TV and did not attend and 4.5 million listened to jazz on radio, but neither attended events nor watched jazz on television.[46]

There is a National Jazz Archive, which safeguards recorded jazz music (although not publications), a number of magazines dealing specifically with jazz, together with more specialised journals covering particular areas (eg *Big Bands International*).

Only 7.4% of current attenders are aged between 15 and 34. This appears to be a better record than for ballet, opera and classical music, but it does suggest a need to encourage young people to interest themselves in jazz. Such local jazz information as there is is tilted towards 'white' youngsters and tends not to cater for the black community. Jazz Services, which was formed more than 10 years ago to promote the growth and development of jazz, sees education and training as key priorities in its work. Its educational strategy (in association with Access to Music, an independent music support service and training organisation) focuses on information provision and networking; training; developing materials for the national music curriculum; and providing advocacy for jazz throughout the educational system. There is a National Youth Jazz Orchestra and a Young Jazz Competition, as well as a number of youth jazz orchestras in the regions, such as the Doncaster Youth Jazz Orchestra. There are also black youth jazz groups – among them Quite Sane and Tomorrow's Warriors.

Jazz Link 96 toured showcase events to groups of schools. A training programme for musicians to gain diplomas (NVQ Level 4) to enable them to work in the classroom with teachers has been set up. A report on jazz education techniques in relation to the curriculum and a materials pack is in preparation for dissemination to schools.

Opportunities for young people to play jazz outside school are unsatisfactory and Jazz Services argues: 'What is needed is a network of rehearsal studios and recording facilities that are easily and economically accessed.'[47]

46 *Arts and Cultural Activities in Great Britain*, Research Surveys of Great Britain (Arts Council of Great Britain, 1991) pp.7 and 135.

47 *Striking a New Note*, Jazz Services' response to the Arts Council of England's Green Paper, *Striking a New Note*, (London, Jazz Services Ltd, undated) p.4.

Jazz Services, supported by ACE, also organises tours and events, runs a comprehensive jazz database, offers marketing services and publishes a national magazine, *Jazz UK*. There are three regional jazz organisations in England (South West Jazz, Jazz Action and Jazz North West), the Welsh Jazz Society and in Scotland Assembly Direct Ltd, all of them receiving public subsidy. There are a number of specialist jazz societies throughout the country relying on voluntary help and self-funding.

The distinction between professional and amateur is more than usually complicated in jazz. A few top-class musicians are not full-time professionals; some amateurs have earned a living from time to time from jazz and there are a substantial number of 'pro-ams'. About a thousand professionals and semi-professionals are members of the Musicians' Union and perhaps a similar number in the same categories are not. The amateur sector (that is, those who play for pleasure and do not make a living, or part of their living, from music) is proportionately smaller than in (say) classical music. It is estimated that amateurs make up perhaps two-fifths of jazz musicians. Jazz is performed in a wide variety of settings including concert halls, arts centres, village halls, ballrooms, restaurants, coffee houses and public houses.

According to Chris Hodgkins, director of Jazz Services, jazz is to certain extent a victim of its own success. Because its vocabulary has infiltrated other genres, there is a risk that it will fail to be sufficiently differentiated from other kinds of music. So, for example, orchestral musicians experimenting with improvisation often use jazz techniques. There is a defensive feeling in the jazz movement that it is important, both for artistic and for marketing reasons, to preserve the integrity and authenticity of jazz as a musical form.

Participation in rock and pop is a largely uncharted field. Anecdotal evidence suggests that in every part of the country young people – especially young men – see listening to and playing music as a central feature of their lives. It is part of what constitutes youth culture. Young people see the arts in a rather different way from their elders. Together with fashion and various forms of mass entertainment they are a means of asserting a particular lifestyle. As Paul Willis observes:

> 'In amongst the plethora of expressions which help to constitute the different cultural fields of the young are some which are made to "come alive" to some degree: a particular pop song suddenly evoking and coming to represent an intense personal episode or experience; a dramatic situation paralleling and illuminating dilemmas and problems in the family, with friends, or at school or college; a look in a fashion magazine sparking new ideas for personal style or adornment. Such items can be symbolically appropriated to produce a cutting edge of meaning which not only reflects or repeats what exists, but creatively transforms what exists – previous personal experience and hopes for the future being reorganised, made more understandable or handle-able; externally provided expressions changed by being made to signify in new and personally "significant" ways. Thus charged, both experience and representation can further change, interact and develop through the processes of creative consumption, creative perception and re-perception.'[48]

It would be wrong to suppose that that there is a single, universal youth culture. In fact, there are many and plenty of young people have less interest in music than in sport, which they enjoy as participants and spectators. Also, it is a little surprising to note that, according to the National Foundation for Educational Research's (NFER's) recent survey into youth participation in the arts, dance, drawing and sketching, and photography are more popular leisure time activities than music-making, in which just 23% of respondents indicated 'a great deal' or 'some' interest.[49]

48 Willis, Paul, *Moving Culture, an enquiry into the cultural activities of young people* (London, Calouste Gulbenkian Foundation, 1990) p.14.

49 Harland, John, Hartley, Kate and Kinder, Kay, *op cit,* p.70.

Nevertheless, a substantial number of teenagers and men and women in their early twenties actively engage in the musical process and a high proportion of them are attracted to rock and pop (if not exclusively). NFER reports: 'Bands and groups of all types were a focus of enthusiasm for most young musicians and boys very commonly formed rock and pop groups, often when still at school.'[50] The study shows that the general imbalance of involvement in favour of those from higher socio-economic classes across the art-forms applies in this area of musical activity as well.

> 'Even rock music, which was expected to be associated with working-class cultural creativity, was often found to be more accessible to those who had benefited from middle-class upbringings which offered the resources and positive attitudes to encourage musical and artistic involvement from an early age'.[51]

Despite this evidence of limited access for some sectors of the population, arts funding agencies find it difficult to know whether or not they should intervene in what is for them largely unknown territory – and, if so, what they should do. They fear that in what is a ruthlessly competitive commercial field it would be only too easy to clog the market with unwanted bands and recordings.

The exception is Northern Ireland where rock and pop bands often join Music Collectives which provide rehearsal space and studio equipment; three of them are directly funded by the Arts Council of Northern Ireland (ACNI). It also supports two groups, Songwriters' Session and the Songwriters and Composers' Guild, both of which are involved in rock and pop. As I mentioned above, the North-South organisation, the Federation of Music Collectives, based in Dublin and with funding from the Irish Arts Council, is an umbrella body for the island as a whole and has a responsibility for encouraging work in this field. In fact, although strictly speaking this falls outside my remit, the Irish Arts Council has a distinguished track record in supporting popular musics and created a Popular Music Officer post in 1988 with the support of the group U2. Later the post was transferred into a new, independent organisation, Music Base, funded by the Council.

In England, things are not quite so far advanced. In the Northern region, a serious effort has been undertaken to find out what is going on. A local University of Newcastle survey gives an estimate of the scale of rock and pop activity. About 500 people are employed in music industry services and there are about 500 full-time musicians with (it is guessed) at least another 1,000 part-timers. Of the 150 live music venues, about 70 are major halls, pubs and arts centres and the remainder social clubs, clubs or occasional pub venues. Twenty management and promotion companies and 34 recording studios support the rock and pop scene and there are 10 locally-based recording companies.[52]

In the East Midlands the picture appears to be much the same, according to an East Midlands Arts handbook.[53] There are 75 different venues, 16 managers, agents and promoters, 31 recording and rehearsal studios and 14 locally-based recording companies.

The RABs in these two areas of the country have adopted different approaches. Northern Arts conducted a review of music in its region in 1995. The review team acknowledged that previously the RAB had had 'little direct contact with the popular music industry' on the grounds that it was 'commercial in nature' and, where it was not, was more properly the responsibility of local authorities or local arts development bodies. But it was now time to become more actively involved. A proposal to establish a regional agency was considered but rejected because it was feared that the rock and pop constituency would be suspicious of what they would see as undue centralisation.

50 *Ibid*, p.90.

51 *Ibid*, p.91.

52 *A Review of Music in the Northern Arts Region* (citing a study by the Cultural Industries Research Unit of the University of Newcastle-upon-Tyne's Centre for Urban and Regional Development Studies) (Northern Arts, Newcastle-upon-Tyne, October 1995) p.36.

53 *Guide to Rock and Pop* (Loughborough, East Midlands Arts, undated).

The review took a cautious line on recording:

> 'In the Contemporary Popular and Rock music area there is a continuing demand for assistance with the production of demo discs. However, markets for locally produced products are very limited and contrary to popular myth fame and fortune are not usually found by an A&R scout in London or New York finding a locally produced recording irresistible ... The Review Team recommends that Northern Arts should leave the recording business to the commercial marketplace at the present time.'[54]

Certain (one senses) only of its uncertainty, the team very sensibly proposed the appointment of a Venue Development Officer on a fixed-term contract, whose task would be to prepare a venue development strategy. However, Northern Arts has not yet been able to muster the resources to put this recommendation into effect. At present, it is restricting its efforts to modest support for Generator, a not-for-profit arts organisation which provides training and other services for rock and pop musicians in the Newcastle-upon-Tyne area.

By contrast, East Midlands Arts boldly determined to make a direct intervention. In 1994 it identified a gap in its arts provision for young people and decided that an investment in rock and pop would not only be a good way of filling it, but would enable it to address questions arising from the rapid development of new technology. It appointed five rock and pop development workers to help musicians at the grassroots level. It has also published a handbook with contacts listings and a section of practical guidance for musicians; a number of funding schemes have been put in place to encourage regional touring, audience development and support for gig promotions and recordings.

Marcel Jenkins of East Midlands Arts told me:

> 'What's needed is not enthusiasm, but access to skills and career development. Regular showcases are presented every three months or so which tour around the region. The lack of good venues is a major problem and we are trying to persuade brewers and so forth to provide them. We are trying as hard as we can to make the system as non-bureaucratic as possible.'

Unfortunately, although there is evidence that bands are calling for the appointment of more development workers, the RAB has not yet fully evaluated the success of its new policy. This is an urgent task, for study of the handbook suggests that the Board is not as street-wise as it could be; both in its advice – which does not always seem consistent – and its listings, it seems insufficiently aware that rock and pop is a field not always noted for sound business practices and financial probity.

It is hard to avoid concluding that there is a case for a national study of the rock and pop scene followed by a debate among the funding bodies, the industry and musicians. It may well be that this is an area where public support is not needed, although if it is true that there are difficulties of access to skills and facilities for some young people, modest schemes like those in the East Midlands may well be timely and useful. At present, though, too little is known to make a judgment.

There is rather more activity in the educational and training field. A music service and training agency such as Access to Music (which was formed in 1992 by a former local education authority senior music adviser 'to provide a range of services which would continue some of the good work established by the Music Advisory Service') specialises in the field of contemporary and popular musics and offers a two-year foundation course in Contemporary Popular Musics in association with the Colchester Institute. From this kind of course it possible to progress to degree and diploma courses (for example, in Media and

54 *A Review of Music in the Northern Arts Region, op cit*, p.25

Popular Music or Popular Music and recording at University College, Salford; Popular Music Studies at University College, Bretton Hall; or a BTEC Higher National Diploma in Musical Instrument Technology or a Postgraduate Diploma in Jazz, Contemporary and Popular Music at the City of Leeds College of Music).

Folk and traditional musics

Towards the end of the 1800s, it was realised with dismay that the old musics of the British Isles were facing extinction. Folk and the traditional musics of the countryside were threatened by the movement of population into the industrial cities and by the growing mechanisation of agriculture. After the Great War suburbanisation, fuelled by rising mobility and demands for higher-quality housing in more pleasant surroundings, stimulated a reverse trend with city dwellers moving out into rural areas and urbanising the countryside. A folk movement, institutionalised in the Folk Song Society founded in 1898 and the English Folk Dance Society (1911), followed by their amalgamation in 1932 as the English Folk Dance and Song Society (EFDSS), sought to halt the decline of the old performing arts. Wales has its own National Folk Song Society, Cymdeithas Alawon Gwerin Cymru, which was founded in 1908; the National Folk Dance Society of Wales; and, from 1996, the Society for the Traditional Instruments of Wales, Cymdeithas Offerynnau Traddodiadol Cymru.

Despite a major internal dispute in the 1980s, the EFDSS, with a small regular grant from the Sports Council, is still the largest of the folk dance and song societies, with nearly 6,000 members in 1990. In essence, its mission is to rescue and record as much as possible of what survives of the mainly oral folk tradition and to revive its practice. Morris dancing is supported by a number of societies; the Morris Ring, the Morris Federation and Open Morris. In Wales there is the National Folk Dance Society and in Scotland the Traditional Music and Song Association of Scotland, supported by the Scottish Arts Council (SAC), the Royal Scottish Pipe Band Association with a playing membership of around 400 bands in the United Kingdom, and the Royal Scottish Country Dance Society with a world-wide membership of nearly 30,000. There is a host of other amateur federations and societies, some operating internationally, which support different aspects of folk music and song: they include The Bagpipe Society, The West Country Concertinas, Northumbrian Pipers' Society, The West Gallery Music Association, Hands On Music, the Yorkshire Fiddle Club, the whole Irish music scene supported through the UK branches of Comhaltas Ceoltoiri Eireann (often linked to Irish Centres) and many more.

More recent initiatives have sought not just to preserve the past but to re-invigorate folk so that it could become an expression of contemporary concerns. At the BBC in Manchester before the Second World War, Joan Littlewood learnt the dramatic value of popular music hall song and in the 1950s and 1960s Charles Parker's radio ballads used folk and popular tunes and songs to celebrate the achievements and sufferings of the industrial working class. Under the inspiration of musicians like Ewan McColl and others, a large number of folk music clubs mushroomed in the late 1950s; although some argue that the folk club movement began to decline in the late 1980s, there are still more than 800 in Great Britain which regularly book guest performers. Ros Rigby of Folkworks writes:

> 'At the heart of the clubs' ethos was, and still is, the opportunity for local people to perform in an encouraging atmosphere, often at the start of an evening prior to an invited guest. Although there are not the number of clubs in existence now, there are still some very effective ones, and there is no doubt that this movement has provided a

way into folk music for tens of thousands of people over the last 40 years.'[55]

Similarly folk festivals, sometimes organised by folk clubs, started to spring up from the late 1950s onwards and also provided opportunities for informal playing and singing alongside their concert programmes. Many now run programmes of workshops, notably Sidmouth and Whitby.

In the last 10 years the arts funding system has recognised the contribution folk arts make to the arts as a whole and has supported a range of 'folk development agencies' with one or more staff. This has enabled musicians to do more educational work and has stimulated the development of innovative touring projects. Some of today's activists believe that a tradition is only really alive if it creates new work which adds to and enriches material from the past. Roger Watson of Traditional Arts Projects told me:

> 'The musical material shows whether or not there is a distinctive tradition. But it is the effects of process on that material that determines whether or not the material is alive. I'll give you an example with a particular song. In 1814 you could have bought a broadsheet of *The Dark-Eyed Sailor*, which is part of that family of songs called the "broken token ballads" that date from the Crusades. A year later you could have found a song with the same storyline and even some of the same lines, called *The Plains of Waterloo*. That is what I mean by process. The first song didn't cancel out the second, but now we had another option. The process of tradition is life, death, life. Once a piece of musical material loses its relevance, it is time to put it in a museum.'

Folkworks is a fine example of this attitude of mind: founded eight years ago by Alistair Anderson, the Northumbrian pipe player and composer, and Ros Rigby, with the active support of Northern Arts, it set itself the aim of involving as many people as possible in the folk arts. Based in the North of England, it has gradually become an influential force on the national scene. It promotes tours, festivals and a variety of training and education courses. It places its emphasis on music in a traditional idiom, interpreted broadly as 'people's music', and, although in its early years it focused on British traditions, it has since widened its scope to embrace other parts of Europe and the world.

Folkworks has always seen its role both as raising the profile of folk arts and offering opportunities for participation. Its educational work now includes in-service teacher-training (INSET) projects and collaborations with schools, colleges and universities – among them a GCSE composition module for 10 year-olds at Gosforth High School, a module in world musics for a BEd music degree course and a module in Northumbrian music at the University of Newcastle. It seeks to develop young audiences, especially outside conventional venues, and sees a future as the holder of a specialist instruments bank. Mainly funded by Northern Arts, the Arts Council and northern local authorities, it is increasingly attracting sponsorship by local and national businesses.

Folkworks' motto or sub-title is 'Tradition in the making' and they are concerned to encourage new music. A songwriting project and tour in autumn 1996 was characteristic of their approach: this was a series of workshops by leading songwriters who introduced participants to the skills of song writing in 10 selected communities nation-wide. They culminated in a concert at which some of the songs were premiered.

Folkworks is by no means unique in its work or policies. A number of other agencies up and down the country act as promoters and developers of traditional musics, collaborating with schools, presenting festivals and encouraging local musicians. One of these is Folk South West, set up by South West Arts and based in Somerset. Another,

55 Letter from Ros Rigby to the author, 27 March 1997.

TRADS, a folk development project in East and West Sussex, pays special attention to local folk arts. In their view, 'the reviving of a once regular, but now long forgotten, local event can both remind those who are local-born of their own heritage and teach newcomers something of the area in which they have chosen to live.' In recent years, TRADS have put two events back onto the East Sussex calendar – the traditional November Blacksmiths' Procession in Mayfield and the wassailing of apple trees in Waldron. A key priority is to persuade the relevant communities to take over such events and repeat them in successive years.

In Lincolnshire, where the composer Percy Grainger cycled from village to village collecting folk songs on phonograph cylinders at the beginning of the century, South Kesteven District Council has appointed a folk arts community worker, Sally Brown, who works on a range of education, community and general arts projects. The EFDSS has an education department (supported by the Sports Council) which works with teachers and in schools with a special emphasis on giving children opportunities for active participation in folk music and dance.

BBC Radio 2 has played an important part in encouraging traditional musics through its weekly *Folk on Two* programme and the annual Young Tradition Award.

One of the most striking aspects of the Scottish musical scene has been the renaissance of traditional Gaelic musics. In the past they were divided into separate, self-sufficient 'worlds', such as Highland dancing, social and country dancing, piping, accordion and fiddle clubs, Reel and Strathspey societies (fiddle) and folk music, and tended to encourage individual prowess rather than music as a social function. However, today there is greater interaction among the different genres than ever before.

Many Scottish musicians and cultural campaigners place a high priority on attracting young people's participation in traditional musics through training and work in schools. The Fèis (festival) movement is a case in point. It started on the Isle of Barra in 1981 where parents decided that their children were not being taught about their language and culture in school. According to its umbrella body, Fèisean nan Gàidheal:

> 'A fèis is an opportunity for young people to come together to be taught skills in Gaelic arts, such as singing, dancing, drama and traditional music instruments. This is done in a fun, but nonetheless meaningful and professional way, with most fèisean taking place over a week. There is however a tremendous amount of follow-on activity now being generated to ensure that the work is not limited to that one week per annum.'[56]

It is one of the country's most successful community arts initiatives and there are now at least 25 tuition-based fèisean every year; in 1995-6 1,972 students received training from 356 tutors. Fèisean have received little support from the formal education sector, but are an influential component of a wider movement to promote Scottish national identity. According to a recent study, fèisean can be shown to contribute to individual and personal development, social cohesion, community empowerment, local image and identity, people's sense of creativity and, even, to their health.

> 'The fèisean have a galvanising effect of participants' sense on identity and their interest in Highland culture, especially among young people who sometimes express newly-positive feelings about the area.'[57]

Edinburgh's Adult Education Project (ALP) was formed in 1988 as part of Lothian Regional Council's Community Education Department and launched a programme of classes and events under the heading 'Scotland and its People'. Its philosophy owes a good

56 Fèisean nan Gàidheal, *Fèis Facts: An information leaflet for the Highland Council* (Portree, 1996).

57 Matarasso, François, *Northern Lights: The Social Impact of Fèisean (Gaelic Festivals)* (Stroud, Comedia, 1996) p.3.

deal to the ideas of the Brazilian educator and Christian Marxist, Paolo Friere. The programme concentrated on historical, political and cultural topics (such as land issues, adult literacy and women's history). ALP is managed by its participants (unlike many adult education projects) and their debate-based investigations led to the formation of the ALP Music Group six years ago which runs a large number of training workshops and performance events, grounded firmly in the perception of a national culture needing to free itself from its neo-colonial past.

The Music Group set itself a radical agenda. According to its statement of aims:

> ' ... in deciding how to set up the music programme, [it] debated a number of issues relating to the ... state of Scots music: the question of [why] it had moved so much to the social margins, being perceived as a hobby rather than (as in Ireland, for instance) a vital part of the national culture; historical factors such as the repression of music by the church, the militarisation and privatisation of pipe music, the Victorian upper class colonisation of the land and culture, the music's transition from an integral part of everyday life and celebration in the community to a minority commodity found largely in a closed world of clubs and societies each imposing its own orthodoxy.'

A key question was how to maintain 'purity, respect and continuity with the past' while encouraging accessibility, innovation and contemporary relevance. There is surely no single answer, but what can be said is that, in the setting of a resurgent Scottish culture, the music scene is various and hybrid, traditional musics mingling with rock and professionals with amateurs. Stan Reeves of ALP writes:

> 'It would seem a warm wind of change is blowing into the stoorie neuks of the music. Scots bands like Runrig and Capercaillie dip into the well of the music and bring in huge audiences looking for a new way of identifying themselves as Scots.'[58]

A study has been conducted into the desirability of creating a Traditional Music Development Agency, and the SAC may establish an in-house function with a view to making it independent once it is safely up and running.

Cultural nationalism is a vital force in Wales too, but takes different forms and places special emphasis on the Welsh language (which unlike Gaelic is an officially recognised language in the United Kingdom). A key element is the institution of the eisteddfod – a competitive festival which encompasses all the arts – music, dance, drama, literature and the fine arts. Evolving from bardic tournaments in the remote past, today's festival – with its Celtic apparatus of Druids and Archdruids, white robes and golden regalia – stemmed in large part from the eighteenth-century re-invention of the antique Gorsedd of Bards. The first recognisably modern national eisteddfod took place in 1861.

Today the Royal National Eisteddfod of Wales (RNEW) is one of Europe's largest competitive festivals and attracts annually about 150,000 visitors. More than 200 competitions are held, many of them musical, and about 50 to 60 choirs take part. An International Musical Eisteddfod takes place annually in Llangollen. RNEW sits at the top of a pyramid of county and local eisteddfodau (some in better health than others, but all of them active) which can be seen in part as preparatory to the RNE. Amongst other things, the eisteddfodau celebrate the Welsh tradition of amateur music-making, bringing together folk, hymns and other choral singing and form a key focus for the assertion of Welsh identity.

It will surprise few readers that the political divisions in Northern Ireland have left their mark on traditional music-making in the province. As in Scotland, the popularity of folk traditions is not only an artistic but also, in some eyes, a cultural and political project. This

58 Reeves Stan, *Scottish Traditional Music and Song – Beating the Cringe!* Alpworks (in-house ALP magazine), issue 2, May 1993, Edinburgh, p.6.

is especially, but by no means exclusively, true for the nationalist community. So far as the Loyalists are concerned, marching bands are a crucial feature of their cultural identity, although it should not be forgotten that they also play a role among the Catholic population. Three points should be borne in mind. First, much traditional music reflects Irish culture as a whole and does not necessarily reflect state frontiers. A second and related factor is that, beneath the noise of political rhetoric, many believe that both public and players see traditional musics as part of a common culture. Thirdly, there is less interest in 'hybrid' forms than on mainland Britain, a possible consequence of the fact that traditional music has always been a living force and did not need to be 'revived' in quite the same way as in Scotland and England.

National sentiment is also a feature of the musics of other European countries, some of which can be sampled in the United Kingdom. If the twentieth century has been one of war and revolution, it has also, and in consequence, been one of migration. Refugees from Europe's two great wars, from the Soviet revolution and the Nazis and other political or economic crises have found shelter in Britain. Many British cities are home to settled communities from various European nations, including the Ukraine, Poland and the former Yugoslavia, for whom traditional music and dance are a means of recalling and celebrating their cultural identities.

In conclusion, for all their abundance and variety, Britain's participatory musics have been regarded at best with indifference. Little valued or noticed except by those involved and in the back pages of local newspapers, they become invisible. However, the climate of opinion is growing much less wintry. A picture emerges not simply of bustling activity and tireless self-sufficiency, but of change and self-improvement. We see artistic and practical collaborations among different genres and groups. Amateurs are coming to believe that they make music not just for the love of it, but, through educational projects, to stimulate love of it in other people. Regenerated folk happily joins hands with rock, brass bands emerge largely unscathed from the collapse of the industrial communities that brought them into being. Composers work for non-professional ensembles.

This is not to say that everything in the garden is as it should be. If one does not come from a family or a local community with music in its tradition, it is not so easy to make the right contacts or to know where to go to find like-minded enthusiasts. The falling away of interest in music after school or college is a problem that few are successfully addressing. The key issue is one of information and publicity and, as I argue in the final chapter, a priority for those concerned to promote the cause of participatory music must be to create some kind of information network within the reach of all. There are other more specialised difficulties that need to be overcome. In rock and pop young people struggle unaided to make music, while in choral singing (with the exception of black gospel music) they are conspicuous by their absence. There is a widespread lack of training on the practical business of fund-raising and management. Rehearsal and performing spaces are increasingly hard to come by at a reasonable cost or of a reasonable quality and in some fields the high price of instruments is an obstacle to progress.

None of these challenges in insurmountable. In, fact a good deal of energy is being spent on tackling them. Music activists and, as we will see, the arts funding system, fuelled by the National Lottery, are turning their attention to finding sensible and affordable solutions. Although much remains to be done, it is hard to resist the impression, when surveying the scene, of a sleeping giant stirring itself into life.

photo: Anne Rogers

3 TRANSFORMING
THE CURRICULUM

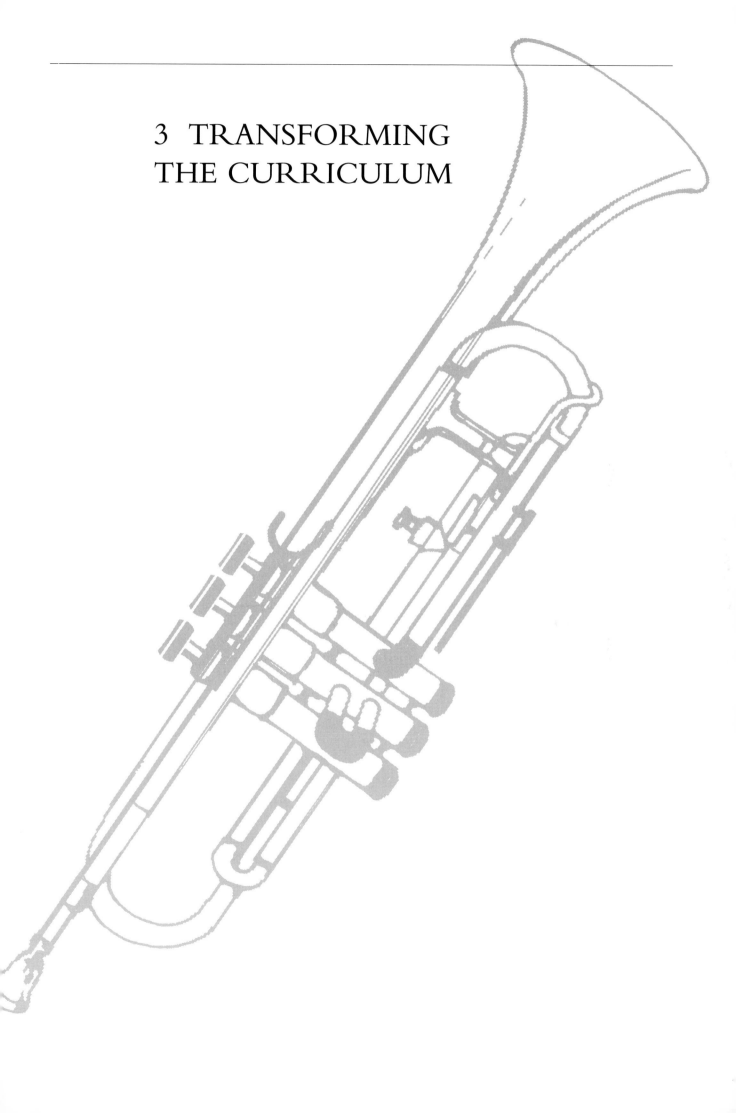

I believe that only actual participation constitutes socially valuable learning, a participation by the learner in every stage of the learning process, including not only a free choice of what is to be learned and how it is to be learned but also a free determination by each learner of his own reason for living and learning – the part that his knowledge is to play in his life.
                    IVAN ILLICH, *AFTER DESCHOOLING, WHAT?*

The purpose of music education, as Kodály frequently emphasised, should be to help individuals to develop their aesthetic experience and understanding by exercising their powers of discrimination.
                    JOHN BLACKING, *A COMMON-SENSE VIEW OF ALL MUSIC*

Music in public education

A curious conclusion can be drawn from the preceding chapter about young people's involvement in music. A good number of them shy away from the dominant Western tradition if we can judge from the ageing memberships of music clubs and choral societies. They seem to be to some degree disillusioned with how they were introduced to the subject in school. However, the omnipresence of rock and pop in their lives, the vigour of new, hybrid forms invented by young blacks and South Asians, suggests that it is not music they are turning from, but particular approaches to music.

Families no longer sing to the piano in their front parlours and, although some infants doubtless learn the principles of rhythm and harmony at their mothers' knee, for the most part the classroom and the assembly hall offer the first serious opportunity to engage with and make music. The educational reforms of recent years have stimulated a new approach to teaching the subject in future.

The Education Reform Act of 1988 (followed in due course by the Education [Schools] Act of 1992 and the Education Act of 1993) has revolutionised teaching and is having a profound effect on the arts in schools. Aiming to provide a 'broad but balanced education', it established a National Curriculum for England and Wales for all pupils throughout their compulsory schooling (five to 16 years), with three core subjects, English, mathematics and science, and with seven foundation subjects including music and art. Scotland has its own more discretionary arrangements for education; the Scottish Office offers guidance to local authorities, which includes advice that they incorporate music in the curriculum. A review in 1993 by Sir Ron Dearing, Chairman of the Schools Curriculum and Assessment Authority (SCAA) (since October 1997 the Qualifications and Curriculum Authority) sought to make the new curriculum more flexible and led to a slimming down of the foundation subjects. Music is a compulsory subject for every maintained school in the country, but only up to Key Stage 4 (ie 14 years). A recent study suggests that only a quarter of schools require pupils to undertake at least one arts subject thereafter.[1]

The music curriculum is the culmination of a long period of rethinking by educationists and has shifted the emphasis in schools decisively in the direction of participation. It is significant that leading figures in the music profession, among them Pierre Boulez, Sir Simon Rattle and Sir Charles Groves intervened in public to make the case for a balanced approach which should incorporate the musics of many cultures. This helped to improve the curriculum and contributed to the widespread approval with which it was received when it eventually emerged. It is based on two attainment targets, Performing and Composing, and Listening and Appraising, and one of the main intentions is to give ' ... pupils the opportunity to participate in practical music-making in schools'.[2]

1 Rogers, Rick, *Guaranteeing an entitlement to the arts in schools* (London, Royal Society of Arts, 1995) p.12.

2 Eric Forth MP, Minister of State, Department for Education, in the introduction to the Music for Youth Conference Programme, 1995, p.5. Cited in Shuker, Margaret Jill, *Live Music-making in Rural Areas – A Dying or a Flourishing Tradition?* major project submitted as part of an MA in European Cultural Policy and Administration, University of Warwick, September 1995.

In a contradictory trend, affecting students beyond 16 and outside compulsory schooling, the government has shown much less interest in courses which aim to encourage personal and creative development than those with a strong vocational content. A White Paper on education and training in 1991 made it clear that financial support should be made available only for areas of study that lead directly to qualifications.

> 'The government expects that public expenditure on education for adults will be concentrated on the courses that can help them in their careers and in daily life. It is not intended that colleges should receive explicit funding from the councils for courses catering for adults' leisure interests.'[3]

For as long as there has been a public education system, educationists and teachers have been worrying about the state of music teaching in schools. In 1871 a member of the Board of Education excused the neglect of music in schools and universities because 'the musical education of the upper and middle classes had been neglected, and it was difficult to find gentlemen competent to examine in the notation of music.'[4]

The practice of music in schools, especially group singing, made rapid advances when the Tonic Sol-fa notation came into general use in the classroom and revolutionised sight-singing. However, in the years that followed the Great War an important study, the Cambridgeshire Report on Music in Schools, reported that:

> 'music still gets grudging treatment in many schools, with curtailed time and "tired" periods in the timetable. The music class is sometimes used as a dumping ground for children with insufficient intellect to learn more reputable subjects.'[5]

The emphasis was less on the practice of music than on musical appreciation — a state of affairs for which the BBC was given a large share of the blame. Sir Henry Hadow wrote in *The Times* in 1932:

> 'It will be a national loss if we allow ourselves to be satisfied with listening [to the wireless] and let our practice fall into desuetude.'[6]

The report is a sharp reminder of just how foreign a country the recent past can be. 'Good voice-production in singing', opine its authors, 'has far-reaching effects on speech, and pure speech helps to lower class barriers.' They have little time for folk song or popular music; music education should be based on the classics (although 'teachers should not exclude modern music, even if they are not attracted to it'). Like Sir Henry, they have serious doubts about broadcasting, which they discuss as if it were a form of cultural self-abuse:

> 'The growing habit of turning on the wireless set or gramophone as an accompaniment to conversation or on other sociable occasions seems wholly bad: it is bad for the social intercourse, worse for the nervous constitution and worst of all for the musical growth of those present.'[7]

The document is a cautionary tale for writers — and readers — of books on music, for it is a demonstration of the speed with which taste and theory can change. However, it does identify a number of themes that are still current today, if in different terms. There is an acknowledgment, albeit expressed with distaste, that 'children and adults are continuously battered by music on all sides.'[8] The impact of the globalised culture, still new at that time, is duly registered:

> 'The influence of the picture palace is enormous ... Over 30 million people attend the cinema every week in the British Isles ... The cumulative effect of the music they

3 Department of Education and Science White Paper, *Education and Training for the 21st Century* (London, HMSO, 1991) p.60.

4 *Music and the Community, the Cambridgeshire Report on the Teaching of Music* (Cambridge University Press, 1933).

5 *Ibid*, p.178.

6 *Ibid*, p.179.

7 *Ibid*, p.14.

8 *Ibid*, p.149.

hear cannot be overestimated. Music is an essential part of the film show ... At present the hearing of much cinema music cloys the musical palate because of the high proportion of emotional and highly coloured music.'[9]

It is also worth noting that advocacy of the classics was influential with Kenneth Clarke, when, as Education Secretary, he was taking the National Curriculum Order for Music through the legislative and consultative processes. The notion of a 'respectable canon' is strong again in some circles in OFSTED, the schools inspectorate, and the Schools Curriculum and Assessment Authority, as well as in right-wing think-tanks.

The main burden of the report was to change the balance between practice and appreciation. In the authors' opinion, the current unsatisfactory state of affairs was in good part due to a general increase of leisure and the omnipresence of recorded or broadcast music. While this reflected the growing importance of music in people's lives, it placed at risk advances in the earlier part of the century in the growth of 'ear-training, and sound aural foundation, in place of the old basis of "theory"'.[10] The report placed great weight on the importance of the study of notation, although it accepted that it is far more difficult to interest children in this than in music appreciation. The debate between the virtues of practice and of understanding and the importance or otherwise of notation in school music teaching remained live issues in the years after the Second World War.

The great education legislation of 1944 set out a completely new approach to teaching and how it was to be planned and managed. Public education was to be a national service, locally administered. Comparisons between Britain and other countries suggested that its education system had taken too narrow a view of success and failed too many people; it was accepted that there were many kinds of success and that everyone had talents. The Act established, for the first time in England and Wales, secondary education for all by means of the 'meritocratic' tripartite system of grammar, technical and secondary modern schools, together with the 11-plus selection exam at the end of primary schooling. The 11-plus had the effect of dictating a narrow primary curriculum.

In the early post-war years there was an exciting, even heady, sense of entering a new age. The spirit of the Victorian poet and schools inspector, Matthew Arnold, was abroad; his definition of culture as 'the acquainting ourselves with the best that has been known and said in the world, and thus with the history of the human spirit'[11] was seen to have a special relevance to the work of schools.

As the tripartite system gave way to comprehensive schooling through the 1960s and 1970s, selection naturally disappeared. The result was that the primary curricular range exploded. The philosophy was child-centred and, in that context, the experience of the arts would play a significant role; the discovery method of teaching and learning was epitomised by the primary education mantra: 'We teach children, not subjects.'

Local education authorities (LEAs) appointed powerful chief education officers with their own inspectorates and banks of specialist advisers. Some of them spearheaded a revolution in the arts, building up the teaching of music and establishing the system of peripatetic music specialists – among them Peter Newsom in Hertfordshire, Alec Clegg in the West Riding of Yorkshire, Stewart Mason (followed by Andrew Fairbairn) in Leicestershire and Robin Tanner in Oxfordshire. In some parts of the country schools profited from a strong local tradition of music in the community – choirs, brass bands and competitive festivals. An important consequence was the emergence of youth

9 *Ibid*, p.147.

10 *Ibid*, p.172.

11 Arnold, Matthew, preface to the 1973 edition, *Literature and Dogma*.

orchestras and choirs across the country, often playing to high standards and ultimately feeding into the membership of professional orchestras.

The 1944 Education Act did not set out a national curriculum and while this encouraged diversity it led to some uncertainty about standards of attainment. Although the 11-plus exam was a potentially constricting factor, its comparatively rapid decline opened up the curriculum at the primary school level to allow many different pedagogic methods. To bring some order into their work, LEAs set up their own curriculum development centres and in the 1960s the Schools Council was established to ask from a national standpoint what needed to be taught in schools. Its task was to review the curriculum and to oversee examinations such as GCE and CSE. It encouraged a move away from what was widely perceived as over-academic syllabuses and teaching methods in favour of a closer involvement in process. The arrival of the CSE in 1962, which catered for students who were not sitting GCEs, had a positive impact in this respect, involving as it did course and classroom assessment as well as formal examinations.

However, so far as music was concerned, it took time for the effects of these developments to be felt on a national scale. Until well into the 1960s, music tended to be a narrowly focused subject, with comparatively little in the way of involvement and performance, especially in secondary schools. For most children it figured among the academic rather than the practical subjects. To illustrate the general point, Eric Bolton, former Senior Chief Inspector of Her Majesty's Inspectorate (HMI), recalls a secondary school in Kennington in the early 1970s where a typical music lesson entailed pupils studying on paper the notation of an Elizabethan song, *The Knot Garden*.

This reflected a way of thinking with which many of the LEAs were sympathetic – namely, that:

> 'pupils are inheritors of a set of cultural values and practices, needing to master relevant skills and information in order to take part in music affairs. Schools and colleges can be seen to be important agents in this process of transmission. According to this theory, the task of the music educator is primarily to initiate students into recognisable musical traditions ... children should at least come into contact with "good" music, should have some idea of how staff notation functions, should acquire some ability to aurally and visually recognise standard instruments and should know something about important musicians and their work.'[12]

Transmission was rigorously tested through competition and examination. It was an approach which went hand in hand with a general move in schools, colleges and higher education to give the arts a higher degree of academic standing.

The trouble with this was that, although thoroughly Arnoldian, it was not very obviously 'child-centred'. It offered only one aspect of what a modern liberal education could be and was unlikely to engage children who were far more interested in popular music. An alternative theory emerged which stressed creative expression and involvement. Its musical progenitor was the composer Carl Orff, for whom the experience of music should be instantaneous and universal (many school cupboards throughout the land are full of Orffian percussion instruments, put aside as fashions changed). Notation and the business of learning to play an instrument well were of far less importance than stimulating the musical imagination.

From the late 1960s one of the most influential advocates of this point of view was John

12 Swanwick, Keith, *Music, Mind and Education*, (London and New York, Routledge, 1988), p.10.

power of LEAs and in the size of their centrally held budgets. The responsibility for arts education has in effect been devolved to schools and the day of the influential local authority arts and music advisers has ended. According to the Royal Society of Arts (RSA), local authorities have abolished one-third of their advisory posts and just over half of their advisory teacher posts; only a quarter of authorities have a full complement of full-time advisers or inspectors for arts subjects.[22] By 1993 more than three-quarters of LEAs had devolved, or were in the process of devolving, funding for their music services, often to a business unit, agency or trust. This has had potentially damaging consequences for the provision of instrumental teaching in schools. Schools find it difficult to take up projects on offer from arts organisations because of their cost. Instrumental and music teaching sometimes falls into the hands of private companies, where the range of instruments on offer is frequently restricted to the cheapest and the most popular (resulting in a surfeit of flutes and clarinets and a dearth of bassoons, trombones and double basses), and there are widespread fears that quality as well as coverage may be suffering. Furthermore, the 1988 and 1993 Acts allowed schools (or LEAs) to charge for instrumental provision if it is designed for individuals or small groups of up to four pupils and is not part of a public examination syllabus.

Evidence is mounting that the number of students being charged for lessons is rising, that free access to instruments is falling, and that more and more parents are filling the gap with their own financial contributions. If the cloud has a silver lining, it is that, for those who can afford it (schools or individuals), the range of peripatetic teaching appears to be as wide as ever — some argue, wider — and in certain areas of the country more accountable than in the past.

That part of the budget for instrumental music which comes from public funds, having been passed down from LEAs to schools, has declined from 70% to 63%, while the average hourly fee rate has doubled, according to a recent RSA report.[23] Also, one-third of primary schools and one-third of secondary schools are not properly equipped with good quality instruments for performing and composing. It is also claimed that there are too few music teachers, especially in the primary sector, to deliver the curriculum. A recent MORI study suggests that funding changes have not had an adverse effect on the number of pupils receiving tuition across the country. However, others disagree: members of the National Association of Music Educators (NAME) in the Northern region claim that so far as they are concerned the situation is far worse than has been described; they are concerned by the increase in the number of pupils whose parents have to pay for tuition and confirm that cost is deterring children (especially those from poorer families) from learning to play the larger and more expensive instruments.

The key point to be made is that those aspects of music-making are suffering most which, to be done well, need to be done at a level wider than that of the individual school; for example, coherent teams of local instrumental tutors; music centres; instrument loan banks; youth orchestras, bands and other kinds of ensemble. LEAs are finding they are no longer in a position to maintain them. In this respect, the story of the London-based Foundation for Young Musicians is instructive. It was founded to take over the school and youth music arrangements of the Inner London Education Authority when this was abolished, and was intended to be supported by all the new borough education departments which pay for students to attend the Centre for Young Musicians, play in the London Schools Symphony Orchestra and so forth. The Foundation has also raised £3 million in sponsorship. None of these monies are given for core funding expenses, which are covered by the Department for Education and

22 Rogers, Rick, *op cit*, (summary version) p.3.

23 *Ibid*, p.12.

Employment to the tune of £100,000 a year. Now this core funding subsidy is to be withdrawn and, because no one else is likely to pick up the bill, the survival of the project is now threatened.

In the long run, the fall-out from the decline of the LEAs may, if uncorrected, have a knock-on effect on the general orchestral scene. It would not do to exaggerate this, for, in the absence of a public service, it is perfectly possible that parents would pay for musical training and experience if it came to the crunch. Nevertheless, the Association of British Orchestras estimates that 75% of the players in major orchestras benefited from free instrumental teaching and from performing in youth orchestras run by LEAs. In Sir Peter Maxwell Davies's words:

> 'without the British youth orchestras, the tertiary music colleges and professional symphony orchestras around the country would not be able to recruit musicians. Without the county youth orchestras the national youth orchestras would not be able to recruit players. Without the school orchestras the county youth orchestras would not be able to recruit players. Without instrumental teaching in the schools, school orchestras will disappear.'[24]

Many teachers were not trained across the full range of the music curriculum and are finding the delivery of some aspects to be difficult. In primary schools, 41% of new teachers feel ill-prepared to teach music, according to the RSA.[25] They also argue with some justification that music and the arts are given insufficient timetable space. Teacher training is also no longer centrally managed, having been mostly devolved to individual schools. Not unnaturally priorities vary, although some large, better funded schools do have substantial professional development budgets. Up to 80% of training time is spent inside schools rather than elsewhere, making it harder for teachers to acquire the range of musical and knowledge they need. The decline in funding for advisory and support organisations with expertise in arts education at national and regional levels, combined with the withering away of the LEAs' advisory structure, means that many teachers are largely left to their own devices at a time of change and challenge. It may be no accident that music has the highest teacher vacancy and teacher turnover rates of all the National Curriculum foundation subjects.

Facilities for the practice of music in schools, where they exist, are often inadequate technically and acoustically. Timetabling constraints inhibit their best use in school hours and they tend not to be readily (or cheaply) available out of school hours. Lack of finance and the need to levy 'commercial' letting charges mean that the ideal of the community school which is open to local organisations as well as pupils is potentially under threat.

This is a serious matter for, although the delivery of the curriculum in the classroom is important, we should not undervalue extra-curricular music-making out of school hours, such as school choirs and orchestras, end-of-term musicals and even nativity plays. Although unfortunately not always related to curriculum work, it gives those youngsters involved the chance to develop their talents. Without more resources this kind of activity is at risk and there is even less incentive than there was to build bridges between music in and out of school.

In this connection, we should not forget the substantial number of private or commercial tutors. They offer a range of services, although clearly only for those who can afford their fees. The code of practice drawn up by the Incorporated Society of Musicians' Private Teachers' Section and its Music in Education Section Committees

24 Spoken during Sir Peter Maxwell Davies' presidential address given at the north of England Education Conference, 2 January 1985.

25 Rogers, Rick, *op cit*, p.3.

suggests that relations between the public and private sectors are not all they might be:

> 'This code of practice acknowledges a need for more communication on all "sides" for it to become apparent that there are, in fact, no sides ... Communication and elementary courtesy provide the very simple key to a good professional relationship between music teachers working within and outside schools ... Too often pupils are the unfortunate go-betweens in a tussle of authority and will.'[26]

This initiative to reconcile disagreements, or at least differences in attitude, is surely the right course of action. Boundaries between the two camps are blurred in that a private teacher may well play a part in publicly funded organisations (music groups as well as educational establishments). Not only can such a teacher provide additional out-of-hours tuition for keen or talented students, but they also represent a valuable specialist resource which hard-pressed schools can make use of to bolster sometimes generalist provision in the classroom.

For all the difficulties, more young people are taking public examinations in arts subjects and achieving high grades. In 1993, 70,000 young people took an A-level in art, design, media studies, music, the performing arts, photography or theatre studies. In 1994 there were more than half a million secondary school entries for arts subjects at GCSE, although there is a low take-up in music. Nine out of ten 11 to 16 year-olds take part in at least one arts activity inside school and about as many participate outside school. Nineteen per cent play a musical instrument on their own inside school and 24% outside. However, for children from the lower socio-economic levels, charges for music tuition for groups of four or fewer pupils is a barrier to development. A quarter of young people say they never engage in imaginative or creative activities. Music-making in the daytime is fractionally higher among female teenagers than male, although in leisure time this picture is reversed, doubtless due in part to the male orientation of much rock and pop.

So far as further and higher education are concerned, art and design, the performing arts and media studies are the third biggest programme funded by the Further Education Funding Council. Almost 200,000 people have some form of artistic qualification and the younger they are the more this is likely to be the case. An indication of the popularity of the arts in tertiary education is that applicants for drama training outstrip the places available by 14 to 1. One in five creative arts graduates goes on to further studies – a third of them into teacher training who comprise 17% of all music graduates.

Adult education has played an important part in arts development, but is itself facing considerable pressures from government reforms. The results are unquantifiable at present because it is a decentralised field and no comprehensive research on recent changes has been conducted. Universities led the way in adult education from the early nineteenth century, followed by local authorities, who became involved in the late nineteenth century, and the Workers' Educational Association, founded in 1903. In 1985-6 a survey of local authority adult education classes showed that there were an estimated 600,000 enrolments for arts and crafts classes in England (excluding dance).[27]

In the decade that has followed the situation has deteriorated, although in the absence of hard evidence we cannot say for sure to what extent. According to a national study carried out by the National Institute for Adult and Continuing Education for the Arts Council of England (ACE), the arts are increasingly a leisure interest for many adults alongside sports, reading and gardening. Almost a third say that they enjoy the arts and crafts (9% play a musical instrument), but report growing difficulties in pursuing such

26 *Shared Music Teaching, A code of practice agreed by the ISM private teachers' section, for school and private music teachers who teach the same pupils*, ISM Information, 01/2, London, 1995, unpaginated.

27 Rogers, Rick, *op cit*, p.19.

interests,[28] since the general squeeze on local authority budgets has led to decreasing programmes in many parts of the country. Those that remain are shorter and charge higher fees. This falling away has been especially damaging in rural areas where general arts provision is, in the nature of things, thinner on the ground. University providers are also short of cash. Government policy is focusing public resources on vocational rather than recreational training.

Despite these difficulties some observers claim that attendances at music courses have risen in recent years. It is hard to be sure exactly why, but there are a number of possible reasons. Local authorities have increasingly targeted their provision at disadvantaged communities and the traditional student profile is changing. There is evidence that young Asians are enrolling to gain music qualifications which would enable them to work in their communities. Also more young Afro-Caribbeans are taking part. In general, there is greater interest than previously in music involving new technologies and in pop or rock. Another important factor has been the franchising of courses by established colleges and institutions to other organisations; this has enabled arts centres and community music projects to join the adult education world and they have brought a fresh approach to the work. Unfortunately because of various problems (managerial and financial) with some franchisees, the Further Education Funding Council has replaced franchises with longer-term and more closely monitored partnerships: this is an understandable reaction, but it may make it more difficult in future for smaller music organisations to bid into the system.

An important feature of continuing education, although not necessarily part of the publicly funded sector, is the wealth of summer schools and music courses which is on offer in every corner of the country and makes a valuable and varied contribution to the development of participatory music-making. The magazine *Classical Music* does not overstate the case when it observes:

> 'There are summer schools which cater to people with every musical taste and ability. From professional opera singers to budding recorder players, from string enthusiasts to brass band aficionados – there is a course to suit you.'[29]

Although most of the courses focus on the Western classical tradition, a number specialise in other genres, Some adopt a catholic, intercultural approach; perhaps the leading exemplar is the Dartington International Summer School which presents a programme of concerts, courses, masterclasses, workshops and lectures on more or less every kind of music you can think of, including African drumming as well as chamber music, flamenco as well as choral singing, baroque dance as well as 'The Rock Shop'.

28 Tucket, Alan, and Sargent, Naomi, *Creating Two Nations? – headline findings on lifelong learning from the NIACE/GALLUP survey* (The National Organisation for Adult Learning [NIACE], 1996).

29 *The Classical Music Guide to Summer Schools and Music Courses 1997* (London, Rhinegold Publishing Ltd, 1997) p.3.

The educational system has passed through a period of wholesale change, which has led to a waning of the powers of those bodies that used to be charged with providing authoritative planning, guidance and 'disinterested' long-term funding (most notably, the LEAs). Business sponsors and the National Lottery are neither willing nor able to provide the basic administrative and running costs of youth orchestras and the like. It is not at all clear how this financial gap can be filled unless LEAs are given back the resources to do so.

On the credit side of the ledger, there is a growing acknowledgment of the contribution which artists and arts organisations have made to education over the last 15 years. This contribution was in large part a response to the Arts Council of Great Britain's (ACGB's) entry into the field when its Secretary-General, Sir Roy Shaw, established an education department and policy in 1978. ACGB argued, and won, the case that artists (working as artists not as teachers) can make a valuable contribution to the teaching of arts in schools. Most theatres, dance and opera companies and orchestras have education departments of their own which run extensive programmes. In financial terms their input is not inconsiderable; for example, in 1995-6 ACE and the English Regional Arts Boards (RABs) spent £4.25 million on education and training. About £1.6 million went to artists, arts organisations, venues and promoters and £2.6 million towards education and training projects.

There are signs that the Arts Councils and the RABs are moving in to fill the gap opened by the educational reforms and to offer both practical support and a theoretical overview for which the LEAs used to have the monopoly. This is confirmed by ACE's Green Paper on education and training.

> 'Much innovative work in arts education has come – and still does come – from LEA initiatives and policies, and there is an urgent need to rebuild or underpin the networks which can guarantee the continuation of resources for arts education in schools. Some of this work is already under way, particularly in the RABs which have strong partnerships with LEAs ... Work is under way to develop standards of practice in training, planning, management, and evaluation of projects. To address the current patchy provision, the [arts funding] system aims to develop a network of agencies across the country which can play an effective role in developing links between professional artists and arts organisations in the education sector. The arts funding sector has a critical role to play here in complementing and adding to arts education.'[30]

What is emerging is a confluence of thinking between the arts and education sectors that is now increasingly expressing itself in joint action. Despite many differences of emphasis, the body of ideas which underpins the education programmes of many arts organisations has a great deal in common with the development of educational theory which led to the establishment of the arts components of the National Curriculum. The workshop-based practice of professional music groups and community musicians functions along the same lines as the principles underlying classroom practice with a shared emphasis on eliciting creativity as much as the imparting of knowledge. There is a common understanding of the need to promote cultural diversity and of the ways in which music can contribute both to social and personal awareness. Necessity, in the form of inadequate public funding across the board, is speeding up this process of collaboration and interaction.

Although this book is not primarily concerned with schools, the future of participatory music is in large part dependent on what is taught in them and how it is taught. In the brave new world of league tables and competition for students, ambitious schools regard music as an important component of their work, or at least as a useful adornment. A school orchestra, a choir and public concerts are attractive selling points. Most parents and teachers are not familiar with recent research, such as the Swiss study I report in chapter 1, *The case for participation* (see page 31), but the canniest of them have a strong suspicion that children who learn music are often good at other subjects and that there is a link between the study of music, mathematics and languages.[31] They value the self-discipline required in learning to play an instrument – the ability to sustain practice and the persistence to overcome difficulties.

Unfortunately, it tends to be middle-class parents who place a value on music teaching, since they are able to offer the space and the encouragement to practise at home. Although some local authorities still provide free or cheap access to musical instruments

30 *Consultative Green Paper for Education and Training in the English Arts Funding System* (London, Arts Council of England, June 1996).

31 It is good news that the Royal Society of Arts' 'The Arts Matter' programme is funding research by the National Foundation for Educational Research into links between a healthy arts scene in schools and good academic performance generally.

and lessons, coverage is patchy. In schools which are unable or unwilling to make music a priority, the opportunity to take music as a GCSE subject is unavailable. Music teachers can find themselves reduced to one class a week and what they offer pupils is often scrappy and unchallenging, bitty and eclectic. There is a tendency to focus on the musically able (usually those whose families can afford out-of-school tuition) at the expense of the rest.

All the political parties have stressed the importance of education in children's early years. If progress is to be made on this front, policy-makers must understand that music should be a building block of the curriculum right from the outset. Teacher training in music should be improved, especially at primary school level, for both specialists and generalists. Music should be a substantial feature of nursery education. More time should be given to music for all children in primary schools (with an emphasis on choral singing and music at school assemblies). GCSE in music should always be on offer for those who are interested. Schools need to be furnished with freely available instruments, facilities and dedicated rehearsal and practice spaces so that every pupil who wants to has an equal chance to develop musical skills. If resources of this kind are also open to use by the local community (I discuss the role of community schools in chapter 4, *The re-creation of community*), children will find it easier to make the imaginative and practical link between school work and music-making in the world at large: this may help to ensure that they maintain their musical interests after leaving school.

Further discussion on classroom teaching methods is required. Techniques intended to encourage self-expression are not always practical in today's conditions and should perhaps be complemented by more traditional approaches to the acquisition of particular skills. Group learning can be as constructive as individual learning. Good practice in the use of new technologies would ensure that expensive electronic equipment is put to the most effective use.

These are complex issues and, although education is hardly a discipline deficient in committees or working groups, there is a case for establishing one more to look into the practicalities of delivering the music curriculum at early years, primary and secondary levels, to explore the potential synergies between adult participatory music-making and the education sector, and to help schools to be resources not simply for the children in their care but for the community at large.

4 THE RE-CREATION OF COMMUNITY

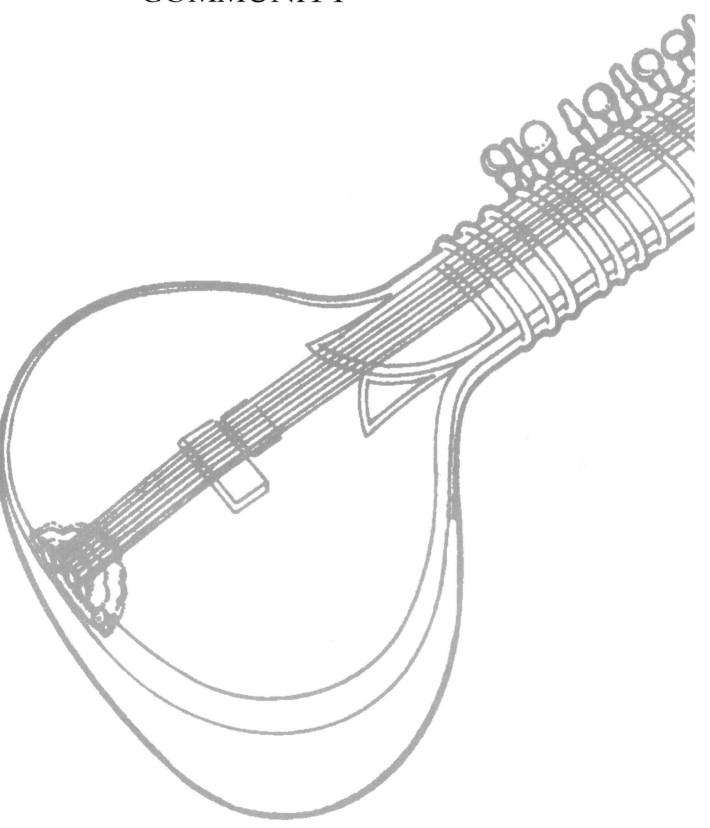

*Our descriptions of our experience come to compose a network of relationships, and all our
communications systems, including the arts, are literally parts of our social organisation. Since our
way of seeing things is literally our way of living, the process of communication is in fact the process
of community: the sharing of common meanings, and hence common activities and purposes; the
offering, reception and comparison of new meanings, leading to the tensions and achievements of
growth and change.*
      RAYMOND WILLIAMS

(On the out-of-tune singing of an old stonemason.) *Watch him closely and reverently, look
into his eyes and hear the music of the ages. Don't pay too much attention to the sounds – for if you
do you may miss the music. You won't get a wild, heroic ride to heaven on pretty little sounds.*
      CHARLES IVES, *MEMOS*

The origins of community arts

The story of choral singing in the Potteries in the nineteenth century is an illustration
of how a deracinated community was able to rebuild itself through art and how
'ordinary people' were able to make a significant contribution to the onward march
of contemporary music. It also shows that, while there was certainly no communal Golden
Age, geographically defined social groupings were in a position (almost within living
memory) to assert their own, authentic cultural values.

They set something off – an ethos, an energy – which spread and continued across the
country throughout the following 100 years. Choirs, brass bands, music festivals and, later,
music clubs of all kinds sprang up, thrived, sometimes faded only to be reborn or renewed,
in the Welsh valleys, the Northern mill towns, the churches and village halls of the shires.
Little of this activity has been documented, but in the archives of every local newspaper in
the land there will be records of concerts, operettas, marching bands and the like. They are
the only remaining traces of a nation-wide cultural movement which touched the lives of
every class and every human settlement.

This movement was characterised by the fact that it was often led by individual musicians
or music-lovers with vision, drive, ambition or local pride and, above all, a delight in
music-making for its own sake. Such people still exist. They play the organ, teach the
clarinet, run the local choir, organise and perform in festivals and performances and work
in pubs and clubs. They are to be found at weddings, barmitzvahs, discos, raves and street
festivals. But this is only one side of their work. Many also encourage people to value
music through participation and other forms of engagement; they work with community
groups in disadvantaged neighbourhoods as well as developing education-based activity in
or out of schools.

Paradoxically, at a time when real communities existed and embodied real community values,
the term did not have the connotations it possesses today. Indeed as far as music is concerned,
the 'community musician' is a distinct species which derived its name and ethos from a
philosophy which was rooted in a particular time and political stance – one that reflected
political and social concerns throughout the Western world during the 1960s and 1970s.

For many in the early days of the community arts movement, an explanation of what had
happened rested on a socialist critique of capitalism. The proposition was that art had been
appropriated by the ruling classes and was deployed as a means of bolstering their authority.
The critic and writer John Berger, spoke of the 'illusion' that:

' ... art, with its unique, undiminished authority, justifies most other forms of authority, that art makes inequality seem noble and hierarchies seem thrilling. For example, the whole concept of the National Cultural Heritage exploits the authority of art to glorify the present social system and its priorities.'[1]

This echoes the influential views of the German literary critic and theorist Walter Benjamin, who flourished in the 1930s, but whose work attracted the attention of community artists some 30 years later. For him the vision of history as a progressive continuum, the gradual 'becoming' of truth and freedom belonged to the victors – 'the continuum of history is that of the oppressor.' He developed the notion of 'redemptive criticism' which would interrupt this continuum, unveiling moments of discontinuity in history and making it possible to restore what continuous, progressive history has dominated and suppressed.

Su Braden was a community artist of note who co-founded 'Pavilions in the Park' in 1967, an attempt to persuade local authorities to use parks and open spaces to take the full range of arts to random audiences. She put together a conceptual approach by which it would be possible to examine the role of artistic expression in everyday life. She wrote: 'It is only through actively engaging with society that artists may acquire a perception of reality which matches that of ordinary people in local contexts.'[2]

She saw the history of social and economic development over the last two centuries through a form of class analysis.

'Since the beginning of the Industrial Revolution, the middle and upper classes have been able to continue their art-forms almost unchanged. But the vernacular culture of rural populations – who were to become the future industrial working class – suffered considerably in the course of the Industrial Revolution and has subsequently received even more deadly blows at the hands of industrial and city planners. There is today a large population of working people who had to be educated to fit themselves to the industrial life of the cities, while the middle classes have been able to retain their culture – albeit with less and less direct participation.'[3]

This account was complemented by a view of personal (as distinct from social and political) development which reflected the work of the psychiatrist R D Laing. He argued that what was understood as sanity and madness was 'degrees of conjunction and disjunction between two persons where one is sane by common consent'. The denomination of sanity he saw as a social construct and madness was best understood as an understandable reaction on the part of those estranged or excluded from the outside, 'real' world. This neatly linked the notion of individual creativity, or the lack of it, to external pressures very similar to those of the politico-cultural analysis of a Braden or a Berger.

1 Berger, John, *Ways of Seeing* (London, BBC and Penguin Books) 1972.

2 Braden, Su, *Artists and People* (London, Henley and Boston, Routledge and Kegan Paul) 1978, p.133.

3 Berger, John, *Ways of Seeing*, op cit, p.8.

4 Nettel, R, *op cit*, p.108.

One may surmise that these ideas would not have had so vigorous an outcome in practice had it not been for the intervention of another factor. The birth of community arts coincided with that of rock and pop. This was important for a number of reasons. Firstly, so far as Britain was concerned, pop music (although exploited for purely commercial ends by the music industry) was of great cultural significance because it was led by a generation of working- or lower-middle-class musicians, many of them trained in art schools (institutions which offered unprivileged adolescents a unique ladder up into professional creativity). They produced what seemed to be a new and original form of urban industrial folk and of the ballad tradition. R Nettel's description of the Potteries in the nineteenth century as a 'commercial society in the throes of an artistic urge'[4] could, it seemed, be applied with equal force to the Britain of the Swinging Sixties.

Secondly, the arrival of rock and pop coincided with the economic 'coming of age' of young people who for the first time in history had sufficient funds at their personal disposal to become an economic force in their own right. Music was at the heart of a new autonomous youth culture and, with the coincident invention of more effective birth control and a loosening of family hierarchies, was closely linked to a revolution in sexual *mores*.

Thirdly, these new forms of music-making seemed to modify the conventional relation between active performer and passive audience. Rock concerts were (and still are) communal celebrations with quasi-religious, sexual and political overtones. In other words, they were digging up the lost roots of music long since overlaid by the polite manners of the classical music experience.

Jim Morrison, of the primal American group The Doors, summed up his contribution in a way that characterised the general mood:

> 'When I sing my songs in public, that's a dramatic act, but not just acting in theatre, but a social *act*, real action. A Doors concert is a public meeting called by us for a special kind of dramatic discussion and entertainment. We make concerts sexual politics. The sex starts with me, then moves out to include the charmed circle of musicians on stage. The music we make goes out to the audience and interacts with them; they go home and interact with the rest of reality, then I get it all back by interacting with *that* reality. When we perform, we're participating in the creation of a world, and we celebrate that creation with the audience.'[5]

The language may seem hip-ly dated, but it is easy to see the resonance this kind of claim had in the ears of community artists and musicians.

Bob Dylan's songs were hugely influential too, for some of them combined an up-to-the-minute political consciousness with wide popular appeal. Another witness from the time, although speaking in equally over-the-top terms, was not far wrong when she said:

> 'Dylan is a mass poet. People follow his work and wait for his latest releases with an eagerness no poet has received in this country [ie the USA] since at least the Industrial Revolution. People talk about his work and his changes as if they had participated in them. They see his poetry as *process* – a living growing thing – not as a mysterious product in an aesthetic universe apart from life.'[6]

Fourthly, and more practically, rock and pop brought with them a huge surge of interest in guitars and drums. Not only were these instruments relatively affordable by young people, but it was possible to achieve more than adequate musical results without years of formal training. This is not to make a comparative judgment of the ease or difficulty with which they can be played compared with other instruments, nor of the artistic quality of the best rock and pop. I simply mean that they were readily available and usable expressive tools in a way that the keyboard or the violin, with the cultural expectations they arouse, were not (much the same point can be made of the brass band movement to explain its enduring popularity among amateur musicians; the use of treble clefs throughout, except for bass trombone, and identical fingering means that instruments are easily taught and playing skills readily transferable).

The 1960s also saw the rise of the arts centre movement. With their commitment to 'empower' the disenfranchised, their intermingling of art-forms, their willingness to give house-room to rock and pop, their sense of art as a search or a voyage of discovery and the simple fact of accessible facilities, arts centres were helpful to community artists. But Su Braden, writing in the late 1970s, was probably right when she sensed their lack of a radical edge.

5 Cited in Baxandall, Lee, 'Spectacles and Scenarios: a Dramaturgy of Radical Activity' in Baxandall, Lee, ed, *Radical Perspectives in the Arts* (Harmondsworth, Penguin Books) 1972.

6 Tax, Meredith, *Introductory: Culture is not Neutral, Whom Does it Serve?* in *ibid*, p.28.

'Beaford ... is not unique. Other arts centres where residencies have taken place recently are the Brewery at Kendal, South Hill Park in Bracknell, and the Old Town Hall in Battersea, London, and all of them suffer from many of the same problems noted in relation to the *Maisons de la Culture* in France, which were founded with the idea of bringing the "arts" to the people. This proposition was based on very little analysis of either the arts themselves and the forms of expression which have developed in more formal contexts, or the "people" and the reasons why the working class have become alienated from those forms of culture which the middle class term "art".'[7]

Community music did not make such rapid advances as the performing arts and aspects of the visual arts (especially the print media), although it often appeared in multi-art-form presentations or activities. However, community-based workshop practice began to become widespread. 'Workshop' is a term that can mean many things to many people. Andrew Peggie has provided a carefully crafted definition. In his words it is:

' ... an activity, part of which would consist in the "audience" working with musical material presented by the group or session leader, and usually under the direction of a group member or leader. While various degrees of preparation may have been undertaken beforehand, the emphasis would tend to be on improvisation or on material created at the time. Workshops are (by and large) predicated on the notion of exploration and experimentation, the assumption being that the participants are there because they wish to broaden their horizons, expand their knowledge and experience (both self and musical) and learn new skills.'

The object of this work was not that community artists should feel that their job was to take their art to the people, for that in essence is the relationship of professional to amateur; rather, believing that many people's power of creative expression was stunted or suppressed, their task was to place their talent at the disposal of others and to collaborate with them on a basis of equality – even if this equality (at least at the outset) was one of intention and comradeship rather than of skills.

John Stevens, a drummer, visual artist and co-founder of Community Music London wrote *Search and Reflect*, which became a treasured handbook for practitioners. As I have already observed, some educational thinkers, among them John Paynter and Keith Swanwick, were proceeding down similar avenues and their work percolated through to the community music sector. Other influential figures included Peter Wiegold who ran Gemini, a contemporary music performing group with a serious commitment to working in community and educational settings; and Trevor Wishart, the composer. Disenchanted with the estrangement of contemporary classical music from its audience, he argues that 'good art is both accessible and profound.' He told me in an interview:

'My work springs from a commitment that there's no point doing art if you don't speak to people. It matters to me as an artist who deals in universals. I'm not purveying material for a niche market which six professionals in Switzerland will enjoy.'

Su Braden's *Artists and People* is one of the few published texts which attempt a rigorous evaluation of community practice and it raises issues from the 1970s which are still current today. Evaluation is, in fact, the first of them, together with the linked debate about 'artistic quality'. The question of what was or was not good art (whatever that might mean) was side-stepped by an emphasis on process rather than product. To offer a 'product' was to enter the capitalist world of production and to accept the very notion of professionalism which it was the community artist's task to subvert. In those early days, it was an

7 Braden, Su, *Artists and People, op cit*, p.111.

understandable approach, for it was necessary to wean workshop leaders away from an over-concern with their own work and from the implicit attitudes which their conventional training may have inculcated.

Other themes emerged from Su Braden's survey of a range of community projects and schools residencies: in particular, the need for community artists to settle on a clear aim, to establish appropriate support systems and to discuss plans carefully and openly with all those involved, whether directly or indirectly.

A question of particular relevance to music was raised in a couple of the residencies; namely, the literary character of British culture echoed in the academic bias of the schools system which places an undue importance on 'writing things down'. The notation of music, it was felt, can distance people from the experience of making music.

The arts funding establishment was uneasy about community arts. Their anxieties focused on the unresolved question of artistic quality. Richard Hoggart, who was a member of the Arts Council of Great Britain (ACGB) and chairman of its Drama Panel for a number of years, expressed typical reservations:

> ' ... you have to believe that some works of art are better than others, that some music is better than other music, some novels are better than others and some paintings better than others. Even if such a view can never be incontrovertibly proved, there is no refuge in the "good of its kind" fog which invites you to settle for saying that a best-selling crime novel is in its way as good as *Middlemarch,* and that the Beatles in their own way are as good as Beethoven.'[8]

In part, this is a persuasive argument. No doubt the *Oresteia* has something over *Eastenders.* No doubt too, unfortunately, some community-based practice has been unsatisfactory within its own terms and for those taking part, let alone anyone looking in from the outside. Community artists at the time probably missed a trick because their neglect of product made it difficult for them to deliver an effective riposte. But it does not follow that things cannot be good of their kind, whatever one may think about the kinds themselves. Human creativity and tastes are diverse, both generally and for individuals: that is, it is possible for one and the same person to enjoy opera and soap opera.

The trouble with Hoggart's remarks is less their content than their tone. What someone with a democratic perspective might recognise as a new egalitarianism where different types of creative opportunity are becoming available for all, he saw dismissively and pejoratively as 'levelling-down'.

In any event, it was this negative point of view which helped to turn ACGB away from community arts. Largely as a result, their full potential was smothered by lack of funds and of serious attention, although their basic tenets came to be taken up (if often in diluted form) by local authorities, which were beginning to pay increasing attention to arts provision. Meanwhile, of course, the musician in and of the community, who was practising music for music's sake, was largely if not completely overlooked. Being a mere 'amateur', he or she was neither a threat nor a serious competitor for such public finances as were available for the arts.

At the end of the 1970s and in the early 1980s Roy Shaw was ACGB's Secretary-General and superintended the devolution of responsibility for supporting community arts to the regional arts associations. He regarded them as little concerned with artistic excellence and suspected, darkly but not altogether inaccurately, that some of them saw the arts as a way of conducting politics by other means. But then, having booted them out by the front door he

8 Hoggart, Richard, 'False Populisms, false Elitisms', *Arts Express,* 12, February 1985.

inadvertently let them return through the back. With a background in the Workers' Educational Association and in adult education at the University of Keele, he believed that the funding system should develop explicit links with the world of education. In 1978 he founded a small education department at ACGB, an important and timely innovation with long-lasting consequences. Over the years that have followed the application of discreet pressure has persuaded the main arts organisations which the Council regularly funded – the regional theatres, orchestras and so forth – to appoint education officers and establish educational and outreach policies. Unsure how to proceed, many adopted the methodology of community arts practice.

The participatory musician today

The debate widened and moved on, although, as we shall see in contemporary debates about the nature of artistic quality, Hoggartian voices are still to be heard. The word 'community' became increasingly problematic. A loose working definition in the 1970s was:

> ' ... a variety of social contexts in which groups of people recognise a relationship between each other and a defined geographical area or administrative structure. Within the meaning of "community" used in this sense [are] the hierarchical communities of schools and hospitals and the working teams that compose a new town development corporation, as well as the communities who simply recognise the pervasiveness of local/environmental and economic conditions within a geographical area.'[9]

The complexity of today's social realities have made this position difficult to maintain. At a seminar on community music in 1994, participants found themselves in difficulties:

> ' ... despite much discussion, there was no consensus on the definition of "the community", or indeed, who should define it ... Boundaries are contestable and difficult to set: communities can be small, large, isolated, concentric or overlapping ... Generally, people thought it better to resist such definitions as they could become straitjackets.'[10]

Peter Renshaw of the Guildhall School of Music and Drama, whose main concern is to relate community practice to a reform of orchestral practice, takes a tougher line. 'Community music is too much rooted in locality, to place in a narrow sense,' he told me. 'This means that it doesn't really "empower", for it locks people into their cultural relativity, even if it does politically empower. There is little sense of wider standards.' In other words, if I take his meaning correctly, he is arguing for giving people access to a larger cultural 'community' where aesthetic standards and critical understanding are hammered out and exchanged rather than for a localist approach which will generate only local results.

Now while of course it remains true that many projects are still geographically based in neighbourhoods, schools and the like, this is not always how people today regard their social relations. A person's loyalty to a neighbourhood can be strong, but may often be much less significant than that to other non-topographical networks – for example, those which represent Black consciousness or disability culture or the environmental movement or indeed their friends. A follower of traditional Gaelic music may be celebrating a sense of locality, but could equally well be asserting his or her national identity and political loyalties.

Sound Sense, the community music umbrella body, accepts that definitions have moved on over the years. In its view, ' ... community music ... involves musicians from any musical discipline working with groups of people to enable them to develop active and creative participation in music[;] is concerned with putting equal opportunities into practice[; and]

9 Braden, Su, *Artists and People, op cit*, p.107.

10 *The Voice in Community Music Seminar, The Report, 30 August-2 September 1994* (Norwich, Community Music East Ltd, 1994) p.15.

can happen in all types of community, whether based on place, institution, interest, age or gender group, and reflects the context in which it takes place.'[11]

For an increasing number of us, place is simply where we happen to be for the time being, as traditional family structures weaken and social and job mobility grows. The growth of individualisation and 'active consumption' means that we tend to make opportunistic use of multiple communities to construct a confident, customised sense of ourselves, as distinct from defining ourselves in terms of a fixed community of which we are fully paid-up members. The all-pervasive globalised culture, transmitted through the mass media and other forms of modern communication, enables people to leapfrog traditional social structures to attain a sense of togetherness, a sense so abstract and non-topographical that the process is perhaps best likened to an electronic bran tub into which we dip for material that suits our tastes; or even as a protection from our local context when it becomes oppressive. That many millions of other people around the globe may share these tastes is 'cool' and creates a comforting feeling that individuals are not alone and do not need to regard themselves as antisocial or eccentric, but it does not usually create functional loyalties that lead (as in the case of traditional communities) to common social or political action.

Community music, defined as a discrete movement, today reflects these trends, sometimes speaking less to identifiable social groups than to *ad hoc* gatherings of deracinated individuals for whom it may be a ladder to the attainment of a personal aspiration as well as a means of personal empowerment in the context of a wider social movement. So (to choose two examples more or less at random), although Raw Material, the community project in Kings Cross, London, which introduces young black people to new music technologies, has social objectives to help alienated and unemployed youth, its 'selling point' lies in the fact that it offers potential entry into the commercial music business for ambitious youngsters.

Overtones, a London project specialising in new technology, has gradually softened its originally rigorous feminist agenda in favour of the more pragmatic aim of providing training opportunities for women who want to enter the recording or music presentation business. Originally named Ovatones, it was founded in 1983 as a separatist collective to produce music made by women and, thanks to the Greater London Council, was able to establish an eight-track recording studio. Insurance from a robbery enabled an investment in 16-track and, under pressure from funding bodies, it became a constitutionally more conventional arts charity. The organisation operates as an interface between the worlds of community and commercial music. Lesley Willis, who administers Overtones, told me:

> 'Our essential task is to enable women to have a higher musical profile as technicians and engineers. We made a fundamental decision to teach them how to use technology in their particular musical areas; we don't teach people how to compose. A third of our time is spent on teaching women; another third on producing top quality recordings of women's music (whatever the gender make-up of their bands) and for the final third we are "out there" running events.'

The issue of quality has been directly addressed in recent years. Community musicians are laying greater stress on projects leading to specific artistic outcomes. Other sectors of the music world, for example, amateur music societies, folk musicians and orchestras, have adopted community-based practice the primary concern of which is with the development of the art-form rather than with socio-politico-cultural aims where music may be more the servant than the master. It is beginning to be accepted that when professionals and non-professionals meet in joint endeavour, the results can attain high artistic standards. A telling case in point is the educational work of the Glyndebourne Opera Company, an elite

11 See *Sounding Board*, Sound Sense, Bury St Edmunds, spring 1995, p.29.

establishment if ever there was one, whose community operas have both embodied social objectives and produced work remarkable in its own right, as most of those who attended *In Search of Angels*, a 'community opera written and composed with the people of Peterborough', would attest.

As I will describe in the following chapter, following the pioneering example of Sir Peter Maxwell Davies over two decades at the St Magnus Festival in the Orkneys, more and more contemporary classical composers are finding that community work is not merely a way of paying one's social debts but a rewarding method of creating new music. The old debate between 'good in itself' and 'good of its kind' is looking increasingly out-of-date and irrelevant to contemporary practice.

The ideology of community music has opened out with the years. Community Music, a 'training, education and performance centre' in central London, for example, is one of the key agencies working in the field. Founded by John Stevens and David O'Donnell 15 years ago, its thinking has grown and developed over time. It has positioned itself, with considerable skill and flair, at an intersection where 'traditional' neighbourhood-based community practice, commercial popular music and the formal education sector meet. Stevens, who died prematurely in 1994, was one of the progenitors of community-based music, but he and his colleagues have always been able to rethink their practice. The project expanded massively in the days of the Manpower Services Commission, but found in its disappearance a welcome opportunity to consolidate and focus their activities. Community Music runs a range of courses, performances and outreach projects across the capital. Its annual turnover is between £350,000 and £400,000, of which about £100,000 comes from grants.

Its staff are missionaries, having helped to establish other important projects elsewhere in the country, such as Community Music East in Norwich, Community Music Wales and Musicworks. Aware that lack of continuity and poor national coverage are two of the greatest threats to community-based practice, they have made their Music Tutor Training Course the cornerstone of their work and established structural relationships with the Open University and Kingsway College. In association with the London Arts Board and Solotec (the training council for South London), they are currently administering The Arts Apprentice Initiative, a government-funded job-creation scheme offering an Arts National Vocational Qualification (NVQ).

Community Music also offers a direct address to various forms of pop and rock and enters into partnerships with commercial music organisations. It runs workshops in funk and rock as well as the Brouhaha Multi-Music Club where jazz, techno, classical, dub, jungle and bhangra intermingle and seasoned professionals play opposite teenagers from youth clubs. Last year a group of composers including members of Asian Dub Foundation, the London Musicians' Collective and the Bhangra band ALAAP were commissioned by the London Arts Board to write a suite of pieces entitled *The Journey*. This was performed at Community Music and other venues.

The Lewisham Academy of Music in South London is another community project that focuses on popular musics, mainly for young people. Founded in 1981 as a music wing of the Albany Empire, it became independent five years later. Occupying a former mortuary, it is managed by a seven-member collective and offers a wide variety of courses ranging from Latin American to death metal. It targets beginners and about 25 tutors offer courses in instrumental teaching, improvisation workshops and music technology.

The fact that new ideas or modes of activity are being explored is not to say that the past has been superseded or that community music has always abandoned its moral and political grounding. When I visited Community Music East, based in Norwich, Ben Higham, one of its founders, told me: 'Writing a community opera? It's a contradiction in terms.' So far as he is concerned:

> 'I work through music on a larger project of understanding. Community Music East is a medium for people to develop a high level of critical understanding, unifying communities in themselves and so contributing to diversity. We stem from the old community arts idea of "giving people a voice".'

In the last resort, the arts cannot exist in isolation, but must function in the world. Alison Tickell of Community Music in London commented:

> 'If you're a community musician, you can't avoid bringing your own sense of values with you, for they are what gives you a passion and a language. You have to come clean about these things; community music is explicitly anti-racist and committed to equal opportunities. These kinds of policy are not simply just, but also value-laden; they come with an idea of the society one's working towards.'

In other words, because music is part of broad social processes and is both universal and ubiquitous, it can be a metaphor and a mechanism for a comprehensive social and political enterprise.

Interculturalism

A time-traveller from the 1960s to the present day would probably say that the single most obvious difference between community music then and now has been the introduction of non-European musics. There are a number of reasons for this. By the mid-1980s a generation of British-born Afro-Caribbean and South Asian people were coming of age and were eager to develop their own forms of creative expression. Angered by exclusion, they brought pressure to bear on local authorities and the arts funding system for both money and esteem. At about the same time, public interest in what came to be called World Music began to grow; the WOMAD festival and Anne Hunt's World Circuit Arts came into being in 1982 and a handful of recording companies began to feature world musicians, especially from Africa. The British public was introduced to choral singing from Armenia, the Silk and Bamboo ensemble from China, religious song and dance from Ethiopia, mask dancers from Indonesia and much else besides. Indigenous musicians began to see rich opportunities for making multicultural links. Cultural Co-operation, founded by the late Robert Atkins and Prakash Daswani, is another important promoter; its Music Village series of festivals began in 1987 and paid special attention to participatory music-making among many world cultures. As I have already noted (see page 54 and following), much pop music has its roots in Black American culture, and new forms have continued to emerge from the Caribbean, such as reggae and rap; meanwhile, young British Asian musicians experimented with different types of 'fusion'. At the same time, black jazz musicians (on both sides of the Atlantic) and others look to Africa for inspiration, visiting the continent to relearn African rhythms, melodic structures and techniques of improvisation.

We should pause to consider the significance of these developments. In the long struggle to attain equal opportunities for members of all the diverse cultures in the United Kingdom, and especially those of the non-European communities, 'multiculturalism' has been a commonly used term, with an apparently beneficent connotation. As a principle, it has the advantage of implying the rights of cultural minorities to express themselves. This is all right so far as it goes, but it does not go very far. As the Council of Europe's report on European culture and development points out:

> 'Perhaps diversity policies should do more than guarantee due respect for minorities. Would it not be logical for them to be available to every kind of cultural grouping, large or small, each of which has a legitimate interest in promoting subsidiarity and counteracting centralisation? In fact, it is worth questioning the relevance of the terms "majority" and "minority": belonging to a minority implies being marginal, being exiled in an enclave, whereas all cultures are, in a sense, central and deserve to be seen as such, whatever the political consequences. ... The defence of cultural pluralism goes hand in hand with cultural exchange, or "interculturalism". By interculturalism, we mean that the co-existence of different cultures entails dialogue, not confrontation. It is not a matter of de-limiting, but of opening up. The circulation of people, ideas and projects allows cultures to "breathe".'[12]

What is interesting about the British musical scene is that it is acquiring intercultural characteristics in the course of spontaneous development and not under the pressure of public policy. Musicians, including many in the participatory field, are, like jackdaws, appropriating material and ideas from the gamut of available musics. The habit of interaction and exchange is also increasingly becoming a feature of music teaching in schools. Traditional musics are mingling with jazz, rock and pop; white pop musicians, such as Peter Gabriel, Sting and Paul Simon have learned a great deal from the musics of Africa, Asia, Latin America and the Caribbean. The classical styles of India, whether directly or through intermediary forms such as Asian film music, are contributing to new, hybrid forms. Much the same can be said of Western classicism. There is a growing amount of two-way musical traffic.

There is much to be said for this new tolerant and inventive spirit of sharing, but we should acknowledge that gains can be accompanied by losses. When music is transplanted from one culture to another, there is always the risk of rootlessness: that is, it can be torn from its original social context and, in the process, we find that its meaning has been weakened, lost or transformed. Does that matter? Opinions vary. Purists simply wish to conserve while progressives argue that everything changes and that we should welcome the new riches of interculturalism. Many opt for a *via media* where excitement at innovation is moderated by respect for origins, a dislike of cultural looting and a concern to retain a link, however attenuated, with authentic roots.

Community musicians are in the forefront of events. Traditional Arts Projects (TAPS), founded in 1989 to develop traditional British musics and based at the South Hill Park Arts Centre, is an interesting example of what is being done. At Sound Sense's 1996 *Cut and Blend* conference, I attended a remarkable multicultural workshop which was part of a project described in TAPS' latest annual report:

> ' ... developing the theme of common ground between two cultures, an exploratory meeting between Kiranpal Singh and Roger Watson ... led to the launch of a new project Millan. Millan is a Hindi/Punjabi word which translates as meeting or reunion, in this case a meeting between the east and the west, a coalition of two distinct musical traditions. It emerged that many of the earlier English and Celtic tunes in Roger's repertoire fitted very nicely with the structures of the older folk ragas – not just the scales but even the predominating notes and phrases ... Building on this discovery Millan was formed with Kiranpal Singh and Roger Watson joined by Davinder Singh on tabla, supplying the Indian rhythmic development and Andy Baker [of the Bournemouth Sinfonietta] on double bass, giving a western harmonic structure to the whole.'[13]

12 *In From the Margins*, op. cit. p.44.

13 *TAPS Annual Report, 1 April 1995- 31 March 1996*, (unpaginated).

South Wales Intercultural Community Arts (SWICA) offers another illustration of what can be done. Founded in 1990 as a breakaway organisation from Theatre Taliesin Wales, it sees its task as essentially developmental. Working with people of all races, it runs workshops in carnival arts (and an annual Mas Camp), as well as in steel pan, tabla and samba. Samba is rising in popularity, although it attracts little public attention or support from the funders: SWICA runs the largest samba band in Wales, with a substantial annual gig list. It also presents ambitious theatrical spectacles (eg an outdoor multimedia interpretation of a Celtic myth).

The musics of exclusion

The notion that arts practice is not only valuable in itself but can contribute positively to personal and social development has been influential far beyond what one might call the arts community. All kinds of public and voluntary agencies have taken it on board and included the arts among their programmes of activity. Music is one of the most commonly provided art-forms, either alone or in association with other performing arts. For those who have made use of the arts for a long time, the community arts philosophy has helped them refine their thinking. This beneficent plagiarism has been so widespread that it is almost beyond monitoring and assessment. As we have found in other areas, we simply do not know what, or how much, is going on.

The youth sector is a case in point. Whether it be in the field of the treatment of young offenders, or the general provision of social services, or urban regeneration, the arts have been a useful way of working with young people. Probation services have found the arts a handy addition to their armoury of rehabilitation; thus, the Birmingham Probation Service has invested in The Cave, an arts centre for young black people, and a senior probation officer in Surrey established the Surrey Music Initiative as an exercise in crime prevention.

According to Nick Randall of the Youth Arts Network, most local authority youth services have designated one of more of their centres as having a special arts function. Music, because of its significance in youth culture, often has pride of place in provision (this, of course, has always been the case in the 'uniformed' sector – eg the Scouts and Guides, and the Boys' Brigade). In order to get a grasp of the extent and range of activity, the Prince's Trust and the National Youth Agency have commissioned Randall to produce a survey of youth music and his report, to be entitled *Mapping Hidden Talent*, is to be published during 1997.

At the other end of the human lifespan, public authorities and welfare agencies are uneasily aware of the demographic 'time bomb' which is set to go off when the post-war 'baby-boomers' reach pensionable age. The chances are that health, welfare and economic services will be under even greater pressure than they are today, but with earlier retirement, whether voluntary or enforced, and longer lives, a large proportion of the growing number of old people will have the potential to enjoy a more active life if they have sufficient resources. There is a growing recognition that, while not everyone aspires to be an artist, people need creative experience at all ages and in all circumstances. Psychologically, the arts assist people to deal with the ageing process. They can help them to find purpose and understanding about the past, about the loss of youth, and show the way to new, life-enhancing perspectives.

ActiveAge, a European network of organisations, arts bodies and policy-makers, issued a number of recommendations for action to promote the contribution of older people to the arts at its second European meeting on Older People and the Arts, held in Dublin in 1995.[14] They included the need: to explore and exploit the capacity for self-expression through the

14 Cited in *In From the Margins, op cit*, p.125.

arts to give older people a voice and help define their role in society; to promote and acknowledge the value of older people's economic contribution to the arts; to build on the social, enjoyable side of the arts to help to re-establish links between different sections of society; and to prepare for an active and stimulating later life by providing opportunities to develop creative interests, before retirement.

Music, because of its powerful links with memory and its encouragement of socialisation, is popular among older people, as a number of voluntary sector bodies have acknowledged. There is a good deal of musical activity on offer, much of it traditional in nature and reflecting the tastes of former times. More challenging projects which promote empowerment are fewer in number. Examples of good practice on recent years include the work of Heyday across the art-forms at the West Yorkshire Playhouse in Leeds and David Sulkin's extraordinary composition project, promoted by English National Opera's Baylis Programme, for a group of old people suffering from dementia. In 1987, the South Bank Centre launched a Senior Centre which enabled old people to work with the London Sinfonietta and symphony orchestras and be introduced to playing the gamelan.

Unfortunately, despite all this good work, progress is slow; Age Concern, on of the leading agencies in its field, is only now beginning to address the need to develop an arts policy. Once again, a key problem is that an unco-ordinated mass of music-making needs to be mapped: a survey, commissioned by Age Concern, has been completed and will hopefully go a long way towards filling the gap. It will probably be published later in 1997.

Artists of all kinds have been concerned to introduce an experience of the arts into 'closed' institutions, chief among them hospitals and prisons. There is now a substantial record of arts activity in the healthcare field. The value of such work was well described by the art critic, Richard Cork, writing in *The Listener*, in 1985:

> 'The medical profession is at last beginning to realise that a hospital should care for the *whole* person, not just the specific illness. To try curing people in surroundings which demonstrate an appalling lack of sensitivity is to betray the whole basis in which hospitals should rest. How can anyone possibly justify treating patients' ailments in a building shabby and dehumanised enough to depress them still further? Incarcerating them in such places is bound to alienate people who are already depressed and desperately need assurance. Artists can help to provide this consolation.'[15]

Of all the art-forms, music is often said to be the one that has the most profound power to affect patients. Medical science has long believed in music's therapeutic powers and recent scientific advances have tended to confirm its power to reach the deepest recesses of our being (see page 28 and following). It was also the first of the performing arts to be used in any systematic way in British hospitals.[16] As long ago as 1948 a group of concerned people took a wind-up gramophone and some 78 rpm records into a psychiatric hospital. The success of this experiment led directly to the establishment of the Council for Music in Hospitals. It was soon recognised that live music, with its potential for patient participation, would be preferable to recordings and soon concerts by professional musicians were being organised. The rise in the number of hospital concerts has been phenomenal, reaching nearly 3,000 performances in 1991.

Peter Senior, director of the leading national body Arts for Health, is an experienced pioneer in the field. In 1973 he founded the Manchester Hospitals' Arts project. Its early emphasis lay in the visual arts, but by the end of the decade a strong performance programme was set in motion. Gradually, the work began to attract national attention and hospitals around the country began to experiment with arts activities of various kinds.

15 Cork, Richard, 'The Art of Healing', *The Listener,* 11 July 1985.

16 I am indebted for the following paragraphs to Senior, Peter, and Croall, Jonathan, *Helping to Heal: the Arts in Health Care* (London, Calouste Gulbenkian Foundation, 1993) *passim.*

Meanwhile in 1976, the dancer Gina Levete founded SHAPE with the aim of bringing professional artists into contact with groups isolated from the rest of the community, including elderly and mentally ill people and those in hospitals, day centres and residential homes, and established a network of regional agencies throughout the country. Some years later the Attenborough Committee of Inquiry into the Arts and Disabled People, which reported in 1985, took the view that the arts in healthcare was one of the largest areas of activity to be considered. It recommended that the government should require health authorities to develop the use of the arts; within a couple of years the Department of Health and Social Security formally acknowledged the importance of the arts within its sphere of responsibility. By 1992 it was possible to identify at least 300 hospital projects around the United Kingdom, with new ones starting all the time. The NHS reforms do not appear to have had a negative effect on the development of arts in healthcare; in fact, according to Peter Senior, 'the loosening of thinking which the changes has brought about has introduced a climate of positive thinking and openness to new ideas. This has benefited the arts.'

Many musical ensembles encourage patient participation, which can vary from requesting a piece of music to singing a favourite song. The Council for Music in Hospitals continues to be a leading promoter and has been joined by Live Music Now (which also organises performances in schools, prisons, offices, factories, churches and other community venues). Where general arts programmes have become a settled part of hospital life, many patients are given the opportunity to make music themselves either in groups or on a one-to-one basis. The opportunities for real participation in music-making as distinct from the presentation of concerts are greatest in mental health and some specialist fields, such as spinal injuries. They depend on the availability of continuous arts expertise and an estimated 150 hospitals now employ arts co-ordinators on a full- or part-time basis.

A distinction should be drawn between the contribution artists can make *as artists* in healthcare and the work of arts or music therapists. Their skills are complementary and their common interest is communication with the patient, but musicians do not make music to heal, even if it does heal, but for a variety of other less direct reasons. Creative therapy is a particular skill with a specialised, medical purpose, whereas what an artist has in mind is the creation of a work of art.

Participation in the arts can be a powerful confidence-building measure and it is surprising that it is not used more as an instrument to help those in prisons or correctional institutions to make creative use of inmates' time in custody and to equip them to rejoin society once their custodial sentence is over. Prison routines are usually stultifying; they repress individuality and this can lead to pent-up frustration and anger, which may well affect security. The arts can provide a creative and fulfilling channel for prisoners to express their feelings and, if sensitively handled, can reduce social tensions in prisons. Music-making can be a valuable tool in enabling them to discover paths to personal change and rehabilitation.

A striking example of this is the work of Pimlico Opera, a small-scale touring company which began working in prisons in 1990. Starting out with a brought-in production of *The Marriage of Figaro* at Wormwood Scrubs, the company graduated to joint productions with inmates and a few prison staff at the Scrubs and Wandsworth of *Sweeney Todd*, *West Side Story* and *Guys and Dolls*. These were received with enthusiasm in all quarters. A prisoner commented: 'Given me a high which I have never had before. Not from drugs or anything.' For a prison governor Pimlico Opera had 'brought forward the prison 10 years'. Of the larger opera companies, Glyndebourne Opera has run highly valued projects in prisons.

The London Sinfonietta/Opera Factory was one of the earliest music groups to undertake serious work in prisons, presenting an opera by Brecht and Hindemith at Holloway in 1988. Gillian Moore recalls that, when during a courtroom scene a judge sings: 'All rise', the prisoners stood up *en masse*. The incident revealed the ambiguities and difficulties of making art in such a context, the confusion between reality and fiction and the highly charged atmosphere of creative activity in a closed institution.

The Hallé Orchestra's education department is interested in prison work and ran a popular one-week residency at Risley where 10 prisoners (who had already shown interest in music-making) worked with some of orchestra's musicians to devise and record the sound track for a silent film.

The essential challenge concerns the honesty and the clarity of motive among those undertaking creative activity in prisons. What exactly is it that the artist or arts group has in mind to achieve? And how is it possible to make a useful contribution when prison projects are almost inevitably one-off? The most convincing answer to these questions is to produce a work of art which can have some kind of external 'life' outside prison and so will add to the self-esteem and confidence of those taking part. In the minority of prisons which employ arts co-ordinators in the education departments, continuity is possible and visits by musicians and musical groups are designed to complement ongoing artistic activity.

Artists and writers in residence, music performances and short courses in the development of creative skills have been increasingly employed in prison settings. One professional writer, commenting on his experience, observed that his early fears about patronising and exploiting prisoners proved groundless: 'They ignore you if you patronise them and they discuss openly the ways in which we exploit each other.'[17] Although arts in prisons appear to lack systematic resourcing, specialist training and adequate research to enable evaluation, there is goodwill on the part of the Prison Service, in token of which it established a Standing Committee for the Arts in Prisons in 1995. However, the need to make savings, the huge rise in the number of inmates, problems of security and political pressure for more austere regimes is leading to a reduction in arts provision.

It is increasingly accepted that participation in creative activity is an essential right of disabled people. This does not necessarily mean 'special' provision, but 'ordinary' provision made truly accessible. Employers and the general public need to be encouraged to accept disabled people on an equal basis whether as artists, administrators or audiences. Until policy-makers fully accept this point, disabled people are caught in a double-bind. That is to say, they are unable to attend arts events or take part in them as professional or amateur practitioners because of inaccessible buildings or the absence of such aids as induction loops for partially-hearing people, signing for deaf people or tactile signs and large clear print signs for sight-impaired or blind people.

I was given access to an early draft of a Music and Disability Audit which is being conducted for the music department of the Arts Council of England.[18] It commented:

> 'Conservative estimates put the number of disabled people in Britain today in the region of 6.4 million. Many of those people are still denied access to arts experiences – as audience, as participants, as creators, as performers. Those who have physical access – because of their specific disability or because of access having been provided – still rarely have the opportunity to fully enter arts experiences *as disabled people*.'

The survey showed that disabled musicians come from every age group, that as a group they cover the full range of musical interest and that most kinds of disability are represented

17 Peaker, Anne, and Vincent, Jill, *Arts in Prisons: towards a sense of achievement*, a report for the Home Office and the Arts Council of Great Britain (London, 1991).

18 Verrent, Jo, and McGinty, Terry, of East Midlands Shape, *Music and Disability Audit for the Music Department of the Arts Council of England*, first draft (unpublished, 31 July 1995) p.2.

among their number. Thirty-two per cent of the disabled musicians surveyed were earning less than 10% of their income from music-making and only 10% were earning more than 90%. Most of them are very poorly paid.

Groups of disabled people in Nottinghamshire and Northamptonshire were surveyed to find out what contact they had with music. Many respondents reported that they had opportunities to listen to music. So far as participation was concerned, a majority had had opportunities 'in-house' but a far lower proportion externally. We can deduce from this that many disabled people are ghetto-ised inside the disability community.

Facilities are one thing, but training in music-making and the arts is another. Music is often a component of many disability projects, but the number of those which 'lead' on music is far smaller. The issue is not therapy or opportunities for diversion; like anyone else, disabled people want the chance to play a full part in the musical life of the country. In the case of physical disability, new technologies are offering solutions to once intractable difficulties. As I report in chapter 6, *The electronic soundscape*, on the impact of the digital revolution, organisations such as the Drake Music Project and the Soundbeam project are making good headway on this front.

Opportunities are opening up at the instigation both of specialist organisations and of general community music projects. The Association for the Development of Open Opportunity in Recreation (ADOOR), for example, which has worked extensively in the leisure field, has been running a series of arts training programmes. In 1996 one of these was a music and disability training day. Chris Rodin, who leads most of ADOOR's arts-related projects, stressed the importance of empowerment. The seminar was not just a matter of how to run music activities for disabled people. 'That sounds a bit passive on the part of disabled people. The training will explore how people with disabilities are sometimes excluded within a musical activity, and how it can be more inclusive.'[19]

In the same year there was a festival of disability work at London's Albany Theatre, featuring performances and workshops by some national and international disability arts companies, a disability Arts Mart in Leeds with stalls, videos and exhibitions on arts activities from local and national disabled people's groups, and a variety of courses concerned with a variety of disabilities.

The related field of special needs has also attracted the attention of community musicians, with animateurs working on adult training courses and in special schools. It has also been an important strand of some orchestras' and opera companies' outreach activities. For example, in the late 1980s the social services department of Strathclyde Regional Council engaged the Scottish Chamber Orchestra to provide special needs projects in adult training centres in each division of their region. The aim was to bring in musicians with good communications skills to act as catalysts for creative activities over a period of months,

Heart 'n' Soul at the Albany Empire celebrated its 10th birthday last year and focuses on people with learning disabilities. At its core is a 10-strong performing company of performers with learning disabilities. The project runs training courses and two years ago launched a bi-monthly nightclub/cabaret where people with learning disabilities are the performers, the DJs and the musicians. It provides a much-valued social focus and helps to counteract the isolation into which the NHS's Care in the Community policies have plunged many people.

The 13 year-old Ark, based at the South Hill Arts Centre in Bracknell, offers programmes of creative performance work for people with severe learning difficulties, and physical or mental disabilities. Its founder, Penny Sanderson, works with a team of three musicians,

19 *Sounding Board*, Sound Sense, Bury St Edmunds, November 1996, p.12.

three dancers and an actor, all of them non-disabled. The two key features of their work are improvisation in a pre-constructed 'set' and the linking of music with movement. 'We dance our musical instruments.' Projects do not culminate in public performance ('voyeurism and hang-ups within public perceptions are problems we avoid'), although on occasion there are public rehearsed workshops. The Ark collaborates with social security and education services in Berkshire. It is not run by disabled people, on the grounds that the level of disability among those they work with would make it inappropriate and 'unfair'.

The contrast between the philosophies of Heart 'n' Soul and the Ark is instructive. Both care deeply about the problems faced by people with learning difficulties, but (to put it simply) one seeks to empower and the other to provide. It is hard to make a judgment between them – although critics of the latter would argue that, even if particular groups of disabled people are unable to take part in the governance of the projects they work with, there are others with experience of the field and with less severe disabilities who would be able to represent their interests.

Sounds of Progress, an ensemble of disabled musicians in Glasgow, is an illustration of the excellence that is attainable by disabled musicians. Originating during the city's year as European City of Culture, the project now receives support from the Orpheus Trust. Led by Gordon Dougall, it has set its sights not only on training disabled musicians, but also on teaching non-disabled professionals 'that it is easier than they think to work with disabled people. We are not interested in therapy – but in integration and the creation of good music. We see ourselves quite simply as a music production company.' Sounds of Progress runs a wide range of workshops and training courses as well as developing the skills of the ensemble.

The diversity of these projects gives a taste of the variousness of practice in music by disabled people. As in other areas of participatory musics, a great deal of excellent work is being done. What is less clear is the precise extent of practice. This has not been measured or quantified, much less evaluated. In fact, there seems not to be a well-debated consensus about aims and standards. There are some knotty questions that need answering: for example, is there a necessary correlation between disabled control of projects and organisations and the development of disability culture? Is public performance invariably an appropriate ingredient of music and disability work? Is there always a clear understanding among providers of the difference between music therapy and music-making?

Arts and disability is a field (cynics might say a minefield) where 'good intentions' are not enough. In Sheffield plans are well advanced for the creation of an arts centre equipped with state-of-the art facilities for disabled people, Genesis – Arts for All. It has an all-embracing philosophy and is not in sympathy with the separatism of many disability arts activists. As a result it has aroused a degree of local opposition which threatens its future.

To sum up: we find in this field two broad strands of thinking. The one supports the provision of a cultural service to disabled people by non-disabled artists and organisers, while the other (in my view more authentically) supports the idea that disabled people can and should run their own cultural events by and for themselves. It would be desirable to have an in-depth discussion of this issue, but at present no mechanism exists for such an exchange to take place.

Music resource centres

The picture I have drawn of the world of participatory musics is of highly active individuals and small groups coming together spontaneously in creative combustion. This is indeed the case, but two reservations need to be entered. Firstly, it is not so easy as might appear for individuals who want to become involved in participatory music-making to find the advice and connections they need. Secondly, music project leaders and independent musicians tend to be lone operators who have little time to engage with other people's work. Many are young, idealistic, but comparatively new to the field, for, over the years, inadequate resources have led to a continuing drain of talent and experience.

At the national level, there is a clear role for bodies such as Sound Sense, the community music movement's umbrella organisation; founded in 1989, it has 250 members including animateurs, both freelance and attached to projects and arts organisations; community music projects; and the community and education departments of orchestras and opera companies; together with other bodies and individuals which support its work. It publishes a bi-monthly magazine, *Sounding Board*. It is working on a professional development programme and hopes to establish an interactive archive. A review has been conducted of the desirability of establishing a Scottish Sound Sense. At the time of writing (February 1997) it is possible that a Sound Sense support group will be established, with funding from the Scottish Arts Council towards the costs of an office and a worker. As the concept of community music gives way to the broader idea of participatory music, perhaps the time is approaching when Sound Sense will be able to bring all kinds of musician and music-making inside its catchment. Working alongside other more specialist agencies (eg the National Federation of Music Societies and Jazz Services), it would be an invaluable clearing house for information, the exchange of ideas and the dissemination of good practice.

Another practical means of making life easier both for experienced practitioners and absolute beginners is through established music institutions in the field offering themselves as a resource, providing advice, facilities and opportunities for networking. There is evidence in different parts of country that this need has been identified, and it is worth pointing to some examples of good practice.

In Scotland, the Skye and Lochalsh Young Music Makers has been created to encourage the development of musical skills and enjoyment among young people in Skye and Lochalsh. The project will involve the appointment of a Music Development Officer for a three-year period. A range of ambitious tasks has been set, among them that of increasing the number of young music participants from 300 to 600. These goals will be realised through such activities as networking with other areas and initiatives, a regular newsletter, improved access to venues and instruments, workshops, musical weekends and so forth. In short, the aim is to be a contact point and support for whoever wants to make use of it.

To move from a rural to an urban setting, the Hackney Music Development Trust (HMDT) was formed in 1995 to create new opportunities for music-making among the inhabitants of Hackney. Music is an important force in the borough cultural industries and substantial sums have been invested in the physical regeneration of the area. Believing that real cultural vibrancy comes from people, not buildings, HMDT aims to be a catalyst for creative activity. It has raised funds to support various local bodies or projects, including Hackney's Centre for Young Musicians, the Hackney Youth Orchestra and Jazz Ensemble, local schools, a Music Business Training Course at the Hackney Community College and a programme of short course and demo clinics for local musicians.

Neither of these projects is building-based. It is interesting to note that a number of participatory music organisations have their own centres and are committing themselves to major building schemes (often substantially financed by National Lottery grants). Community Music East, Overtones and the Lewisham Academy of Music are all in the throes of ambitious capital developments that will give them the space and the technical equipment to expand the services they are able to offer.

Community Music in London is planning to move into a new building at a cost of about £5 million. This will allow them to develop access to new technology, will provide more space for performance and for rehearsal and training. It will also mean that they will be on more equal terms with the commercial music industry as regards their scale of activities and range of facilities.

Outside London there are few community music projects large enough and sufficiently well-established to act in this way as a major resource across the musical forms both for professionals and amateurs. In Birmingham, though, a major arts centre, *mac* (formerly known as the Midlands Arts Centre) is filling this role with energy and skill. Its success is instructive, for it shows how a large-scale conventional cultural institution can be an 'open' facility, non-bureaucratic at the point of delivery, for musicians of every kind.

mac was founded in the 1960s as a centre for young people and music has always played a large part in its activities. Dorothy Wilson, Programme Director, told me:

> 'Our policy interlocks professional production (mostly in touring) and participation. The ethos is the same as it was when the centre was set up – to make the arts a part of daily existence.'

Many performers and musical groups began their artistic days at *mac*. So, for example, the City of Birmingham Touring Opera, one of the country's finest small-scale opera companies, originated in the centre's music department where for many years Paul Herbert ran his pioneering Birmingham Music Theatre group.

Nearly 100 arts organisations see *mac* as their home. The centre is old enough to demonstrate the power of intergenerational loop-back: that is, people who used the place in their childhood and teens have now grown up and send their children there. Some have become professional musicians and teach at the centre or use it as a base. Others form part of its loyal audiences.

Music groups that are associated with *mac* include the community music project, Sound It Out; Xango, a Latin percussion and wind group; the Maestro Steel Orchestra, now in its eighteenth year; and the Jammers' Caribbean Jazz Band. SAMPAD, the South Asian music and dance community development organisation, works out of the centre.

The question arises whether the formal education sector can help support the unplanned patchwork of arts centres and community music projects by opening its facilities to their local public as arts resources. One interesting example of what can be achieved is the work of the Estover Community College in Plymouth. Estover is a large, bleak housing estate in the outer ring of the city with a population of 14,000 and few amenities of any kind. It has a large number of older teenagers and above-average levels of youth unemployment.

In 1992, the College's Community Education Department founded the Estover Percussion Project. This was consistent with its academic mission, but was also a conscious contribution to the local community. The Project has grown from small beginnings and now actively involves more than 200 adults and young people. It consists of a number of musical ensembles – an all-female youth steel band, an adult steel band (which emerged from an adult education class), two junk funk bands, a street samba band, a youth *a capella* group and a percussion group for adults with learning difficulties. The project runs an annual festival, Street Rhythms; this hosts a number of internationally known bands, delivers educational workshops to schools and community groups, brings professionals to work and perform locally, facilitates inter-agency co-operation with national youth associations and environmental groups and is engaged in the design and development of low-tech, easy access musical instruments.

There are three features of this work that merit special attention. First, the Project has succeeded in making links with media and one or other of its ensembles has frequently performed on national and regional television and radio. This is significant, for it is rare but telling evidence that amateur and community-based product can be more than a little-noticed full stop at the end of a process, but can attract substantial numbers of listeners. Secondly, with a National Lottery grant, the College is constructing a performance building which will be managed for the most part autonomously and will be an interface between the College and the local community. Thirdly, once it had proved its staying power, the College made the Percussion Project a fully independent institution. It will stand or fall according to its ability to reflect and celebrate the values of the Estover community and the local people who run it. It will not depend on the life-support system of the College.

Community schools – that is, secondary schools which offer cultural and other services to its local community – were pioneered as long ago as the 1940s in the shape of Village Colleges in Cambridgeshire. The policy was further developed after the Second World War, with local authorities such as Leicestershire, Devon and Coventry taking the lead. By the 1960s and 1970s, perhaps about 10% to 12% of the country's schools had developed community programmes and facilities. One of the models for the community school is Stantonbury Campus in Milton Keynes, which has an outstanding record in the performing arts. Like many of its counterparts in other areas of the country, it has survived the education reforms of recent years and, indeed, is thriving. Around 1970 Leicestershire applied the same principle to primary schools. Today funding for the community aspect of schools' work comes from the Further Education Funding Council rather than from local education authorities, as used to be the case in the past.

The concept is now taking on a new lease of life. This is in good part due to the impact of the National Lottery: educational institutions are eligible for arts capital grants, provided there is public access. Also, the success of the BRIT Performing Arts and Technology School in Croydon, which was one of a number of pathfinder institutions under the City Technology College scheme, has shown the potential of an arts-centred secondary education. The Department for Education and Employment (DfEE), which launched its Specialists' Schools scheme in 1993 to enable secondary schools to specialise in such areas as technology and languages, decided in 1996 to open it to sport and the arts. Stantonbury Campus is bidding for specialist school status and may receive as much as £1 million for the further development of its arts courses for pupils as well as improving community access (applicant schools have to raise £100,000 from the private sector to be matched by the DfEE, which will also contribute about £100 per pupil per year).

In the light of these opportunities, a number of schools across the country are now planning the development of substantial arts facilities. The Latymer School in Enfield, for example, is applying for Lottery funds towards the construction of a £5.6 million performing arts centre. This grant-maintained state secondary school had originally simply intended to install facilities for the exclusive use of its pupils, but recast its ideas when it found that it would qualify for a Lottery grant only if they were open to the public. What is now being proposed, after a feasibility study, is that the centre be independently managed. It will not only serve the school's needs, but is also likely to be the headquarters of two professional arts bodies; the arrangements have not yet been finalised, but they are likely to be the

Young Persons Concerts Foundation and the well-known young people's theatre company Theatre Centre. In addition, amateur societies and local artists will be invited to use the centre. So far as music is concerned, there will be 19 practice and teaching rooms, three rehearsal studios, a percussion studio and a media suite with a sound recording studio.

The school recognises that this development will inevitably transform its 'culture'; both teachers and pupils will find themselves engaged in artistic activities both within and with the community, and scholarly isolation will have to give way to interaction with all kinds of professional and amateur practitioners.

One can only respond to such schemes with enthusiasm. If a geographic spread of schools, focusing on the arts and open to their local communities, were gradually to emerge throughout Britain, we would be going a long way to resolve the present inadequacies in the resourcing of participatory musics.

I discuss in the following chapter, *The turn of the tide* (see page 101) another scheme, this time promoted by an orchestra, which promises to create a local resource for participatory music-makers; this is the Northern Sinfonia's plan to establish a centre in Gateshead. The argument I want to advance is that there should be a network of such centres, whether they be independent arts organisations or community schools and colleges, to encourage musicality of all kinds, at every age and in every social class.

Some musicians may be suspicious of becoming over-dependent on building-based institutions on the grounds that, as experience shows, they can easily become bureaucratically hidebound and artistically unadventurous. Although this is indeed a danger, well-run, transparently administered centres can be an invaluable resource for an art-form where facilities, instruments, equipment, training and advice are in short supply.

There are also some planned initiatives at national level which seek to advance the development of British music-making. In the expectation that proximity will lead to synergy, a number of umbrella bodies and national service organisations are proposing to work together in shared headquarters buildings. Thus, Sound Sense has taken over the resources of the defunct National Music and Disability Information Service and restored its operation. Six London-based organisations working in the field of new music – the British Music Information Centre, the British Academy of Songwriters, Composers and Authors, the Association of Professional Composers, the Composers' Guild of Great Britain, NMC Recordings Ltd, Jazz Services and the Society for the Promotion of New Music – are planning the establishment of a custom-built centre for composers and creative performers. This would both be a resource for professionals and be accessible to the general public. As well as offices, it would include an extensive collection of contemporary music scores and recordings as well as information about contemporary British music, and a concert venue, studios and workshop spaces.

In a similar enterprise, the Association of British Orchestras (which already cohabits with a number of other national music agencies) is engaged in a feasibility study with a view to creating a national orchestral centre. This would not only offer a range of services for the 'industry' and foster artistic as well as administrative interaction, but also be a public resource (perhaps including catering, IT facilities, studios and rehearsal spaces). It is likely to concern itself with amateur and professional music-making. Initiatives of this kind, when they have a wide remit and welcome all kinds and levels of practice, could be of great assistance to local musicians, music teachers, young people, community projects and amateur societies throughout the country.

In summary, community music has widened out like a river approaching the sea. Some of its basic ideas have penetrated every corner of the musical world. Its origins lie in a socially-committed, oppositional project to retrieve a lost sense of community, but now, as we approach the millennium, it has divided into an estuary of many different streams and islets. The notion of 'community' has been extended to all kinds of interest groups and there are signs that agencies with general social objectives, especially those concerned with exclusion, are devising arts development strategies. There is a growing understanding of the need to foster synergy between the music education and community music sectors. There is much to be said for encouraging schools, colleges and arts centres to act as open resource centres for local musicians, whether professional or amateur. In the course of time this could lead to a national network of institutions which would stabilise and enrich a creative activity that is both massively popular and massively under-financed.

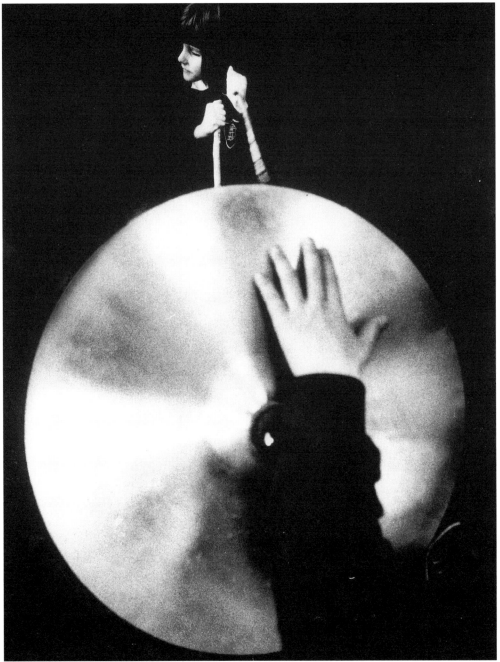

photo: Marcus Tate

5 THE TURN
OF THE TIDE

success, there is no doubt that *The Turn of the Tide* was a landmark event in that it raised awareness of orchestral educational work, supported the newly established music curriculum and encouraged orchestras which were new to the field.

If McNicol's objective was to introduce children to classical music through creative practice, others (among them Maxwell Davies) saw the role of the composer in a wider perspective. Were there ways in which he or she, Janus-like, could look simultaneously in two directions, developing their art in community settings and then feeding the result back to the concert platform? Perhaps this would be a solution to the public's lack of interest in contemporary classical music and might also inspire composers to produce work closer to people's lived concerns.

Of course, this is not an altogether new line of thought in the history of twentieth-century classical music. Elgar, who spent most of his life in Worcester, was at one stage the bandmaster of a local lunatic asylum and, as we have seen, much of his early work was written for local amateur competitive festivals. The largely forgotten Rutland Boughton, whose opera, *The Immortal Hour*, had the unique distinction of a long, unsubsidised West End run, attempted to establish an English Bayreuth in Glastonbury which depended entirely on local community involvement and for which he wrote many community operas. Gustav Holst was happy to a be a schoolmaster at St Paul's Girls' School and he wrote music for his pupils. Benjamin Britten had similar community and educational ideals and composed many pieces for local children and amateurs (among them, *St Nicolas*, *Noye's Fludde* and *The Little Sweep)*. Michael Tippett was Director of Music throughout the 1940s at Morley College.

Vaughan Williams epitomised this tradition. He once said: 'The composer must not shut himself up and think about art, he must live with his fellows and make his art an expression of the whole life of the community.'[13] He was closely associated with the annual Leith Hill Music Festival in Dorking, where he conducted amateur groups and wrote music for them. He gave his *Concerto Grosso* for triple string orchestra (1950) in which the third section may consist of 'those players who prefer to use open strings'.

Sir Peter Maxwell Davies is one of the latest standard-bearers. In 1977 he launched the St Magnus Festival on the Orkney Islands with his *Martyrdom of St Magnus* as its centrepiece. In its first years the festival was a controversial innovation, disliked by many islanders. But it gradually gained the trust of the small, closely knit community. The islanders organise and produce the festival on a voluntary basis. A hundred or so artists are billeted in local homes; amateurs are in charge of stage management and backstage production. The islands' schools, where there is a strong musical tradition of fiddle playing and Scottish folk, are heavily involved with children as singers and musicians. In 1996, the six-day festival (which now also includes drama, dance and literature in its programme and has extended its musical bill of fare to incorporate rock, jazz and folk) attracted an attendance of 18,000, a remarkable feat by any standards.

The role of the composer has always been central to the festival and during its history nearly 100 new works have been commissioned. However, the number is less material than the context in which many of them were written – a self-confident, self-helping community where amateurs and professionals, children and adults intermingle on equal terms. Maxwell Davies told me:

> 'The composer should not be a separate being. All young people are perfectly capable of composing, given the right tools. The training of composers baffles me. They get a piece of paper awarding them a degree in composition without ever having conducted

13 Vaughan Williams, Ralph, from his essay *Who wants the English Composer?* 1912, cited in Foss, Hubert, *Ralph Vaughan Williams* (London, 1950) p.200.

incidental music for an art or drama college, say, without ever having gone out into the community or done something for a local radio station.'

Two remarkable examples of what the St Magnus Festival can achieve were a production of *A Midsummer Night's Dream* in 1993 when a group of children with professional guidance produced the score, the sets were designed by a local secondary school, again with professional input, and the music performed under the direction of a musician-in-residence, Steve King of the SCO; and a revival of *The Beggar's Opera* with music devised from original airs by practically a complete generation of young Scottish composers who had studied under Maxwell Davies. The production featured the local St Magnus Players and the Scottish Chamber Music Ensemble.

Later, Maxwell Davies became the SCO's Associate Composer/Conductor. With the support of the now defunct Strathclyde Regional Council, the orchestra embarked in 1988 on the ground-breaking *Strathclyde Concertos* project. Maxwell Davies undertook the composition of 10 concertos, specially written to suit – and to test – the skills of its principal players. The plan was that the series would be completed by 1995 (in fact, the final concert took place in 1996) with all the works broadcast, recorded and, hopefully, taken up by other soloists and orchestras across the world. But the aim was not simply to commission new music.

Each concerto was adopted by one of the educational divisions of the Strathclyde region and a younger Scottish composer-in-residence (for example, James MacMillan and William Sweeney) was hired to work alongside the teachers, the soloist for the concerto in question and other SCO musicians. The scheme was devised by Kathryn McDowell (who, in the same way as Gillian Moore in England, had a profound influence on Scottish orchestral education work). What emerged were either distinct compositions involving students and local bands of musicians, or 'framework' pieces (along the lines of *The Turn of the Tide*) into which pupils inserted their own work. The material they produced, based on the Maxwell Davies concerto, was assessed as part of their curricular activity. Also they had the chance to perform it in their local community with the full SCO a week or so before the Glasgow premiere of the *Strathclyde Concerto* itself.

One of the umbrella bodies for composers, the Society for the Promotion of New Music (SPNM), has seen the way the wind is blowing and is doing its best to encourage innovative forms of practice as well as fostering links with a wide range of 'commissioners' of new music, including amateur organisations and the formal education sector. In recent years it has explored a number of unusual areas, having run projects for musicians in association with architects to explore the analogies between music and architecture, for steel pan composing and in 1996 an ambitious collaborative project with one of the country's leading brass bands, the Black Dyke Mills Band. In 1996 it launched a pilot Adopt a Composer scheme (a notion first invented by the City of Birmingham Symphony Orchestra with its Adopt a Player scheme in the late 1980s) to enable young professional composers to develop a working relationship with amateur choirs. In the same year it ran a seven-month composing project with 28 A-Level and GCSE pupils and four teachers at a Welsh comprehensive school which ended with a professional performance at the Vale of Glamorgan Festival. The SPNM has launched a nation-wide training initiative to help music teachers with the compositional demands of the National Curriculum.

A consequence of the widening role of the composer and the demands of the music curriculum, with its new emphasis on composing, is that more and more teachers are generating their own music. In the past, their task was essentially pedagogic, but today many see themselves as artists in their own right. If this trend continues, we may be on the point of a remarkable flowering of musical talent. This is intrinsically a welcome development; but it is also a model of renewal, based on the retrieval of live links between people at large (in this case, especially the young) and the business of music-making, between a professional caste and amateur creativity.

However, too exclusive a preoccupation with composers underestimates the contribution of orchestral players. To be more precise, improvisational techniques are beginning to subvert the notion of the composer as a distinct specialist. Of course, this is no new phenomenon, for composers have always made use of improvisation as part of the creative process. But a change in degree is becoming a change in kind and is having a knock-on effect on a class of professionals whose traditional job has been to interpret the music of others. The pianist Veryan Weston commented on the rising status of improvisation in 'serious' new music:

> 'Over the last 30 years, some musicians in Europe have been developing ways to bypass notation and enter each moment as a performer with ideas that have been carefully, personally and consciously developed over years of practice and preparation ... There are obviously many profound political ramifications with this process of music-making. For a start I feel it is naturally addressing our culture which still reflects an infrastructure with feudal origins. So a composer is like a landlord accruing property in the form of notations (PRS registered in his name only). These get performed by well-dressed servants, themselves victims of the system, who are carefully trained and then supervised by the landlord's policeman – the conductor.'[14]

Some claim that these well-dressed servants are so estranged from their individual creativity goes that their psychological health is affected. This is a delicate area, but it is reasonable to conjecture that the ability or otherwise to express one's creativity is likely to be connected with a satisfactory lifestyle (satisfactory, that is, to the person conducting it). Those interested in a full discussion of the relationship between personality and musicianship will find much of value in Anthony E Kemp's recent study, *The Musical Temperament*.[15]

The perception of the need to foster the personal growth of musicians is the starting point for one of the most interesting orchestral experiments currently being undertaken. The Royal Philharmonic Orchestra (RPO) is emerging from troubled times, when its financial stability and artistic quality have both been in question. There has been a long interregnum between general managers. However, for all its difficulties, it established a long-term relationship in 1994 with Nottingham and Nottinghamshire and, one of the last orchestras to do so, developed an ambitious education and community outreach programme in partnership with the Guildhall School of Music and Drama.

14 Weston Veryan, 'It's time to recognise the creative strengths of improvisation' *New Notes,* SPNM, November 1996.

15 Kemp, Anthony E, *The Musical Temperament* (Oxford, Oxford University Press, 1996).

It is perhaps no accident that its Head of Education, Judith Webster, comes from a background in music therapy. Her view on arrival in 1993 was that it would not be possible to engage in effective participatory and community work unless the players' approach to music-making had been transformed first. She is worried about the way in which their training and career over-emphasised technical virtuosity. She told me:

> 'When musicians choose their path in life, they tap into the opportunity to be excellent in some field. This often leads to a feeling of insecurity and lack of personal recognition. It is possible to get submerged by the orchestra as an

institution and to lose touch with what set them off in the first place. It's possible to become quite screwed up.'

The RPO, working with Peter Wiegold, Sean Gregory and Paul Griffiths of the Guildhall School, devised a training programme for a core group of players, taking as its basic tenet that musical, social and personal goals are separate but interdependent facets of musical development. There have been some remarkable outcomes. The players are now confident enough to take part in community-based projects, many of which they organise themselves rather than handing them over to workshop leaders. The core group has set itself up as a musical ensemble called Sharp Edge, with its own artistic identity, sometimes working with composers and on other occasions producing new musical pieces themselves, based on improvisation.

A project with clients of the Nottingham Probation Service in 1995 was successful in many ways, but suffered from a characteristic weakness of this kind of scheme. When it was over, it was over and, having aroused expectations, the RPO was unable to offer continuity. This issue was addressed in a subsequent project, this time in association with a Nottingham 'street' organisation called Open Door which concerned itself with support for drug abusers. A local community musician, Mat Anderson, was co-opted at the outset to work on a follow-up programme once the project had finished. The project worked, at least in the sense that it is still running and the RPO players have paid a return visit. But Judith Webster admits that there were difficulties, especially in the relationship with the community musician. The essential problem, familiar to many community musicians, was how to establish a partnership between the RPO players, the community musician and the participants on unpatronising terms and to get the balance right between periods of high-intensity and low-intensity involvement.

What is notable here is the RPO's long-term commitment to a particular area, thanks to its special relationship with Nottingham and Nottinghamshire, and a willingness to identify weaknesses and address them. Most interesting of all is the possibility that the core group of players may be creating a 'virtuous circle' where the orchestra is not just giving something to the community, but is trying to establish an open way of working that may eventually lead to new music emerging from the core group's creative and community activities which will join the concert platform repertoire. In other words, this could become a model of practice which feeds directly into the orchestra's traditional artistic mission.

I have singled out the RPO for comment because it is explicitly (and unusually) tackling the question of whether community and outreach work can affect the nature of an orchestra. Like all latecomers, it has been able to profit from the experience of those who joined the game earlier. Will its ambitious plans succeed? The jury is out and it will be some years before we know the answer.

A number of other orchestras are ploughing their own furrows. The educational strategy of the Philharmonia pays special attention to the areas where it has residencies – London, Bedford and Leicester. They offer a wide-ranging package of activities, including schools workshops often linked to a visit to a Philharmonia concert or rehearsal; special concerts or open rehearsals supported by preparatory workshops and teachers' packs; and work with a variety of community groups involving older or retired people, young people through the Youth Service and multicultural projects. In Bedford an 'alternative Philharmonia' was created by a group of young people from a disadvantaged neighbourhood who assembled a collection of musical instruments made from recycled or scrap materials. The Philharmonia offers support to the education sector in two ways: it runs teachers' days and in-service training (INSET) to help teachers brush up their knowledge of the orchestral repertoire; and a programme for music students, including schemes to let postgraduate students play in Philharmonia rehearsals and to allow composition students to write for smaller ensembles with the results performed at the Royal Festival Hall.

The orchestra sees itself as operating in a European context and is planning to perform, record and tour the entire opus of György Ligeti. In parallel with this project, it will stage a course exploring Ligeti's music and its relevance to the classroom. The composer Nigel Osborne and the South African musician Eugene Skeef and the conductor Esa-Pekka Salonen will be among those running sessions.

The LSO, which has recruited Richard McNicol as its Music Animateur, has formed a Discovery Department with a comprehensive range of educational and community activities, covering nursery, primary, secondary and special educational schools. These include continuing education with targeted access schemes; teacher INSET; opportunities for music students at the main London conservatoires; commissioning composers to write works for school students, and collaboration with professionals from other art-forms; schemes for the elderly and the infirm; the development of links with local communities, especially in Islington and Hackney; work in prisons; training for the personal and musical development of LSO musicians; and the compilation of a visual and audio archive of LSO education work. The LSO hopes to establish a permanent base for its educational and community work in a redundant church in Old Street in London's East End.

The Bournemouth Orchestras have a well-established Education and Community Unit which runs a 'mixed economy' of activities with a variety of community groups. Schools projects concentrate on the three principal aspects of the music curriculum – composition, performance and listening. The unit stages elaborate cross-art-form projects, including rock music schemes with youth groups and activities with older people based on childhood reminiscence schemes. It also organises children's concerts, community concerts with small ensembles in villages, masterclasses and coaching.

Cross-art-form work and collaboration with musicians working in other genres are specialities. One example was a series of performances of music as part of a project with the North Devon College Band called 'Musical Maps' which took the landscape of the area and its associations, with Henry Williamson's novel *Tarka the Otter* as the inspiration for the music. The Bournemouth Sinfonietta runs Community Music Weeks where the orchestra develops a close relationship with a particular community over three months, culminating in an intensive residential week of activities. As with other orchestras, the Education and Community Unit devotes a great deal of energy to training the orchestra's musicians in the skills needed for outreach work. Plans are under discussion with Trinity College of Music to establish a training programme leading to a professional qualification.

At first sight opera, with its complexity of staging, high cost and (for many people) remote theatrical conventions is an implausible candidate for community-based work. But all the major, large-scale opera companies have community and educational outreach departments. In the mid-1980s Sue Harries and Welsh National Opera, with Phil Thomas as composer-in-residence, pioneered some ambitious community opera initiatives in Cardiff Bay. The idea caught on and some companies mount specially-written, ambitious community operas – for example, the Baylis Programme at English

National Opera's *Arion and the Dolphin* in the South-West in 1993-4 and
Glyndebourne's *In Search of Angels* in Peterborough in 1995. This year Glyndebourne
presented a community-based piece in its opera house for the first time: called *Misper*
(the title comes from police shorthand for missing person), it is an opera for young
people with music by John Lunn and libretto by Stephen Plaice. Less well-publicised
but often equally effective is the work of Britain's smaller touring opera groups. Many
of them exist on a part-time basis and cannot call on revenue funding from the Arts
Councils and Regional Arts Boards (RABs). They have found that it is easiest to fund-
raise for educational or community projects, whether from charitable foundations, the
private sector, RABs and local education authorities.

According to Jean Nicholson, manager of the Opera and Music Theatre Forum,
financial necessity soon yielded to cultural conviction as a motive for working in this
field: 'They found it more rewarding than they had thought it would be and it
stimulated them to think of how to communicate new ideas about opera.' So, to choose
a few well-regarded examples, Mecklenburgh Opera accompanies each production with
a specially devised education project and every two years or so commissions a new piece
of music theatre, often devised through a series of workshops involving the composer,
performers, librettist and conductors. Pimlico Opera specialises in taking opera to
unusual venues and is well known for its work in prisons, involving inmates in all
aspects of production and performance. Vocem Electric Voice Theatre creates new
pieces using electronic technology and works directly with young people in schools and
community groups. Finally, ACE designated 1997 as the Year of Opera and Music
Theatre in the East of England. The programme has a substantial education and
community component.

Stepping back, then, we can see how more and more attention is being given to
fostering the creativity of individual players and their personal growth in the context of
community-based practice. Nobody is claiming that this either improves or diminishes
the quality of their playing of the traditional concert repertoire, although it may help to
sharpen their motivation and job satisfaction. There *is* evidence that it enables them to
broaden the range of their work. This is helpful to their careers in a highly competitive
market and many of them report great pleasure in being able to escape, at least for a
time, from the constraints of conventional music-making. It is possible that with the
passage of time this new, freer approach to musicality will contribute to a development
of the repertoire.

Composers too are finding that working in community settings is an exciting way of
testing their inventiveness. After a long period of relative isolation, contemporary classical
music is regaining contact with the lives and aspirations of people at large and is learning
to make use of other genres. It is as if a breath of fresh air is blowing through a hothouse.

All of this is to the good, but does not mean that the nature of the orchestra is being
turned upside down. Rather its role is being adjusted to suit its present circumstances.
This is no revolution, but gradual reform, and as we look towards the future we can
imagine the orchestral world carrying on much as it is now, but with closer and more
vigorous interaction with communities as well as with audiences. Indeed, audiences which
have engaged in participatory practice should be able to walk into a concert hall without
feeling in the least intimidated, because their understanding of the process of music-
making will have enhanced their critical appreciation of what an orchestra can do and will
have honed their critical faculties.

A more controversial, but widely held, view is that computers make music creation too easy. Sir Peter Maxwell Davies is a composer deeply committed to the democratisation of music, but he believes that an essential element of learning about music is the acquisition of musical 'literacy'. He told me:

> 'It's impossible to think of dealing with Western music without being able to read and write. It's as if you could handle German literature without being able to read German. It's felt to be enough for people to express themselves with the means for doing so being unimportant. This is due in part to a misconceived idea of elitism in music; dexterity is deemed to be elitist. I'm afraid that the electronic keyboard is sometimes seen as a panacea for all ills. Oh, yes, kids can produce respectable work with it, but it bypasses the possibility of relating your skill in creating sound to your body. The core of music is the relation between physical, mental and spiritual abilities.'

Some people have a difficulty with this insistence on difficulty. First, is it actually true that using computers does not demand first-class technical and theoretical skills? This seems implausible. A glance at the equipment in a sound studio or through the relevant literature makes it very clear that a sound knowledge base and considerable dexterity are required of composers. The development of electroacoustic composition is accompanied by experimental research into psychology and the properties of sound with which practitioners are wise to familiarise themselves. Paul Wright suspects that what lies behind this critique of electroacoustic music is a fundamental 'lack of sympathy with the way music is changing from a note-based system to a timbre-based approach through time'. What is at issue is not so much that composing is now as easy as falling off a log as that the necessary skills are not the same as those we use in learning to play an instrument and read conventional notation or in creating music for instruments. If it turns out that these skills can be learnt more quickly than the old ones and that it no longer takes a lifetime of quasi-monastic dedication to compose and present new work, so what? Only those for whom music is a priestly mystery inaccessible to the multitude will have cause for regret. Musical democrats should cheer.

Community musicians are not necessarily wedded to a revolutionary new musical language, as Sonic are, but they too see nothing to regret in the arrival of new, easier ways of composing. Alison Tickell of Community Music in London told me: 'The great strength of the new technologies is the quality of "easiness" because it enables all kinds of people to engage with music as performers and composers as opposed to simply being listeners before.' Technique is no more than a precondition for music; it is not a sacred ingredient.

It is easier to agree with Maxwell Davies when he says that once the music has been created, it is no longer necessary to recruit and train armies of people to play it, so that the traditional social dimension of the concert or, for that matter, the *ceilidh* is at risk. This would be true if we were to suppose that electroacoustic music will become universal and that other forms will die out. At present there is no evidence that this is likely. If we look at the lively diversity of the musical scene, the old and the new look as if they are in a state of cohabitation rather than a fight to the death.

In one area where recording technology has taken a firm popular hold there are interesting indications that consumers are compensating for the absence of players by becoming more proactive themselves. In pop music the rise of the disc jockey at raves and other events suggests strongly that theatricality and improvisation can be combined successfully with recording technology. Those attending see themselves as being at the centre of the stage and develop dancing skills requiring virtuosity and stamina. Both professional DJs and interested individuals manipulate and alter existing recordings through techniques like dubbing and scratching to create 'their own' work which, if they wish, they produce and market to CD standard. A good deal of jungle music has been made this way in back garages and bedrooms. This is no more than speculation, but if musical presentation were ever decisively to abandon the live performer, perhaps we can anticipate the emergence of individual music consumers as 'artists' in their own right.

In passing, it is worth noting that the live performer may be facing a challenge from another quarter. Science is experimenting with computer equivalents to the player and the singer. Computer models at the Computer Music Research Institute in Stamford, Connecticut, have been devised which show that whereas a mathematically perfect electronic clarinet sounds dull and artificial, the introduction of a 5% uncertainty factor creates a result that sounds alive and attractive. By extension, it would appear that human imperfection is an essential component of art (as the poet Robert Herrick observed in a different context when he wrote of 'a sweet disorder in the dress [enkindling] there a loveliness'). Stamford has also created a mathematically perfect 'human' voice:

> ' "Sheila" passes mathematically measured air through her algorithmic vocal chords and because she tends to come up from under each note, just as human singers do ..., she sounds human. "Sheila" is all the more convincing because, in common with her human counterparts, her error factor is greater when she starts singing.'[10]

Meanwhile, a concert pianist and neurosurgeon, Professor Manfred Clynes, noting that emotion is expressed in micro-muscular responses, has invented an interactive computer system, the Super Conductor, whose programme takes over the motor function aspects of playing a piece of music. Computer 'windows' allow the user, whether musical or not, to vary the character or emotional quality of a performance.

The question of ease or difficulty is much more problematic in schools. As I have already noted, well-informed and experienced observers such as Eric Bolton, former HMI Senior Chief Inspector, fear that the child-centred approach to education has been taken too far. The correct move away from an over-academic view of music teaching towards creative expression has led to a disturbing lack of rigour. 'What began to worry me,' he told me, 'was the hegemony of "doing it". Concentrating on doing rather than understanding has become almost *de rigueur* in arts courses.' Of the pillars of the music curriculum, there have been advances in *performing* and *composing*, but less progress, he feels, with *understanding*. Getting the balance right between two schools of thought – those who favour the instinctual or the impulsive and others who argue for the organised or the formal – is perhaps one of the most delicate challenges facing music teachers.

There is general agreement that electronic technology in the classroom has great potential, but that this is not being realised for a number of reasons. Like record players in the old days, an electronic keyboard can be a way of *not* teaching. There is not enough suitable equipment in the classroom and teachers themselves need more training.

A more fundamental problem may be that there is not enough bespoke software available. Some of the best programmes so far enable young children to select melodic modules and join them up into a melodic shape. But they tend to place visual perception and choice first and do little to stretch aural awareness. In neurological terms this means that they favour the left side of the brain rather than the right, while most educationists would prefer methods which develop a balance of skills. Some software designed for children with special needs combines visual with acoustic imagery and new 'paint' programmes are being produced which enable the user to make 'brushstrokes' that create its 'sound' equivalent, thus stimulating both sides of the brain.

For older children, a range of equipment is on the market which links music keyboards and sequencers; keyboards can also be linked through MIDI to computer programmes, a powerful combination which can be operated by children from about seven years old right up to professional studio practice. Unfortunately much equipment is generally unsuitable for the classroom, being mainly designed for domestic consumers.

However, the music industry is aware of the potential of the education sector and supports training not only for individual customers, many of who are young, but also for schools. Manufacturers, such as Yamaha and Technics (part of Polygram), back their sales with training programmes. Yamaha Kemble in the United Kingdom has a Music School Department which offers training for teachers, mainly with a technical rather than pedagogic emphasis, and has also established about 90 music schools for customers, often associated with retail outlets.

Some electroacoustic musicians sees little real value in using machinery that reproduces the sounds of existing musics; the equipment which Sonic Arts believes to be necessary for educational (or community) work could be as basic as a cassette-based four-track recorder, a pair of good loudspeakers, a sound processor, which transforms sound in real time and is programmable for echo, reverberation, pitch shifting and so forth and a sampler (which is a device for capturing sound that can then be altered in a number of ways and 'triggered' by a MIDI keyboard or other controller). Like many educationists and community musicians, the organisation has been much influenced by the writings of John Paynter, for whom learning about music is a voyage of discovery. More than 20 years ago, he and Elizabeth Paynter set out a methodology for which the latest technology provides a perfect means of realisation:

> 'A child making a poem searches for the words that will express succinctly what he has to say. So in making a piece of music he must also try things out, explore and experiment with his materials until he can discover sounds that will have meaning for him and convey the essence of what he feels.'[11]

As Paul Wright points out, there is 'a gulf between music-making with electronic instruments and acoustic sound sources'.[12] The as yet unresolved question facing teachers is how to achieve the right balance between conventional musicianship with instruments and voices, the use of factory pre-set electronic instrumental sounds for composition and the manipulation of electronically created sounds or sounds recorded from nature. At present there is a wide range of practice in the classroom. An interlocking issue concerns the management of the limited equipment to be found in the classroom and the combination of individual work with full class work.

Not surprisingly, inspectors and educationists are worried by unimaginative use of equipment and poor learning outcomes and concerned about the lack of models of good teaching practice and assessment. What ways are there out of the impasse? Firstly, there is an urgent need for the development of hardware and software specifically designed for the classroom and, secondly, for the commissioning of classroom teaching materials which offer teachers examples of integrated work. Also, if we bear in mind the growing importance of the work of artists in schools, the education sector would be well advised

11 Paynter, John and Elizabeth, *The Dance and the Drum* (Universal, 1974). Cited in *The Music Teacher* magazine, September–November 1991, p.22.

12 Wright, Paul, 'New Technology in the Classroom', *Musical Times*, August 1992, p.381.

to involve professional composers in classroom activity in much the same way as they may already be involved in their community-based practice. Taking a hint from Contemporary Music-making for Amateurs, it would be useful to commission new work for conventional instruments and live electronics within the technical reach of young performers and the equipment resources of schools. Sonic Arts has made a start on this approach with Javier Alvarez' *Pyramid of Pianos* (1996) which was prepared with and for school and university students in Kirklees.

Although the new technologies promise their most exciting applications in the field of direct creativity, we should not forget that they can also offer support to the development of 'appreciation'. The invention of the CD-ROM, for example, has led to new ways of improving listening skills. As George Odam points out:

> 'Although some of the early programmes released on CD-ROM did nothing more than transfer the pages of a book plus an accompanying cassette onto the computer screen, within a short space of time the potential for interactivity to enhance musical learning was already being discovered. There is no other medium that can provide an immediate link in real time between music and the visual, either through word, diagram or illustration, together with choice and interactivity with the user. The techniques already learnt through television are now beginning to find their real home in this new medium.'[13]

Not unnaturally, Sonic Arts sees education as a crucial area for its activities. Schools, for all their problems, are the only place where a complete cross-section of the population has access to new technology and the challenge of the new music curriculum offers an unrepeatable opportunity to spread the gospel. Sonic Arts set up 'exemplary' projects with schools to show how it is possible to go back to the raw materials of sound and how these can be structured and manipulated into music. It also provides INSET programmes in various parts of the country.

New programmes are being regularly issued and one example of good practice is Peter Gabriel's *Xplora*, produced in 1995, which introduces music and instruments from many cultures as well as new studio and composing techniques.

This work has not gone unnoticed by the Department for Education and Employment, which has commissioned Sonic Arts to undertake research into ways in which new technology could support the music curriculum. It is giving support to the National Council for Educational Technology, which, by means of a pilot project with eight schools in two London boroughs, is preparing a comprehensive set of classroom materials for teachers, touching on every musical genre from jungle to Baroque music, which is due to be published in 1997.

The techniques of electroacoustic music are as relevant to work in the community as to that in schools. There is great potential, for example, for increasing access to music for people with disabilities. Those working in the field include the National Disability and Music Information Service and the Soundbeam Project. Sonic Arts has consistently involved young people with disabilities and learning difficulties in its workshops. Soundbeam runs a training scheme, SoundAbility, in partnership with other organisations, such as Jazz Services, Community Music Wales, Drake Music Project, Sound It Out and the community music umbrella agency, Sound Sense.

The Drake Music Project is leading the way in the development of customised software and hardware for disabled people. Set up in 1988, it has pioneered the use of computers

13 Odam, George, *op cit*, p.97.

for physically disabled children and adults; its aim is not to offer music therapy (for this assumes that disability is some kind of sickness to be healed as opposed to a condition that can limit access to the usual opportunities of life), but to promote creativity through musical expression at every level of ability, from those taking their first musical steps to the professional composer or player. Currently available standard systems are often inadequate to the needs of people with severe disabilities. A number of interrelated factors can reduce motivation and limit their interest in using them independently of outside help. Computer systems are often complicated to use and in their visual presentation; some people lack reading skills; screens may not be large or clear enough; and systems may be difficult to operate without full mouse or track ball control.

Drake have adopted two approaches to improve disabled access to electroacoustic composition; firstly, by adapting, extending or combining existing software and hardware and, secondly, by creating bespoke or customised solutions. For physically disabled users this has often meant devising suitable switches which can be managed by a person whose voluntary movement is restricted to a few fingers, or the feet, head, chin, elbow or other part of the body; and for those with visual impairment they offer screen-reader or magnifier add-ons. Drake runs regular workshops in several parts of the country, along with residencies, touring workshops (often culminating in performances), taster days and INSET projects.

One interesting example of the imaginative exploitation of technology is the EMS Soundbeam (developed and promoted by the Soundbeam Project), which translates gesture into sound (or, more precisely, is a system of ultrasonic impulses which detects movements and turns them into instructions for controlling electronic musical instruments). This is a MIDI controller, originally designed for dancers: a sonic beam emitted by the instrument can be set to various different modes, including major scale, whole tone scale, chord with portamento and a user note definable mode. The beam can be interrupted by any kind of movement – a hand, a foot or a wheelchair – and so enables the user to explore and experiment with a variety of sounds.

An extraordinary piece of research gives a flavour of what may be possible in the future for those almost totally deprived of motor functions. Richard Bamford, the composer and percussionist with the Hands On Technology Group in Edinburgh, has established that people in this condition may still be able to respond to the world of sound. Even when the eye is all but incapable of registering visual images, the musculature of the eyes remains intact and responds to sound sources. The technology exists to convert eye movement into controllable sound; it consists of an infra-red reference beam illuminating the eye, a video camera to record eye movements, a computer which analyses the information from the camera and a tone or sound generator linked to loudspeakers. Curiously, the Ministry of Defence at Farnborough is conducting research of its own into a similar system for the benefit of pilots in fighter planes. Bamford is seeking support from the Drake Music Project among others and from funding bodies to take the project further.

A growing number of musicians and musical organisations are making use of the Internet. Evelyn Glennie, the percussionist, for example, has established a Web page which gives visual and aural information about her work and is intended to allow her to conduct electronic masterclasses. The capability now exists for musicians in different parts of the globe to 'jam' together in real time, although it is not yet possible to do so at CD acoustic quality. There are many newsgroups on the Internet where people with shared musical tastes can 'meet' and discuss issues of common interest. However, it remains to be seen how important an addition to the creative process all these new possibilities will turn out to be. Although many millions world-wide have access to the Internet via their personal computers or their employers, this is true only of a minority of the British population. While prices for the necessary software and hardware have fallen sharply in real terms, there is a real risk that the new technologies will tend to create two classes of 'haves' and 'have nots' with the poor and the poorly educated cut off (at least once school days are over) from this brave new world.

The future of the Internet is unclear. According to Owen Kelly, some argue that: 'people will create their own unique dataspheres which reveal and reflect aspects of their creators' natures, as any creative work does' or that 'the Internet will be the start of a gigantic communal project in which culture ceases to be made by the few for the many and becomes instead a collective democratic enterprise.' A more pessimistic view has it that 'we can look forward to a digital realm that mimics the format of the industrial mass media: a global web dominated by a few corporations whose idea of interactivity is to offer a limited range of personally customisable packages for subscribers.'[14]

The Internet faces severe technical problems as it tries to accommodate more and more users and threatens to collapse (so to speak) under its own weight. However, it is not implausible to predict that it will in due course become an effective new means of accessing and buying recorded music, whether by commercial companies or by individuals interested in self-publication. Also, it may well be possible in a few years to develop the practice of electronic music workshops with distinguished musicians. All of this could have major implications for amateur, community-based and education work. But these things lie in the future. What is needed now is for the appropriate agencies (funding bodies and umbrella organisations) to monitor the situation as it develops.

14 Kelly, Owen, *Digital Creativity* (London, Calouste Gulbenkian Foundation, 1996) pp.115-7.

It is clear that we are at a cross-roads. The astonishing potential of electroacoustic music, both as a new means of composition and as an educational tool, and the equally astonishing opportunities for communicating information and for music distribution and marketing, have yet to be fully assessed. However, we know enough about what is happening to see that there are immediate applications, whether in the classroom or the community, for which the resources, as well as the political will, need to be assembled.

7 RELATIVE VALUES

Take ... the way in which two people, Jack and Jill, might appear to agree or disagree about a third person, say a Giant. Jill might say that the Giant is huge, eats and drinks a lot, is noisy, a bit rough and ready and very extrovert. She might, being extrovert herself, thoroughly enjoy the company of the Giant and go to all his boisterous parties. Jack, on the other hand, might agree with Jill's description but not with her evaluation. Being of a reflective and scholarly disposition, he might find the Giant an overpowering bore and consequently avoid all invitations to his castle, preferring to spend his evenings more quietly. They each perceive similar features of the character of the Giant but differ in their value response ... So it is with music.
KEITH SWANWICK, *MUSIC, MIND AND EDUCATION*

Creativity is not a way of seeing or distancing, but of being in and constituting, the everyday world. In part this is because in the human 'life world' or 'everyday culture', all artefacts, actions and practices 'signify'; they produce meaning. But this meaning is never strictly contained or given; there is an 'excess of meaning', or potential meaning, which must be selected from, negotiated with, humanly activated in order to produce specific personal meaning in the user/viewer/receiver. In this sense every understanding or use of 'meaning objects' around us is, intrinsically, also an act of creativity.
PAUL WILLIS, *REALISING THE POTENTIALS OF COMMON CULTURE*

Questions of judgment

Making judgments about art is always tricky. This is because they occur in debatable territory, at the juncture where the objective fact of the work and the subjective nature of the responding eye or ear engage with one another. But critical methodologies have emerged with which most educated people are broadly familiar. It is possible to analyse structure and imagery, to determine the relevance of historical context and, at a minimum, to give some account of the experience of a work of art, whether it be a performance, a book or a painting. Over the passage of time a consensus is usually arrived at about the value we place on it, both in itself and in comparison with others. We do not kid ourselves that *the* truth about it can be established once for all as firmly as it can with a scientific hypothesis, but certain agreements can be arrived at, however provisionally and tentatively. As the critic F R Leavis used to ask when discussing his response to a literary text: 'This is so, isn't it?'

Here we have a version, with the rough edges smoothed, of the line Richard Hoggart took during the 1970s debate about the value of community arts (see page 84). The continued vitality of competitive festivals in the amateur music world and the anxieties which are surfacing among music teachers and educationists (illustrated by the recent correspondence in *Classical Music* – see page 71) indicate that it is still a common view. It is one I find I partly share. But it does not seem quite adequate to the variety of the contemporary arts scene, nor does it seem a rich enough response to the various directions which social and cultural change has taken during the twentieth century.

If, with particular reference to music, it is the case that ethical and cultural values are increasingly seen as relative; that the dominance of the Western classical tradition has been challenged by a new interest in, and sensitivity to, the musics of other world cultures and to old and new popular genres; that the distinctions between performer and consumer, and between amateur and professional, are blurring; that we need to pay attention to the social as well as the intrinsic meaning of music; and that scientific advance is demonstrating the multiple synergies of music in the functioning of the brain – if this analysis is correct, then a more complex model of evaluation will be necessary.

The Arts Council of Great Britain's 1993 policy document, *A Creative Future*, makes a stab at identifying the outlines of such a model. It proposed six facets of 'quality': *creator or producer quality* ('the creator's gut feelings, and such standards as "production values" '); *expert assessor/critic quality*; *consumer quality* ('if [this] is to be a useful concept, it must be at least as much about the nature of the artistic experience as about the numbers involved'); *enrichment of the community* ('the arts can be powerful agents for bringing people together in communities defined by geography, ethnicity, gender, religion, or simply shared interest'); *quality in variety* ('the argument runs that in a society of many different interests, cultures and experiences, an essential test of artistic quality is that the arts reflect that diversity'); and *fitness for purpose* ('the essence of this approach ... is that it is not an abstract issue but one which arises from its context').[1]

Most, if not all, of this checklist is relevant to participatory music (that is, amateur music-making, community-based practice and the educational and outreach work of orchestras and opera companies). As Peter Renshaw told me, echoing *A Creative Future*:

> 'In this kind of creative activity, there are different forms of excellence, each with their own criteria of appropriateness – an awareness of context: social, moral, political, artistic. In a music workshop the artistic criteria should be the same as for a Beethoven quartet; you should remember that the other criteria come into play and, in fact, sometimes you might not even reach the artistic criteria.'

One of the striking features of this field of artistic activity is that evaluation of what is being done is fragmented and confused.

It could, I suppose be argued that amateur musicians should be regarded as an exception to this multi-faceted approach; in their case, the only issue is creator or producer quality – or, simply, how well they play the music. The still vigorous system of competitive festivals, one might suggest, is perfectly competent to weed out the sheep from the goats and so, for that matter, is audience response. But this argument cannot be sustained, for it is clear the world of the amateur musician is changing. More and more groups realise that they have a community role and are undertaking outreach and educational work. Thanks to National Lottery money, the arts funding system is set to offer them more substantial financial support than in the past and will want to make sure that they are fulfilling cultural as well as purely artistic functions. Other items on the checklist are also relevant to their work.

So far as the community musician is concerned, an outside observer, aware of the wide range of possible aims and outcomes, of the different bases for evaluation, will want to focus on some practical questions. What exactly are you trying to achieve when you set out on such-and-such a project? And when it is over, can you say with a fair degree of certainty what has actually taken place? Has it made a difference to those taking part and, if so, what kind of a difference?

It is surprisingly difficult to find adequate answers. There is a widespread assumption that participation is a good in itself and that, provided everyone has an enjoyable time, it is unnecessary – and perhaps impractical – to look further. During my researches, I raised the issue of evaluation with all those directly engaged in project work. The almost universal response from those I interviewed could be summed up as, oh dear, yes, evaluation is important and we know we could do it better; it is something we plan to address soon. Many evaluation reports seem to have been composed with at least half an eye on fund-raising from new sponsors or to satisfy the demands of funding bodies; and their dominant characteristic is self-praise. That time-worn device, facsimiles of, or quotations from, enthusiastic letters from eight year-olds or 80 year-olds, is still not uncommon. While it is true that many projects solicit the views of participants, this often takes the form of simple tick-box questionnaires.

1 *A Creative Future,*
op cit, p.53.

Here are two examples of self-assessment which are not untypical of the prevailing tone of voice: I have carefully chosen them from organisations whose work is generally admirable. In an account of a Royal Philharmonic Orchestra (RPO) project for children with severe learning difficulties, we read:

> 'There was a great deal of hugely positive feedback from teachers, and therapists and some parents from the school ... Some children visibly blossomed ... The success of the project was attributable not only to the RPO teams, but to the shared ownership with teachers, with whom we sought to work very closely.'[2]

A London Sinfonietta educational visit to Finland was also a triumph:

> 'The Sinfonia Lahti project was huge success. A young, dynamic and enterprising orchestra with a good relationship to its local community, it seemed the perfect place to begin ... The Tampere Philharmonic was a delight to work with because of the strength of their commitment ... the project rose to an electrifying climax at the final performance and was, as a whole, deemed a very valuable and successful enterprise by all parties involved.'[3]

So, full marks all round.

What we are facing is a failure of critical debate. There is more than one reason for this state of affairs. Some are purely practical and essentially to do with financial resourcing. Unlike public, professional events or performances, most community and education work takes place in small, intimate groups. Neither the funding agencies nor the press are in a position to attend more than a fraction of what is going on in schools and arts or community centres up and down the country. Professional community artists often work individually or in small project teams and, being poorly funded and extremely busy, are seldom able to sample the work of others in the field. There are few critical magazines or journals to monitor and disseminate good (and for that matter bad) practice. Conferences take place from time to time to enable an exchange of views and methods to take place, but demonstrations in an artificial context are insufficient compensation for the direct experience of real-life activity 'on the ground'. Not enough people see not enough work.

By the same token, until recent years amateur music-makers have been left very much to their own devices so far as their nascent social and community role is concerned. It is to the credit of the National Federation of Music Societies (NFMS) that it is seeking to establish models of good practice, but many societies and clubs are inexperienced and some are uninterested in extending the scope of their work.

So far as the education and outreach work of professional music organisations is concerned, much of it follows the methodology established by community musicians. But it is sometimes being undertaken less from conviction than because it has become the done thing. Although there is a good deal of excellent practice, experienced observers believe that standards are variable. It is difficult to be quite sure what the situation is, for as Phyllida Shaw notes in her survey of the education work of British orchestras:

> 'While most education managers recognise the importance of evaluating individual projects, the regular evaluation of the programme as a whole is not undertaken as a matter of course; nor are similar standards, aims or expectations applied across the profession as a whole.'[4]

Andrew Peggie, who has been actively involved in community music since the 1970s, acknowledges that:

> ' ... there has been very little practitioner debate about quality and standards. Many musicians are by their nature nervous of analysing what they do, believing access and

2 Royal Philharmonic Orchestra Community and Education Programme Project Report for the Hamlyn Foundation (unpublished, June 1996).

3 Report – London Sinfonietta Education Project in Finland, second phase, spring-autumn 1995 (London Sinfonietta, 18 May 1996), unpaginated.

4 Shaw, Phyllida, *op cit,* p.3.

engagement to be more important than critical debate. Also a good number of them did not emerge through the formal education or training sector and have neither the analytical tools nor the confidence to engage in debate.'

In this rather unrigorous climate, a little-examined orthodoxy has emerged around the music workshop. According to Gillian Moore of the South Bank Centre:

' ... the formula of the creative music workshop is unhelpful. It can give the illusion of freedom, but in fact it has its own set of rules, but, often because they tend to be thrown together and do not last for a long time, the professionals are firmly in control, not the participants.'

At the 1996 Sound Sense conference Phil Mullen, who trains community musicians for Goldsmiths College in London and is a co-ordinator of the cross-cultural 4 Corners project, led a seminar on workshop skills. He put two questions to the participants: what did they fear most as workshop leaders? And what measures could one take to make oneself and one's group feel safe? The discussion that ensued led to some interesting answers. According to the conference report:

' ... "fear" turned out to be a good word. Its manifestations could take many forms. In some cases fear was acknowledged as beneficial – the adrenalin effect. There was much talk of fear of the unknown, as well as problems of personal insecurity and lack of experience. Leaders could abuse their position, but were worried that participants might walk out or be unco-operative. For their part, workshop members were scared of "what might be thrown at them" or suspected that the event might be a waste of time.'[5]

Workshops tend to be parachuted into a community which is given a taste of what is possible, only to see it instantly withdrawn. They can be a cheap, patronising option for sectors of society suffering from disadvantage. Gillian Moore claims:

' ... [They give] people access, over a limited period of time, to a certain amount of skill. Through these workshops, we are constantly surprised by what people can produce given such brief access to resources, expertise and encouragement – songs, books, poems, paintings, whole operas. In my opinion, we are in danger of creating a two-tier system – the rich get performances and exhibitions, the poor get ... workshops ... We work with people for one day, two days, one week, two weeks. The workshops take on their own momentum and people find themselves hurtling towards an inevitable conclusion – a performance, an exhibition, a publication. But we, the institutions, are very confused about these public manifestations – we want the performances in the concert hall, billed in the main artistic programme, the paintings hung in the main gallery space – and then come the excuses: "It's not really a performance, it's a sharing, a showing ... "; "now you must remember when you look at this work, they only had four days in which to do it"; "it's not the product, it's the process that counts".'[6]

This problem of getting the right balance between process and product lies at the heart of the participatory idea. The acquisition of artistic skills is indeed important and, community musicians increasingly favour the inclusion of some kind of public performance in their programmes of work; however, the process of arriving at an end-product is as valuable as the end-product itself, which, in effect, is an illustration of the process, not its goal.

Some argue that the term 'workshop' should be abandoned. Andrew Peggie, writing in *Sounding Board*, feels it is time to:

' ... consign it to the 1970s retro-culture box ... What the workshop orthodoxy largely ignores are the musical perceptions (and indeed misperceptions) of the ordinary people

5 *Cut and Blend*, conference report, *Sounding Board*, Sound Sense, spring 1996, Bury St Edmunds, p.50.

6 Moore, Gillian, 'Arts Institutions and their Education programme – content and Possibility', speech at British-American Arts Association Conference, 8-9 February 1995 (unpublished).

who are potential participants. Most people's views of musical participation are coloured
by what they see on TV, and stereotypical concepts such as "concert", "rehearsal",
"practising", "conductor", "teacher and pupil". It's with these notions that I believe the
workshop should start. "Let's make a street band – I'll conduct" is surely a more honest
invitation than "Let's explore the rhythms of Samba together".[7]

This is a reasonable point of view. But a distinction needs to be drawn between ditching a
word associated with slipshod and unexamined practice and abandoning a notion of music-
making that is more than simply making music, more than 'just' putting on a concert. At a
meeting in 1989 for Association of British Orchestras (ABO) education managers, Gillian
Moore (then still at the London Sinfonietta) said:

> 'We must always be willing to ask questions about out methods: are they the most
> appropriate to the organisations we work for as well as to the client groups? For example,
> it could be more appropriate to produce a high quality series of learning materials in
> response to the needs of a group and the artistic programme, rather than live workshops.'

Whatever the chosen methodology, the participatory musical process embodies personal and
social as well as artistic development. It is perfectly possible to pay no attention to this and not
to acknowledge its importance, as was until recently the case in the amateur music sector. It
has been the contribution of the community music movement at its best to demonstrate that
this is a mistake.

Ben Higham put it very clearly to me when I visited Community Music East in Norwich,
where he works. 'What we are doing here is to act as a medium through which people can
develop a high level of critical understanding.' He described what this could mean in practice.
In a step-by-step development, the participant in a project first has to acquire the self-
confidence to assert a preference: yes, I like this piece of music, or, no, I don't. The second
step is to determine the basis for this judgment. What meaning in the music drives my
interpretation? The participant sets out to answer this question by engaging in the process of
music-making, of active listening and debate (not only aesthetic but also social or political, on
the grounds that art takes place in the wider environment of life as it is lived). This leads to a
recognition by the participant that his or her ideas have changed or deepened, which in turn
forms the basis of a further enquiry.

The validity of this model will be widely recognised by community musicians (indeed it
could arguably stand as a description of the creative process itself). Of course, people will
view it from their own different perspectives. For some, it justifies the position that music is a
technique for personal growth, for opening up the imagination and becoming fuller and more
complete human beings. For others it is a means of coming to terms with the world around
us and organising to change it. For others still, like Gillian Moore, it describes a revolutionary
new way of making art:

> 'We are constantly flirting with a new kind of collaborative art making, but never quite
> getting into bed with it ... I believe that a new collaborative form of art making is bursting
> to emerge – one in which the professional artist benefits artistically from working with the
> non-professional, and *vice versa*.'[8]

It is possible to hold one, two or all of these positions simultaneously, or to disagree with all
but one. But they share a common factor – the process of community music-making is not
just a way of expressing oneself or of honing unexplored performance skills, but of developing
one's *understanding*. Sue Robertson, former head of education at the South Bank Centre and
now chief executive of the London Arts Board, who has given much thought to questions of

7 Peggie, Andrew, 'It's
time to stop doing
workshops', *Sounding
Board*, Sound Sense,
Bury St Edmunds,
winter 1997, p.9.

8 Peggie, Andrew,
'Cutting Edge Work',
Sounding Board, Sound
Sense, Bury St
Edmunds, autumn
1996, p.11.

creative assessment, told me: 'The task is to create the conditions in which people will achieve confidence about their work and get the critical tools to respond to the music-making of other people'.[9] It follows that evaluation and self-assessment are intrinsic parts of what is a subjective and at least partly internalised process. How is one to evaluate evaluation?

I want to offer two kinds of answer to this question. The first will seek to address ways in which all those concerned can make their necessary judgments and the second will consider improvements to the external circumstances which are at present inhibiting the effectiveness of the participatory process.

Let us begin with the person who has signed up to a music workshop or similar event. From their perspective three processes are taking place simultaneously. They are a translation of the *Creative Future* criteria into individual, participatory terms. The first is the development of musical techniques; the second is the acquisition or refinement of independent social and interactive skills and the third, and arguably the most significant, is the growth of critical understanding – of music both in itself and in relation to its uses, and of oneself.

Now it is perfectly possible, as Andrew Peggie pointed out, to conceive of teaching musical skills by rote, in which case the participant is essentially a pupil or apprentice who could just as well be on a secretarial as a music course. However, if learning music is more than just learning music, even if that is all one thinks one is doing or wanting to do (and that is an underpinning theme of this book), we will still need to take the second and third categories into account. So whether we are talking of a classic workshop or some more conventional means of transmitting skills, active iteration between the participant and the leader or teacher is called for. By the end of a project, assuming it to be effective, they ought ideally to find themselves on an equal footing. One would expect the power relationship in the group to shift from control by the leader to something approaching equal partnership in a common enterprise. While an external eye would be able to assess the objective development of musical and social skills (say at a concert), much of what is taking place is subjective and internal to the person experiencing it. It is a dialectical process where the knowledge and skills a participant brings to a project at its outset are modified by the contribution of the workshop leader and other members of the group; this enhanced understanding is then applied to one's own practice which one then re-introduces to the group, and so on. There is a mutual dependency between doing and appreciating, action and reflection.

This account bears comparison with the notions of 'progression' which have been established for the delivery of the music curriculum in schools. It will be recalled that the *Non-statutory Guidance for Music* issued by the Curriculum Council for Wales (see page 70) classifies progression in terms of what pupils are to do, focusing on the 'development and application of skills and understanding in an increasingly wide range of contexts', and in terms of the nature of tasks which pupils should be able to undertake, emphasising familiarity of the context, complexity of tasks and individual responsibility.

These are necessarily somewhat abstract and abbreviated descriptions of a complex series of interpersonal transactions and intrapersonal events. But a number of practical prescriptions can be derived from them. Workshop leaders should be explicit about their aims, while finding out what they can about the needs and expectations of the group, always being sensitive to its concerns and ready to negotiate. These aims may well not be exclusively aesthetic, but may also be cultural and social (on occasion, even political). The project is worth doing only if a common set of values is hammered out and agreed at the outset. A succession of small goals, giving a chance for discussion and revision, is more consistent with an organic development

9 I am indebted in the following paragraphs to a useful conversation on evaluation which I had with Sue Robertson, although the reader should not hold her responsible for my conclusions.

of joint endeavour than a single large one. It is also the leaders' responsibility to establish a psychologically secure and physically appropriate and congenial space within which a project can take place.

Two conclusions can be drawn from this. Firstly, quality in any debate-led process is a moving target and it is a contradiction in terms to set out definitions in advance and apply them to results which, if they are to have any value, will be unpredictable. To agree aims is not the same as to be certain about outcomes. All an outside observer can do is look for signs of rigour and vigour. Secondly, because the heart of participatory creativity is invisible, it is more practical to assess objective consequences or side-effects rather than the activity itself. An analogy suggests itself with those advanced scientific experiments in which physicists deduce the existence of unmeasurable particles through the effects they have on what *can* be measured.

Tim Joss, in a report on a seminar about the role of community music, identified some of the key issues:

> 'An implication of community music activity being grounded in the real world of lived experience is that the *standards* used to assess the quality of the activity must be appropriate to the context. For communities to achieve ever-enriching change, evaluation of activities is vital but this inevitably entails a move beyond the traditional definitions of excellence as used in formal music education. This is a plea therefore not for non-accountability but rather for standards which, because of the nature of the activity, avoid any excessive preoccupation with the product and do justice to the richness of the process. The evaluation should also create opportunities for the participants to make judgments, including those participants who in more formal settings would lack confidence and sufficient sense of status to make such judgments.'[10]

In the light of such considerations, what is the way forward? Because a number of different parties are involved, there is no single nostrum. What follows is a series of practical but provisional proposals, some of which will add to the costs of participatory practice and so will need to be taken into account by funding bodies when they calculate subsidy requirements. Circumstances vary case by case and I do not argue that they are universally applicable; rather, they should be understood as guides to action, not as a detailed blueprint.

The key element in demonstrating the success of a community project is the 'common statement of aims'. This should be recorded in some succinct form, perhaps on paper or through video or sound recording. If the workshop project leader is a member of a larger organisation (for example, the education officer of an orchestra or someone on contract to an amateur music society), it will be easy to show their employer whether or not this is consistent with its larger strategy. The statement will be the test against which outcomes (and practical/organisational issues) can be described in a written distillation of the project produced by the workshop leader. Such descriptions should be genuinely critical and not double up (as can often happen) as marketing or fund-raising documents. There is a case for arguing that they could be prepared by a participant rather than the project leader and perhaps from time to time by well-informed external evaluators.

10 Joss, Tim, extract from the seminar report *The Role of Community Music in a Changing World* (International Society for Music Education/Commission for Community Music Activity, 1994) p.3.

There seems little real virtue in 'audience satisfaction' questionnaires; most of those I have read have a flavour of the 'Darling, you were wonderful' atmosphere in actors' dressing rooms after a first night. It would be more to the point if participants logged their experiences through written reports or recordings, but not as an additional chore so much as an inherent part of a debate-led process of personal development.

Arts Councils, Regional Arts Boards (RABs), local authorities and business sponsors all have an interest in knowing that their money has been well spent. They wisely tend to steer clear of aesthetics, but over the years the Arts Councils and RABs have worked out systems of evaluation which test the effectiveness of an arts organisation. They ask how clear its objectives are and whether its performance meets them in the event. They keep an eye on its artistic reputation among its peers and professional critics. They check whether its management and financial controls are adequate. Above all, they make sure that its activities are consistent with its own, the funding body's, aims.

However, the elaborate apparatus of formal appraisals which established professional arts organisations undergo is too cumbersome for the subjectivities of participatory music. The best approach for funders is to agree self-evaluation procedures along the lines I have been recommending rather than to intervene directly themselves (except perhaps for occasional spot checks if there are rumours of exceptionally good or bad practice). A light regulatory touch will bring the best results in a fluid and individualistic area of creative work where the object is to free people to make their own decisions rather than follow the prescriptions of others.

A more systematic (but decentralised) address to the maintenance of standards will not be enough in itself to stimulate and enliven the participatory music scene. For that there needs also to be a lively national discussion – or, more properly, ongoing and interlocking discussions – about everything from the nature and value of participatory music to practical problems of marketing and management.

During the preparation of this report, the steering group met to advise me and the report's sponsor and publisher, the Calouste Gulbenkian Foundation. At one of our meetings the group's Chair, the poet Jo Shapcott, asked all those present to speak of their hopes and fears for the future of participatory music-making. The following selection from what they said suggests the range and radicalism of the themes we should all be thinking and talking about in the coming years:

> 'We must explore the ground where professional and amateur meet. We shouldn't eliminate the distinction, but we must arrange a meeting. This kind of work is marked by a lack of intellectual, theoretical underpinning. What sort of art-form are we creating?'

> 'The received perspectives on participatory music must be challenged.'

> 'There should be no inhibition about music-making, nor any questioning whether there is or is not a role for anyone. Creativity is coming from the community rather than artists and policy-makers.'

> 'Music must develop its role as a reflection of contemporary culture.'

> 'Music is an expression of the spirit. Music can change lives.'

> 'We must address a lack of vision – a moral and artistic vision – in a disconnected society.'

It should go without saying that these principles apply as much to amateur music-making as to professional or outreach work. But it is worth emphasising the point because my discussion of evaluation has largely concentrated on orchestral and community-based music, since it is here that self-examination and appraisal are most fully articulated at present. The language one hears applied to amateurs – that they are 'doing their best' and that it is enough if their efforts bring them 'satisfaction' or a 'sense of achievement' – is not exactly inaccurate; in fact, it shows clearly enough that their motives are much the same as those in other areas of participatory music-making. But the terminology has a paternalistic ring.

Brass bands, gospel choirs, folk groups, eisteddfodau, carnivals and rock and pop groups are not only capable of high achievement in their own contexts, but often stand comparison (in terms of artistic communication if not of virtuosity) with their professional counterparts. There is everything to be said for extending the critical debate I have been describing to these areas of music. So, for example, the tradition of festival competition assessment would be enriched by current thinking about community-based practice and, by the same token, has a lot to contribute itself to the general evolution of musical 'standards'.

It is no surprise to learn that NFMS is addressing the issues. According to its Five Year Development Plan, it is committed to 'encourage regular self-critical analyses in order to identify areas where standards can be improved ... to provide member societies with practical assistance in achieving best practice in any aspects of their activities, artistic or administrative [and] to ensure greater and more effective communication of information, opinions and ideas at all levels of the Federation to make individuals feel fully involved'.[11] It won £200,000 in a three-year sponsorship deal from BT for a community development plan, *Making More of Music*, and has run the BT Innovation Awards which reward and publicise examples of best practice among its member societies. It plans to establish a regional network of at least six NFMS officers, each servicing two regions and employed on a part-time basis.

Other umbrella bodies, such as Sound Sense, and agencies, such as Scotland's Adult Learning Project and Folkworks in the North-East, are also doing their best to stimulate debate. Sound Sense, sensitive to a certain disarray and lack of co-ordination among its constituency of community musicians, is gearing itself to a far more proactive role than in the past. At its 1996 conference, the existence of poor quality work was acknowledged, but despite the useful debates on workshop practice, few ideas emerged for repairing this state of affairs. Also, community music clearly has an image problem, stemming in large part from its undefinable diversity. The outside world is hardly aware of the sector's existence. Without status and energetic campaigning, it is no wonder that there is little funding. Sound Sense, convinced of the urgency of the situation, is taking action. It is preparing a research project 'into the nature and meaning of practice amongst community music practitioners'. The purpose is to ask them what they see as the components of good practice. As the project brief states: 'The intention is to support and encourage the practitioner by creating professional common ground, increasing their professional confidence and confirming their professional identity.'[12]

Sound Sense also recognises the need to encourage serious music criticism through developing its magazine, *Sounding Board*, and encouraging the publication of occasional papers. Fund-raising permitting, it hopes to establish a community music archive, to make more use of the Internet through Web pages, to communicate more effectively with its constituency and to proselytise local authorities and higher educational institutions.

In summary, then, coming to a judgment about the 'quality' of participatory music is a multidimensional task and involves a range of different criteria. What these may be in any particular case will depend on the intentions of those taking part, or sometimes on an agreement between those taking part and other stakeholders (say, funding bodies or managers). The failure of critical debate has led to lack of clarity and consensus about these issues and measures should be taken to stimulate discussion and the exchange of ideas about theory and practice. Because much of the value of participatory music lies in internal processes of awareness and understanding, evaluation is most effective when it is a partnership between the external observer and those observed rather than an operation conducted by one on the other. Those outside the creative circle should restrict themselves to drawing up agreed procedures of evaluation and measuring what can be measured – that is, objective outcomes such as the continuation of a music project in being over time. After that, it has to be a matter of trust.

11 NFMS – *Serving Music, Five Year Development Plan 1996-2000, op cit*, pp.16 and 22.

12 See *Sounding Board*, Sound Sense, Bury St Edmunds, autumn 1995, p.12.

'Training the Trainers'

There is widespread agreement that none of the measures I have described so far will be sufficient unless there is also an energetic and coherent development of training. Now in one sense participation in music is itself an exercise in self-training and its encouragement is the whole purpose of the community music movement. In the amateur sector and among those genres where there is a particularly active interface between professional and amateur music-making (eg jazz, and rock and pop), there are a growing number of opportunities for amateur practitioners and groups to improve a variety of skills – not only in terms of artistry but also of administration and marketing.

So, for example, Folkworks, whose aim is to recover lost or failing traditions of popular music and songs, puts a great deal of effort into providing training courses and workshops for non-professional musicians. Ros Rigby, one of Folkworks' two co-directors, told me:

> 'The great strength of folk as a form is its suitability for access by people of different levels of skill. We now run one-day workouts for players and singers of all abilities. We cater for everything from the absolute beginner to the top professional. All playing the same kind of music. One should not downgrade questions of technical difficulty, but all the same almost anyone can produce good work by any standards without supreme virtuosity.'

In 1996 an Absolute Beginners Workout for National Music Day allowed more than 200 people to try a range of instruments, song or dance, all for the first time, under the guidance of experienced tutors. It was a rare chance to experiment with unusual instruments such as the Northumbrian pipe, the melodeon and the Bodhran. In another initiative in the autumn of the same year, Folkworks set up a songwriting project in 10 communities nation-wide. Experienced singer/songwriters introduced a range of techniques to help people develop their songwriting skills. Resident tutors worked with local musicians in a series of between eight and 10 weekly sessions or two weekend courses.

The Society for the Promotion of New Music (SPNM), founded in 1943 by the Romanian émigré composer, Francis Chagrin, in response to a comment made in a BBC lift that 'people aren't writing music any more', has taken recent steps to encourage young people between the ages of 16 and 19 to learn to compose music in a 'wide range of compositional styles'.[13] Run by SPNM's education wing, it offers an extensive programme, led by professional composers, performers and animateurs, of courses, workshops, projects and other events nation-wide. It is to be accompanied by a new magazine targeted at young people which will be distributed to educational institutions, youth clubs, venues, Youth Training schemes and other community and youth groups.

In rock and pop, the Calouste Gulbenkian Foundation noticed a gap in provision for 'a hard core of musicians, on the edge of turning professional, who would benefit from the more sophisticated musical and commercial skills that an "advanced" course in popular music would offer'.[14] In response, in 1996, it initiated Pop 2000, the United Kingdom's first international masterclass programme in popular music. This offered a range of courses in producing and recording, the media and marketing as well as an introduction to the music industry.

NFMS is setting up region-specific training programmes based on research into the needs of its member societies and is considering the appointment of artistic advisers to help it in its work. The following development needs have been identified: concert planning, voice production/choral training, orchestral ensemble/player coaching; and on the administrative side, marketing and publicity, print and design, administration, personnel, chairmanship and volunteer management, finance and accounting, and fund-raising and sponsorship.

13 *New Notes*, SPNM, November 1996, p.3.

14 Richey, Simon, preface, *Pop 2000* (London, European Cultural Centre, 1995).

These are only some of the training initiatives which umbrella bodies and others are undertaking. They are convincing evidence that more and more of those involved in participatory music recognise the need to equip the movement, or perhaps more accurately the network of movements, in order to make a more dynamic input into the arts of this country. One senses a new self-confidence and feeling of self-worth with respect to the professional sector; indeed, a kind of professionalisation of the voluntary impulse.

All of this is greatly to the good, but it does not give a complete account of all the ways in which training can help. As well as looking after the developmental requirements of non-professional musicians of every kind, many of the sharpest minds in community music and music education recognise that perhaps the single most effective means of advancing the cause of participatory music is to 'train the trainers'. If progress is to be made, teachers will have to be properly equipped to deliver the challenges of the new music curriculum; community musicians need a more comprehensive grounding in the methodology of outreach work; unless orchestral musicians' artistic horizons are widened, they will be unable to fulfil the new roles which many orchestras are expecting of them; special skills are demanded of those active in such fields as music and disability; and there are too few training opportunities for those working in non-European musics and in indigenous folk and traditional musics, as well as for peripatetic music teachers and the isolated lone musician out of contact with other forms of practice.

The production of new generations of well-trained musicians and music workers will help to address one of the key factors inhibiting the further growth of participatory music – the patchy nature of expert support across the country, whether it be in the form of too few pro-am local musicians or only sporadic community projects.

Community Music in London, one of the country's most successful participatory projects, has shown how a carefully co-ordinated programme of training trainers can transform music provision in an area and stimulate the setting up of autonomous music groups. It is worth looking at an example of their work in the London Borough of Newham. In 1992 they agreed to run a summer playscheme with 25 low achievers and school refusers. Over two years, they raised £20,000 from the European Social Fund and Newham Leisure Services as well as £11,000 in equipment from Newham Youth Services, and at the same time trained two local youth workers in fund-raising with the long-term aim of enabling any project that was established to become independent. The local owner of a commercial recording studio and an 'apprentice' were trained by Community Music to run a music workshop, concentrating on technology, band work, composition and the creation of a local identity. A group of young people (mainly beginners and many of them at risk) established themselves as the Beckton Music Group, named after a Newham estate. They came from a cross-section of Newham society and were part of the Beckton Drug Awareness Project.

Meanwhile, Community Music ran a series of five public courses to help the Beckton group and widen access to the local community. As a result, two local unemployed musicians, one of whom in particular was unmotivated and had a poor achievement record, came to their attention. They took Community Music's Music Tutor Training Course: one of them began working with the Beckton Music Group and got a job in the project organiser's commercial studio, while the other formed a young women's music project. She also taught elsewhere in London and was hired as music tutor to set up a new Beckton music group. Later she took over Community Music's education programme in Brent.

In 1993, after performing at the National Youth Arts Festival in Devon, the group dispersed as a direct result of their raised skills and confidence. One went onto a music course at a local college, another onto a BTEC course, two set up an independent band and three gained employment with a multimedia arts project in the borough.

In 1993, Community Music was asked to set up a workshop on another estate with serious racial and social tensions. A group was established which has now performed four times at Community Music's West End headquarters, the Community Music House; a purpose-built centre is under construction on the estate and £6,000 has been raised by a local youth worker for musical instruments.

In the following year, Community Music, in association with the London Arts Board and Yamaha Kemble, piloted a major education project to look at how professional musicians can enhance the delivery of the National Curriculum. As a result of the previous youth work, three Newham schools were chosen to take part. A group of young Asian people from Newham came to the Community Music House for a weekly session. Community Music staged a further five open music courses in the borough.

In 1996, the Asian Dub Foundation, an independent group which emerged from work at Community Music, toured the borough and created links with people from the Asian community. Community Music ran classes in a Newham secondary school and an out-of-hours music club at another, which enabled them to keep in contact with young people who graduated to secondary level.

To conclude, the Beckton Youth Project now has four separate music projects, run independently, as part of its mainstream activities.

I have recorded this remarkable story in some detail, because of its virtuous circularity and as an illustration of what one organisation can achieve in a neighbourhood by the careful targeting of limited resources. The policy of training trainers acts like a snowball, gathering more and more community involvement as it proceeds. One can envisage a time, perhaps in the not too distant future, when Newham will be able to look after itself and Community Music can turn its attention elsewhere.

The level of financial investment in the kinds of training so far described, although valuable and ground-breaking, is insignificant when compared to the resources applied to the training of professional musicians in higher and further education. Numerous courses are provided in colleges of further education. Music departments in colleges of higher education offer a variety of degree and diploma courses. These include, in addition to more conventional courses of study: BA (Hons) in Popular Music Studies, HND in Creative Music Technology and BTEC ND in Popular Music at Barnsley College; BA (Hons) in Sound and Image at Bath College of HE; BA (Hons) in Contemporary Musics and in Popular Music Studies at Bretton Hall; BSc in Music and Mathematics at Christ Church College, Canterbury; Modular BA in World Musics and MA in Musical Traditions at King Alfred's College, Winchester; Diploma in Jazz and Commercial Music and BTEC ND in Rock Music at Liverpool Community College and BA (Hons) in Band Musicianship and in Popular Music and Recording at University College, Salford. Fifty-one universities in the United Kingdom offer degree courses in music, usually more conventional in content but often encompassing popular music, film music and the like. The University of Northumbria has taught community music for some 10 years and was the first BA (Hons) Music course of its kind in the United Kingdom. It generates about 25 community music projects a year.

The Liverpool Institute of Performing Arts is a higher education establishment specialising in popular cultural forms and has the backing of leading figures in the entertainment industry, notably Sir Paul McCartney. Founded by the same team that created the BRIT school in

Croydon, a secondary school specialising in the performing arts, it offers BA (Hons) degrees (validated by the John Moores University) in a range of arts/entertainment subjects. The courses are modular and one strand is devoted to community arts (including a music option).

The 11 conservatoires occupy the commanding heights of music education and until recent years have taken a conservative view of their role. The emphasis has been on producing virtuoso musicians to staff the country's orchestras and classical music ensembles. Curtis Price, Principal of the Royal Academy of Music, sees no pressing need to make many changes to this policy although he acknowledges that more effort should be put into equipping students to manage freelance careers in a changing marketplace. He told me:

> 'Our chief function is to train orchestral musicians, although there should not be too much stress on virtuosity. The problem facing orchestras is essentially one of programming; new music should be in every programme and people should be encouraged to look forward to it. To direct resources to training in outreach is ineffective: where help is needed is in schools where instrumental teaching, choral singing and music reading are dying. My ambition for the Academy is that it should be like the Paris Conservatoire as it was in the nineteenth century.'

In an important sense he is correct, in that it will remain the duty of conservatoires for the foreseeable future to ensure a regular supply of classical players and composers. But colleagues at other conservatoires sense that reform is necessary. David Hoult, Principal of the City of Leeds College of Music, wrote to me echoing some of the themes outlined in earlier chapters of this book:

> 'The role of music in society as a *participatory* activity is perhaps the most important issue facing musicians as we prepare to enter the twenty-first century. We have neglected it for too long. As ethnomusicologists such as John Blacking have shown, there are two common characteristics of the arts in developed societies. One is their polarisation into high art and low art, whilst the other is the division of those involved in the arts into producers and consumers, with the art itself as a commodity supplied by one to the other. I do not decry this – I simply point it out. The great flowering of Western art music of the past 400 years could not have taken place, in my view, without creating these divisions. However, we have in this period lost some of what less developed societies have retained: the benefits of social cohesion conferred by widespread participation in (not just consumption of) the performing arts.'[15]

David Hoult supports the enrichment of music training advocated by educationists such as Peter Renshaw of the Guildhall School of Music and Drama (see *Orchestral Variations* above), although he draws a firm distinction between improving access to professional music and encouraging participation by amateurs.

However, there is evidence that other conservatoires are adopting an approach that goes further towards integrating amateur and professional practice. As in the case of the Royal Academy of Music, this is largely inspired by a hard-headed perception of the changing career patterns of musicians, but a more catholic approach is taken than that recommended by Curtis Price. George Caird, Principal of the Birmingham Conservatoire, wrote:

> 'All our conservatoires, while continuing to offer high quality instrumental and vocal training, are working on professional development ... and there are many different and exciting initiatives which provide students with a bewildering choice of specialist courses in, for example, Music Theatre, Community Music, Technology and Recording, Folk Music, Advanced Orchestral Training, Composition and Instrumental Teaching.'[16]

15 Hoult, David, unpublished letter to the author, 19 September 1996.

16 Caird, George, 'UK Conservatoires in a time of change', Music Education Council, Cheshire, summer 1996.

Birmingham, which has developed a range of study opportunities for students interested in disciplines outside Western classical music, is soon to offer new degree routes for jazz and north Indian classical music. A believer in partnerships, it has an association (among many others locally, nationally and internationally) with the Birmingham-based Asian music development agency, SAMPAD. It has pioneered courses with Sound It Out, the community music organisation for Birmingham and a wider area, and the two organisations are now working together on a proposal to establish a community music module at the Conservatoire. When this comes on-stream, the Conservatoire will join a select group of higher education institutions which provide community music options – the Guildhall School of Music and Drama, Goldsmiths College and Dartington College of Arts. Also, from this year the University of York will be offering an MA in Community Music.

Gradual, but significant, changes are taking place elsewhere. For example, at the Royal College of Music a postgraduate Pathway for Orchestral Musicians has been introduced which introduces students to educational work and to the kinds of mental and physical exercises developed by pioneers such as Peter Wiegold, formerly of the Guildhall School of Music and Drama. Gill Graham, the college's orchestra manager, wrote to me:

> 'Addressing the question of being a musician these days is something we are constantly doing. As far as having exemplary playing skills for orchestral playing positions this is taken for granted by most. The skills required, certainly by all the orchestras in this country, in the field of community music, being part of a smaller group that grows out of an orchestra and experiencing repertoire not necessarily related to orchestral life as it used to be etc. are certainly new things to most students coming through our hands.'[17]

Gavin Henderson, Principal of Trinity College of Music, acknowledges:

> ' ... a new pulse in young music-makers – people who will have come with a more creative attitude, fostered through the National Curriculum – a life in which composers are at last regaining the central ground, a mood in which the public may at present choose an evening of African drumming and dance in preference to an orchestral concert, for the very reason that it can engage directly as a social experience'.[18]

The College has launched a new MA (Music Education) which offers professional musicians the chance to extend their skills as educators and animateurs and helps teachers to develop their musical, personal and pedagogic skills. Those taking part can work on curriculum- and teaching-based, community, musical/multimedia presentation, or animateur projects.

The London College of Music at Thames Valley University, which offers students opportunities to study music technology, popular music and world musics, also introduces them to working in schools and to community-based practice.

It could no doubt be argued that the conservatoires are moving too slowly in their programmes of reform and are largely (and indeed properly) motivated by a concern to equip students for their professional careers rather than by any deeply felt commitment to a transformation of the role of orchestras. Nevertheless, even if they are following rather than leading events, we can safely predict that coming generations of orchestral players will be much better trained than their predecessors in making a contribution to the cause of participation in music. They will be able to play a more active part in the creation of new musics and be more interested in working alongside composers and amateurs in the freer, intercultural, improvisatory, interactive musical life of contemporary Britain.

What is striking about the various training opportunities that are available is their diversity. There is an enormous amount of activity with different kinds of expertise often built up over

17 Graham, Gill, unpublished letter to the author, 6 December 1996.

18 Henderson, Gavin, address to the Association of British Orchestras' Annual Conference, Leeds 1995 (unpublished).

years of experiment. There is little overall moderation and no comprehensive overview. Outside the formal education sector nobody has quantified likely demand and related it to potential supply. Colleges, universities and conservatoires are dipping their feet into the water and engaging with areas of music-making previously unfamiliar to them, and many of them appear to be doing excellent work. But their involvement in community outreach and educational projects is not yet a measured response to perceived need. This should be no cause for surprise, seeing that the extent of the participatory music sector and its requirements have not yet been quantified.

A positive sign, though, is the increasing willingness of those concerned to look for partnerships in those areas where they do not themselves have the relevant expertise. The alliance between Sound It Out and the Birmingham Conservatoire is an outstanding case in point. The arts funding system and the education sector have opened a door onto a huge new territory of music-making and, even if the extent of its training needs is unclear, it is not unreasonable to suppose that they will be expensive to satisfy. The principle of making the most effective use of existing resources through collaboration is a good one. It is certainly the best way of making progress at a time when public investment both in the arts and in education is unlikely to expand.

photo: Horniman Museum and Gardens

8 THE SUBSIDY REVOLUTION

'To encourage music-making and play-acting among the people themselves.' One of the aims of the Council for the Encouragement of Music and the Arts.
        CEMA, 1940

The Arts Council believes, then, that the first claim upon its attention and assistance is that of maintaining in London and the larger cities effective power houses of opera, music and drama; for unless those quality institutions can be maintained the arts are bound to decline into mediocrity.
        W E WILLIAMS, THE ARTS COUNCIL: THE FIRST TEN YEARS, 1956

Government motivation used to be that the arts were an ornament of national identity. For instance, part of the glory of Britain was its theatre and – you can see how old I am – the Third Programme. States now have a self-evident reason to promote education and the arts as part of (in the contemporary jargon) the quality of life. It's an ecological argument. We should care to have the arts in a good society.
        SUSAN SONTAG, 1996

The National Lottery is bringing about a historic change to the way in which the arts are funded. For the last 50 years since the foundation of the Arts Council of Great Britain (ACGB), by far the largest proportion of the available resources has been devoted to the development of the professional arts. The participatory sector – amateur and community arts – has received a very small slice of the cake. Regional Arts Boards (RABs) and local authorities have given modest support to community-based practice and have invested in arts festivals which often have an amateur or participatory component. Umbrella bodies, such as the National Federation of Music Societies (NFMS) and Jazz Services, have received annual grants from the national Arts Councils directly or via the RABs. This has enabled amateur societies and associations to commission new music and has been of considerable (if limited) assistance. But that has more or less been that.

Comparisons are not only odious, but sometimes difficult to sustain and misleading. However, one should not forget that other countries have found it possible to do things differently. It is estimated that in 1991 British local authorities spent about £3.5 millions on amateur and participatory arts: a common practice has been to give block grants to local arts councils, leaving them with the task of spreading limited cash among the local societies in their area. No reliable figures are available for the national Arts Councils and the RABs, although they contributed about £370,000 to amateur music societies. The total sum is unlikely to exceed £1 million. Not far away across the North Sea, we find a more generous spirit. In The Netherlands, with a population of only 15 million (as against 56 million in the United Kingdom), the amateur arts receive about £18 million of national, regional and local funding, of which the state contributes directly about £3.5 million. Substantial resources are also allocated from education budgets.

Arts education in The Netherlands is seen as a crucial means of fostering the amateur arts, the purpose being to 'offer high quality education and training by professional artists with a view to promoting the quality of amateur art'. Music education outside the formal schools sector thrives and the huge growth in the number of music schools since the Second World War (in 1990 there were 142 subsidised establishments as well as 66 general Creativity Centres and other Combined Institutions) has made a valuable contribution to today's lively musical scene, both in terms of new audiences and of players and composers.

Why should this be so? The answer is that the state is committed to the importance of culture. The Dutch Ministry of Welfare, Health and Cultural Affairs (a suggestive conjunction of responsibilities) is explicit on the subject. It takes a broad, cultural line, not inconsistent, it is interesting to note, with the underlying purposes of community music as described in this book:

> 'Participation in cultural activities is a manifestation of factors such as entertainment, personal experience and personal development but also of much broader social influences. The dissemination of culture not only means that as many people as possible can profit from and enjoy cultural achievements ("lire, c'est vivre plus"), it also increases the awareness of the citizen, the independent development of original ideas ... By stimulating participation in cultural activities one is able to provide people with the opportunity to compare their own views and opinions with the points of view and experiences of others ... It is for this reason that the dissemination of culture throughout the social spectrum – seeking to achieve a situation in which every member of the community, whatever his or her social origins or position, has the opportunity to participate in cultural activities – serves not only a cultural but a general interest.'[1]

This is not the kind of language we are used to hearing from the Arts Councils and British governments, nor the levels of investment we have come to expect. However, the situation in this country now appears to be on the point of transformation. A new appreciation of the importance of cultural participation is dawning.

With the arrival of the National Lottery in 1995 very large sums of money became available for capital projects, and amateur and community arts groups were eligible for support. During the early months of 1996 pressure grew for the rules to be relaxed to accommodate support for activity as well as buildings. In March the Department of National Heritage signalled its growing interest in participation in the arts with the publication of an important booklet, appropriately entitled *Taking Part*. It advocated active involvement in creative practice in addition to the development of audiences for the professional arts:

> 'Celebrating our shared culture means not just watching sport, but getting out and playing it; not just admiring the achievements of professional actors, musicians and craftsmen, but having a go ourselves ... Amateur participation in the arts and crafts represents a key element in this country's cultural fabric.'[2]

Within a few weeks the Arts Council of England (ACE) launched a consultative document, announcing:

> 'We are ... very grateful to the Secretary of State for the National Heritage for listening to our pleas and allowing us to make Lottery awards for certain kinds of creative activity ... a range of new Lottery programmes will be drawn up – on commissions for new work, access to and participation in the arts and enhancing the creative abilities of young people in particular'.[3]

Events moved at great speed: a rapid consultation phase ensued and before the year's end the national Arts Councils had announced schemes to 'give a very wide range of people throughout [the country] the chance to enjoy high-quality creative activity – either as audiences and viewers or by taking part'.[4]

Cynics have argued that this spurt of activity resulted from the negative publicity which some large grants to major professional arts organisations, such as the Royal Opera House,

1 *Investing in Culture, Netherlands Policy Document on Culture 1993-1996*, (The Hague, Ministry of Welfare, Health and Cultural Affairs) p.25.

2 *Taking Part* (London, Department of National Heritage, 1996) p.10.

3 *New Lottery Programmes, op cit,* foreword by the Chairman (unpaginated).

4 *Arts4Everyone*, Arts Council of England, application leaflet, p.2.

had generated. But, for all the suddenness of the inception of this new policy, there is evidence that over a number of years those concerned with arts funding had been gradually rethinking the system's exclusive commitment to professional excellence.

The pendulum appears to be swinging back to the early 1940s when the principle of state support for the performing arts was first established. During the Second World War it was observed that, while ENSA was responsible for organising entertainment for the armed services, no arrangements had been considered for civilians on the 'home front'. The Pilgrim Trust, a charitable foundation, was approached by the Board of Education (the Department for Education and Employment's predecessor) to create the Council for the Encouragement of Music and the Arts (CEMA). It was to have two broad objectives – to encourage the amateur arts (that is, 'music-making and play-acting by the people themselves') and to ensure that professional artists, their livelihoods threatened by the war, were given work. CEMA's underlying philosophy was rooted in the social idealism of the 1930s and, of its two aims, the emphasis on participation, on the involvement of ordinary people of all classes, took precedence. One typical scheme was the appointment of a number of 'music travellers' whose task was to encourage amateur music-making and to promote concerts.

However, it was not long before the claims of the professional artist began to predominate. Despite the fact that when government funding arrived to complement the Pilgrim Trust's own resources it was intended exclusively for amateur practitioners, a professional repertory theatre company was established to tour the regions. So almost from its beginnings, an ideological conflict underpinned the theory and practice of public funding of the arts. Serious efforts were made to maintain a holistic approach to policy, but gradually the interests of the public as audience, reader or spectator overtook those of the public as doer, maker or participant.

The economist John Maynard Keynes was appointed chairman of CEMA and he went on to plan the ACGB to which the baton would be handed after the end of hostilities. He was, in fact, 'in only limited sympathy with [CEMA's] objectives'. He wrote: 'I was worried lest what one may call the welfare side was to be developed at the expense of the artistic side, and standards generally.' Here we see the origins of the long quarrel about quality which I have shown in earlier chapters to be a common thread running through the debates on participation in the arts over the years.

Although they were revised following opposition from people such as Vaughan Williams who did not want to lose all the gains of the CEMA days, Keynes's draft objectives for the new Arts Council charter make his basic attitude clear. In his view, the organisation should aim:

'a   to increase and widen the distribution of the audiences of the arts
 b   to improve the standard of execution in the arts
 c   to encourage and aid an adequate system of professional training.'

5 It should be noted here that the Arts Council of Wales, sensitive to the traditions of the arts in Wales, has always taken a more active line in encouraging amateur activity.

In the years which have followed the war, the Arts Councils have enjoyed many successes. The arts of the metropolis flourish as never before; in the regions orchestras, opera companies and regional theatres proliferate. Focusing on the needs of the professional artist and usually seeing the public as consumer rather than producer, the Councils have helped to stimulate a great artistic revival.[5]

But this achievement has been a partial one. The state, through the Arts Councils, has tended to focus on what are often called the 'high arts' (or in Raymond Williams' phrase, the 'old arts') and little attention has been paid until recently to traditional folk arts or mass popular culture. While professional arts production has increased together with audiences, the social composition of the arts public has not significantly altered.

Voices of dissent were never stilled. The amateur arts continued on their way, excluded from national policy, although informing local cultures. As NFMS observed, 'the term "amateur" has often been used pejoratively despite the fact that excellence and amateur music were never mutually exclusive.'[6] When the Arts Council closed its regional offices in 1957, the long birth of the Regional Arts Associations (RAAs, now RABs) began: local people came together to form organisations which *they* controlled, not some distant central authority. The arts centre movement spread across the country, bringing all kinds, levels and degrees of artistic activity under a single roof. Then, as we have seen, the community arts movement sprang up from the ferment of the 1960s.

Meanwhile, in 1948, local authorities were given the power to devote the product of a 6d rate to all forms of entertainment and in 1963 were enabled to spend limited sums on general projects (including the arts) to improve their areas and to subsidise organisations outside their own boundaries, so empowering them to contribute to RAAs. The Labour government's famous White Paper on the arts in 1965 gave an impulse to decentralisation when it argued that 'if a high level of artistic achievement is to be sustained and the best in the arts made more widely available, more generous and discriminating help is urgently needed, locally, regionally and nationally.'[7] Slowly, local government interest in the arts grew and began to extend beyond the larger cities; these had long evinced a natural concern for the major arts organisations and buildings that operated in their centres and developed financial partnerships with ACGB (an exception proving the rule were the great Northern cities which, with other local councils, helped to found the North East Arts Association – now the Northern Arts Board – with regional grant-making purposes specifically in mind). Relations began to develop between local councils and the RAAs which assiduously recruited them as paying members. By the mid-1980s there was hardly a local authority not in membership.

In 1976, Lord Redcliffe-Maud published his magisterial report, *Support for the Arts in England and Wales*, in which he argued the primary role of local authorities and proposed substantial devolution of responsibilities from ACGB to the RAAs. In response to the question 'For whose benefit should we support the arts from public funds?', he offered a formulation which was far closer to that of CEMA than that of Keynes:

> ' "The many and the few" is my broad answer. The many, because no one is incapable of some enjoyment or experience of the arts if he has an opportunity to use his own peculiar powers of creation and recreation. The few, because at all times and all places creative talent is rare and genius is very rare indeed. Our society, it seems to me, will not become more civilised if it ignores the claims of either group ... The "many" and the "few" do not together constitute the whole population. They must be thought of, rather, as the largest and smallest of a whole series of concentric circles. The innermost circle consists of the few people of *genius* ... Wider than the circle of genius, is that of *talent*, of many various kinds. Wider still is the circle of those capable of professional teaching of their art (for instance music) though not themselves so talented as the professional performers. Outside that circle are the *active amateurs* – singing in choral societies, playing in orchestras, brass bands and pop groups, acting in drama societies or community art, but earning their living in other ways. Beyond them is the still wider circle of those who enjoy the arts as *audience*, whether of broadcast or live performance. And beyond them "the many".

6 NFMS – *Serving Music, Five Year Development Plan 1996-2000*, op cit, p.3.

7 *A Policy for the Arts: the first steps* (London, HMSO, 1968).

> No circle is at any moment static or exclusive. All of them fade into each other like
> colours in a rainbow.'[8]

For most of the post-war period it has been the local authorities and RAAs, which after initial suspicions have moved into often close alliance, that by and large have sought to pursue this holistic approach and the Arts Councils which by and large have spent most of their resources and energy on the professional arts. What is in essence a battle of ideas was fought with institutional weapons; from the late 1970s in England the RAAs and the Arts Council have locked horns over devolution of funding responsibilities. In 1984 the ACGB published a strategic review, *The Glory of the Garden*, which while applauding the educational policies of the professional arts made no reference to the amateur or participatory arts; however, it announced a programme of limited devolution. In the last decade or so a good deal has been handed over by the centre to the regions, but at the price of closer supervision through a national planning process managed by the Arts Council.

I do not want to oversimplify the picture; while it is true that the RAAs took a wider and more integrated view of the arts than the Arts Council few of them have shown much more interest in supporting amateurs than the Arts Councils (Wales excepted). Lord Redcliffe-Maud again:

> 'RAAs have tended to ignore amateur music unless it involves the introduction of
> "professional stiffening" for an orchestra or a concert. But they are well placed to seek
> ways of actively encouraging and stimulating amateurs. At present few RAAs have any
> sizeable amateur representation on their music panels. If this fault is corrected, the
> RAAs will at least become aware of the needs to be met ... Meanwhile amateurs must
> continue to look to their local authority for aid in the first instance.'[9]

Little has changed in substance since he wrote these words.

Most local authorities have arts and recreation or leisure departments (despite the fact that spending in this area remains discretionary rather than compulsory) with some specialist staff and varying sizes of budget. They own and manage museums and galleries, libraries, performing venues and educational facilities and so are responsible for much of the nation's arts infrastructure. They also promote festivals, concerts and various outdoor entertainment and event programmes. What they do not do directly they often assist financially. Councils also often support the arts from other budgets too (for example, those for economic development, property services and education). This makes it difficult to establish their overall expenditure. No precise calculations exist for their spending on the participatory arts in general, and participatory music in particular.

However, according to the estimates of the Chartered Institute for Public Finance and Accountancy, in 1995-6 total local government spending in England and Wales on the arts as a whole amounted to about £277 million. This is more than the total monies at the disposal of the Arts Councils of England and Wales. Government arts spending is £3.80 per person in England, £5.30 in Scotland, £4.90 in Wales and £4.10 in Northern Ireland. Individual councils spend at very different levels, ranging from Birmingham's £11 per head of population to Solihull's 77p among metropolitan authorities; Leicestershire's £5 to Hertfordshire's 10p among county councils; and Cambridge's £16.50 to Havering's 49p among district and borough councils.

A leading local authority arts official notes:

> 'Many local authorities now provide sustained programmes of participatory arts

8 Redcliffe-Maud,
Lord, *Future Support for
the Arts in England and
Wales* (London,
Calouste Gulbenkian
Foundation, 1976)
pp.21-22.

9 *Ibid*, p.131.

activities within the community. Some of them yield permanent fruit in the form of decorative artworks, whose community origins enable them to tell a more potent story than imported sculptural purchases can hope to match. Not only do these community arts programmes awaken and develop arts interests amongst many people who have no educational predisposition to the arts. They also make far-reaching personal contributions to the lives of people taking part in them, creating within dispirited and fragmented communities a new sense of purpose and hope.'[10]

Local councils have long supported amateur arts groups, often through subsidised facilities, often in schools. But government reforms and financial pressures are reducing the value of this assistance. The complaints of NFMS are not untypical:

'One of the biggest problems ... is the provision and hire charges for venues, both for rehearsals and concerts. There has been a large increase in the cost of hiring school halls in the past few years and a number of societies have moved to church premises in consequence. These are invariably cheaper but often not so well-suited to their needs.'[11]

Community arts, including community music, have been supported by local government, but only spasmodically because funding came from poorly-resourced leisure/arts/libraries departments as opposed to the comfortably financed local education departments. Also, during the 1980s many politicians in major authorities were impressed by the case put for the economic impact of the arts and invested in glamorous city-centre capital developments ('city imaging'). However, there are signs, albeit largely anecdotal, of a revival of interest. Irene McDonald, deputy leader of Kings Lynn and West Norfolk Borough Council, told me: 'One reason it's happening again is because of the widespread appointment of arts development officers in recent years. Some of them are acting as *agents provocateurs*, presenting all kinds of community-based projects.' Unfortunately, because local authority arts budgets often have to be devoted to the management of council-owned facilities (civic theatres and the like), most of this work is poorly resourced and limited to one-off projects.

Two further trends are worth noting. Local government has traditionally (although by no means exclusively) focused on the services it can provide and its own direct promotions, but a combination of declining powers and financial resources, the availability of various kinds of national and European Union grants for economic and social regeneration and a growing debate about the importance of independent voluntary organisations (the so-called 'Third Sector') in civil governance is leading some authorities to see encouragement of the arts less as a discrete activity than as an essential component of community development. As Irene McDonald points out, the emphasis is shifting from high culture to 'our "common culture". That is, you should always start where the people are and then bring in whatever is necessary. You ask "What do you want to do", rather than "This is what we would like you to do".'

This approach harmonises with the philosophy underlying the new Lottery schemes. While traditional arts organisations are eligible, the criterion of professional excellence matched by expanding audiences has been subsumed in five wider aims: encouraging new audiences to experience high-quality arts activity; encouraging and developing participation in arts activity; getting more young people actively involved in arts and cultural activities; supporting new work and helping it develop its audience; and building people's creative potential through training or professional development.

The National Lottery is bringing torrents of cash into the arts world and it looks very

10 Sargent, Anthony, 'More than the sum of its parts: cultural policy and planning in Birmingham', Cultural Policy, Harwood Academic Publishers, vol. 2, no. 2, The Netherlands, 1996, p.310.

11 Letter from Donald Sheppard, Secretary of NFMS South, to Russell Jones, Chief Executive, NFMS, 23 November 1995.

much as if the outcome will be, at long last, a reunion of the two funding traditions that derive from CEMA and Keynes. The four Arts Councils are likely to receive from Lottery receipts an estimated £1.6 billion in total by the year 2000. There really ought to be enough to satisfy everyone's demands and the prospects for the participatory arts look bright.

However, it would be wrong not to sound a few cautionary notes. It is not known for how long the five 'good causes' (the arts, sport, the heritage, the charity sector and the Millennium Commission) will remain the sole beneficiaries of National Lottery proceeds. The Millennium Commission is, by definition, a fixed-term enterprise and, although none of the political parties have yet made it clear how they will dispose of this funding stream after the turn of the century, it appears unlikely that it will be distributed among the four survivors. The new Labour administration has already said that it is interested in extending the number of good causes. The difficulties of financing the Welfare State could well persuade a future government at some stage to divert some or all of the Lottery proceeds to other social purposes. That would leave the arts funding system with wider responsibilities, but without the resources to finance them.

A further difficulty is that, although the Arts Councils are now in a position to subsidise activity as well as buildings, the grants available through *Arts4Everyone* and their Scottish, Northern Irish and Welsh equivalents are not for continuing support, but for one-off or fixed-term projects. There is good reason for this limitation, because otherwise it would be possible for the Treasury to argue that Lottery money was being spent on the same purposes for which their annual grant-in-aid to the Arts Councils is designed – and, accordingly, that the grant-in-aid should be reduced.

Nevertheless, the question arises what amateur and community groups will do once their Lottery projects have come to an end if they are prohibited from applying for further grants for the same purposes. Expectations will have been raised in the short to medium term which may have to be dashed in the long term. This is a difficult dilemma for the funding system, which it will have to address in the next few years.

There are already ominous signs of an incipient and potentially divisive quarrel between the professional and the participatory (amateur and community-based) sectors. Community musicians, for example, are worried that the orchestras, highly experienced as they are in fund-raising and in what one might call the 'subsidy game', will grab the lion's share of resources for their educational and outreach work at their expense. At a conference convened by the National Campaign for the Arts, Peter Finch of the actors' union Equity had a diametrically opposed anxiety:

> 'The Arts Council is looking at changing the way it has funded historically. [Its] Green Paper says that the funding system has wanted for some time to find ways of helping in such areas – amateur theatre, opera etc. Now that does seem to me a fundamental change in the Arts Council of England's funding policy. I totally support amateur arts, but the thread running through this document does seem to me that we should use all the new money to support amateur arts. Now when the whole professional sector is so neglected, in particular, the performers, that must mean we have got our priorities wrong.'[12]

12 *The National Lottery – Whatever Next? op cit,* p.14.

13 From a letter to *The Times,* 3 September 1996.

The issue also boiled over in the letters page of *The Times*, where a former Music Director of the BBC, Robert Ponsonby, wrote criticising ACE's approach: 'At this stage, amateur bodies should not be eligible for support: our professionals must come first.'[13]

It is true that public sector arts budgets are under pressure; local government spending in England and Wales fell by about £3 million in 1995-6 and the Arts Council's Treasury grant for 1997-8 stands at £186 million – the same amount as for 1992-3. But the fears of the arts world regarding Lottery funding are not borne out by the Arts Council's explicit intention to help both the amateur and the professional, although should the resources available fall short of overall demand at some stage in the future it is not unreasonable to foresee trouble ahead among competing interest groups.

An interesting feature of the arrangements for the new Lottery schemes is that the distribution of grants is to remain firmly in the hands of the Arts Councils. Bearing in mind that, as I have said, many local authorities have set up arts departments, that the RABs have a wide range of expertise on their staffs, and that both sets of organisations see themselves as being closer to, and so more knowledgeable about, the activities of many amateur and community-based applicants than the Arts Councils, this seems an odd state of affairs. Some RAB opinion feels that from being relatively autonomous institutions they will be reduced to little more than conduits for, and promoters of, someone else's schemes. If this is to be so, it is hardly in line with the principle of subsidiarity – namely, that decisions should be taken as close as possible to those whom they will affect.

During the period of consultation, a number of agencies suggested that, rather than delegate Lottery grant-giving down the official arts funding structure, it would be better to exploit the potential of the numerous umbrella bodies that speak for the amateur arts. Thus NFMS wrote:

> 'The political dynamic and the only sensible delivery mechanism is subsidiarity via the existing grass roots support networks. The voluntary arts are typically organised pyramidically. Clubs and societies are grouped by region and affiliated to a national federation. Like the pyramid, this structure is enormously strong and the national bodies draw their legitimacy directly from the grassroots activity they service.'[14]

Some of them, including NFMS, have received public sector grants for distribution among their members.

It is an appealing notion. Unfortunately, important sectors of amateur musical practice (eg rock and pop) are not represented by umbrella bodies and not every umbrella body is as well-equipped as NFMS to undertake a funding role. It could also be objected that it would be wrong to hand decision-making to interested parties ('jobs for the boys'), even though the principle of drawing a line between benefactors and beneficiaries has already been breached to no evident harm.

The chief explanation for the present arrangements is that the Lottery legislation and accompanying ministerial directives forbid the named Lottery distributors, among them the Arts Councils, from devolving any of their responsibilities to other bodies. That said, they are expected to consult widely among all relevant interested parties, including local authorities and RABs, before determining grants. It is also worth remembering that many local authorities are themselves likely to be applicants for Lottery funds and their position would clearly be compromised if they were in charge of funding decisions.

14 *New Lottery Programmes – a Response from the National Federation of Music Societies* (London, undated) p.4.

However, this centralisation will place a very heavy administrative burden on already busy agencies and may be a distraction from what has been their function in the past, the distribution of their Treasury grant-in-aid for the benefit of the professional arts. Some also suspect that the press of events will make it difficult for them to engage in the general policy review which the opening up of their policies to amateurs will no doubt necessitate. This is clearly a danger, but the Arts Councils have done their best to devise streamlined procedures to avert it; the 'express' route for applications for grants of up to £5,000 will necessitate a minimum of assessment.

So far as music policy is concerned, ACE's music department is well up with the game. Following its policy reviews for orchestras in 1995 and jazz in 1996, it has recently issued *Creating New Notes, a policy for the support of new music in England*. It adopts a consciously integrated approach to the full spectrum of musics in England, for the first time since CEMA more than half a century ago. Its introduction states:

> 'Music is a fundamental impulse. Whether as ritual, celebration or entertainment, as participation or performance, it has played a central role in the life of every society ... the geographical, cultural and historical barriers which used to restrict people's musical experience have largely disappeared. Recent developments in music education embrace a much more diverse range of musical styles and place creative music-making at the heart of the syllabus for the National Curriculum. And in a society where individuals have increasing amounts of leisure time, there is a growing demand for opportunities to participate in new music, whether through access to recording studios for young people or through amateur ensembles and adult education.'[15]

Its objectives include: 'To enable people of all ages to participate in the creation and performance of new music through voluntary organisations ... ; to work in partnership with the education sector to ensure that creative music-making in schools is extended and developed'.[16] To judge from their literature, the other Arts Councils in Northern Ireland, Scotland and Wales would not dissent from a word of this.

The greatest single obstacle to ensuring that Lottery monies have an optimum impact on the development of participatory musics lies in the government's insistence that the distributors do not target spending according to their strategic priorities or particular policy objectives. It is asserted that this is the inevitable consequence of Parliament's intention, enshrined in the terms of the National Lottery Act, that all applicants be treated on an equal basis and judged on their individual merits – in other words, that there should be a 'level playing field'.

If this approach is to be applied literally, it will not be easy to address some of the challenges I have identified in this book in more than an *ad hoc* way. To pluck out a couple of them at random, one might cite the need to invest intelligently in new technologies and the importance of developing training opportunities coherently and comprehensively.

However, it would appear that in other areas the government is taking a flexible line and allowing a growing degree of prioritisation. The National Lottery Charities Board, for example, whose main aims are to help meet the needs of those at greatest disadvantage in society and to improve the quality of life in the community, has announced a rolling series of targeted programmes: the first was to focus on poverty, the second on youth issues and low income, the third on health, disability and care, and the fourth on 'new opportunities and choices and voluntary sector development'. There is also an International Grants Programme which supports UK-based charities working abroad.

It would be helpful if the Arts Councils, in relation to their new schemes (*Arts4Everyone* in England, *Arts for All* in Wales and *New Directions* in Scotland), were empowered to go down the same road. They would then be able to set out a changing series of favoured

15 *Creating New Notes, a policy for the support of new music in England* (London, Arts Council of England, 1996) p.2.

16 *Ibid*, p.3.

themes or priorities and so address particular challenges or opportunities in the participatory arts. In order to maintain the principle of open application, each theme would run for a set number of years and would not be expected to consume more than a predetermined proportion of overall expenditure.

Funding structures may be seen as no more than a neutral question of administrative detail. The history of arts subsidy in the last 60 years suggests, on the contrary, that they reflect and embody cultural assumptions. The arrangements for Lottery distribution will doubtless continue to be the subject of close scrutiny and sometimes heated debate. However, a system has been set in place and is unlikely to be greatly altered in the near future. The coming year or two will demonstrate how well it works in practice. The Arts Councils and the government would be wise to keep it under close scrutiny and make such changes as seem necessary from to time. They might even go further. The speed with which the new policy has been brought in means that it is being implemented by institutions which were designed for other purposes and it would be surprising if this did not create strains; while I hesitate to suggest yet another overhaul of the arts funding system, there is a case for a review of Lottery funding procedures once they have had time to prove themselves – say, in three or five years' time. The signs are that the new Labour government's arts policy will major on inter-departmental co-ordination across the full extent of Whitehall, on the provision of extra-curricular cultural opportunities and on a possible enhanced obligation laid on local authorities to plan and provide for cultural activities at community level. This may mean that the need for a review will be rather more urgent.

The worst thing would be not to see the wood for the trees. While it is true that the devil often lies in the detail, we should not underestimate the seismic importance of the state's new commitment to the participatory, voluntary, amateur and community arts. This will surely generate its own momentum in the development of artistic practice. One way or another, the technicalities of grant management will be obliged to follow suit.

photo: Horniman Museum and Gardens

9 WHAT NEXT?

I am nearing the end of my journey. And, like Alice in the garden of the looking-glass house, I find I am suddenly at my starting point again – that is to say, the nature and function of participation in society today. In these closing remarks, I want to step back, draw out some of the themes I have argued earlier and bring forward suggestions for what could or should be done to build on all that has been achieved so far.

My key theme has been this. Music is the first thing we 'say', for it pre-dates language and we receive and transmit meanings from sounds before we have mastered words. It emerges from our deepest mental processes. This is the origin of its enduring power throughout our lives and is perhaps the fundamental reason that music is a near-universal accompaniment to the business of existence.

The ubiquity and variety of participatory music in the United Kingdom can be partly explained as the contemporary expression of cultural traditions going back many hundreds of years. But they also reflect the way we live now. For many people, value judgments have become relative and a pervasive individualism is altering our notions both of stable, fixed communities and of stable, fixed ideas of artistic quality. Technological advance has massively expanded the availability of every kind of music and consumers are beginning to play an active rather than a passive role – by having to choose from the multiplicity of cultural material on offer, by exploiting the arts in the construction of their lifestyles and, in some cases, by using technology to modify the works of others. Digitisation is enlarging the possibilities of creativity, for it enables the making of music without instruments.

It is no wonder, then, that music, whether created with a computer in a bedroom, presented in the top room of a pub or crafted for the discrete charm of the concert hall, is becoming more of a solitary pursuit. While, of course, it remains in many ways a vigorously social art, much of it taking place in societies, associations and clubs, a key trend in recent years has been towards celebrating or serving the individual, alone or in a group of other individuals, rather than integrating the individual into the group.

This has meant that we have to redefine the purposes of community music, shifting the emphasis from a territorial definition of community to the multifarious and often provisional forms of socialisation that have emerged in today's climate of shifting allegiances. In fact, it is time to ditch the term and replace it with 'participatory music'.

In a conventional report, this, the final chapter, is where the reader expects to find a neatly tabulated list of recommendations. I would not like to disappoint. There are a number of practical measures that need to be taken and I shall say what they are. But this book is aimed at provoking thought and discussion rather than simply drawing up a blueprint for decision-makers. What is to be done depends in the first instance on what people want to have done.

Participatory music faces no particular crisis. In fact, one could argue the reverse. It is practised by millions and enjoyed by millions. It is one of the success stories of contemporary British civilisation. Whatever the government, local councils and the arts funding system choose to do is unlikely to make a fundamental difference to this unending efflorescence of musicality.

Perhaps the most striking feature of the creative world I have tried to describe is its invisibility. The fact that it is everywhere may be one reason why it is so little regarded. It passes as unnoticed as paving stones or street furniture. Happily, there are signs of change. Perhaps the most encouraging development of recent years is that professional musicians and public authorities are beginning to shift their stance and to accord participatory music the social and artistic status it deserves. My fervent hope is that this process continues.

What those who care about participatory music are rightly demanding of the music world and the state is that they adopt a common vision of music which embraces the rich variety of practice in this country. Anne Hunt put it well when she said:

'My vision is simple. I would like to see created in the United Kingdom a musical climate where no one had any inhibitions about singing or playing an instrument; where collective music-making as a social activity was high on the agenda of hundreds of thousands of people of all ages throughout the country; where individuals would be interested in trying new things musically (from different cultures or different points on the traditional-contemporary spectrum); where people would voluntarily work together to try and develop their skills and their creativity; where a tremendous groundswell of enthusiasm from the community itself, rather than from a handful of professional practitioners, would transform the practice of community music; where the activities of music and dancing would once again become inextricably linked into people's creative practice and in social settings; and where participatory music-making and dance would become as much part of our lives as sitting in cafés or watching football.'[1]

However, this shared vision may take some time to realise and it will come only through more and more people listening to and playing more and more music – in a word, through good practice. In the meantime, a little practical help is necessary – a push here and a shove there. That is the purpose of the suggestions that follow. They fall into nine clusters and, for the busy reader, are summarised in a table at the end.

The most fundamental recommendation is the provision of easy access to music-making within striking distance of everyone in the country. The aim is to help individuals or groups to pursue their own ideas and practice.

The fact that so many people make music might suggest that it is easy for an individual or an emerging music group to know where to go, whom to contact, if they want help or support or even a few basic introductions. I do not believe this to be universally the case. Those who are isolated in the countryside or marooned on a provisionless urban estate, those who are poor, or young, or old, or disabled, do not all have the self-confidence and the basic know-how to join the game. Some may feel that they have left music behind or that it has left them behind.

More particularly, research has shown that there is a musical hiatus in most lifespans. Between the end of schooling and their late 20s or early 30s, many young people lose interest in music-making. No doubt they have other things to do as they set up careers and start families. A good number are unaware of, and do not know how to locate and make use of, established networks.

So we must find ways of making it easier for those who would like to get involved in music to gain a foothold. In appendix one, I list the addresses of organisations which could be of assistance. In some cases, their response to enquiry may well turn out to be still more lists of addresses. This would, of course, be valuable, but many enquirers will hope for something a little more substantial – practical advice and even training. There is no easy answer to this problem. What is needed is a kind of 'one-stop shop' for music-makers, a network of citizens' music advice bureaux which would not only offer good counsel but identify the whereabouts of such resources as musical instruments and equipment, studios and rehearsal space.

1 Hunt, Anne, from a letter to the author, 28 April 1997.

As policy-makers enter the field of participatory music, they will find themselves hampered by inadequate information. The RABs should consider commissioning surveys measuring the extent of participatory musical activity in their regions in order to develop existing provision and identify gaps.

One of my most depressing discoveries when researching *Joining In* was the absence of comprehensive and reliable data embracing the entire field of participatory musics. There are particularly striking gaps in rock and pop, disability musics and community music. Where there are well-established umbrella bodies, a good deal *is* known (for example, about amateur music societies, choirs and amateur operatic societies), but elsewhere information is largely anecdotal. The amount of public sector support (especially by local authorities) for participatory musics has not been accurately computed. It is high time for a quantitative survey of the field. This would involve surveying the extent of independent creative activity across the country (in terms both of active participants and of their audiences), training opportunities both in the education sector and elsewhere, music courses in adult education, festivals, summer schools arts centres, community schools and colleges.

A study of this kind need not be a major and lengthy exercise as some knowledge already exists, but unless it is undertaken, it is hard to see what policy-makers, local, regional and national, will be able to base their decisions on. One cost-effective means of gathering information would be through analysis of material on the proposed information database (see above), assuming that it was established quickly.

It is essential that the music curriculum in schools is made to work effectively. This means ensuring that music is a part of children's lives from playgroup right through to nursery, primary and secondary school.

For most of us, school is where we get our first real chance to engage with music. The discoveries of neurological research have demonstrated beyond peradventure the functional relevance of music to our intellectual and emotional well-being. Educational studies have convincingly supported the claim (long suspected but previously hard to substantiate) that, as well as being valuable and pleasurable in its own right, music in the classroom positively enhances the learning process in other disciplines, especially mathematics and languages.

A potentially excellent new music curriculum is now in place on paper with the approval of most of those concerned with music education. It offers a wonderful opportunity for all children and not just the few who already have access to good music teaching. But in the context of a still struggling education system, where funding for facilities and equipment, let alone adequate timetabling or teacher training, is scarce, its full implementation has been delayed. What is required is hard-headed discussion about how to make the curriculum work in practical terms. Perhaps the best way forward is to set up a short-term working party with a membership drawn from teachers, music educationists, local authority representatives and practising musicians, amateur and professional. The Schools Curriculum and Assessment Authority, in association with the Arts Council of England (together with its Scottish, Welsh and Northern Irish equivalents), should consider convening the group. This is not to argue for yet more talking shops. The working party should set itself a tight timetable to recommend *achievable* aims. Some of the good practice described in this book might provide a starting point.

A number of areas call for urgent attention. The first of these is music in children's early years, in the light of the likely introduction of widespread nursery education; music umbrella bodies and the arts funding system should seek to influence specialist organisations in the field, such as NEYN. More time should be given to music for all children in primary schools. Classroom choral singing should be encouraged and the potential of music at school assemblies exploited, not simply in a religious context but because they are regular occasions when the school comes together as a whole. Music should play a larger part in primary teacher training and, as a long-term aim, there should be a music specialist in every school. Music is already compulsory up to and including Key Stage 3 in the secondary curriculum and should be easily available for everyone throughout the school. There should be a requirement that Music GCSE be available in every school. There should also be an identification of easy routes for progression for children with a particular aptitude for music, whatever their social class. Opportunities for music-making of all kinds outside the curriculum should also be encouraged.

Enhanced teacher in-service training is essential whether for the music specialist, the generalist primary teacher or the visiting instrumental teacher, but there is a limit to what any individual teacher can achieve. A way forward for the beleaguered music teacher is for schools to forge relations with the very many different musicians and music groups, amateur and professional, that already exist in the locality. Greater interaction of this kind would enable staff and pupils to gain access to a wide range of skills and talent. It would probably help to surmount the falling-off in music-making among young people when they leave school for the adult world, as well as giving a boost to non-curricular musical activity at school.

If there are to be specialist arts schools, LEAs should ensure that children in other schools do not suffer from diminished provision; those who develop a serious interest should be given the opportunity to transfer on a full-time basis to such schools.

Another field of knowledge could be helpfully trawled. Because of the advances in neurological and psychological research into music and mental activity, it would aid policy creation and provide invaluable material for advocacy if music educationists as well as music umbrella bodies and the arts funding system kept themselves informed of the latest state of scientific opinion. They would be wise to consider ways of establishing ongoing liaison with the scientific community.

Participatory music will thrive only if all those involved are given the opportunity to improve their skills. This will mean access to a wide range of training opportunities. Everyone working in music should have the chance to attend regular courses or summer schools so that they can improve their skills and exchange good practice.

Learning, of course, is for life. Participatory musicians are well aware that they need various forms of support, many of which involve training. The first of these is the need to improve standards of performance. But how is that best done? There are many ways of learning how to make music – from imitation of one's seniors as a member of a brass band to workshop-based practice. Just as in the classroom, there is no one simple pedagogic ideal and we need a flexible model which suits method to context.

It would be helpful if there were a concerted effort to exploit the full scope of possibilities. One option would be to bring together a range of practitioners to identify access to participation in music by disabled people are considerable and this could be an ideal field for support by the Arts Councils from National Lottery funds in financial partnership with the education sector.

In this difficult and highly technical field, there may be a case for creating a national agency for electronic music, to monitor and test developments as they occur. It should offer support and guidance for schools and music groups in every genre of music from rock to classical; the aims would be to identify the best methods of exploiting new technology, to liaise with the commercial sector and to provide general information and advice.

The network of national and local radio stations and the arrival of cable television channels able to provide local services suggest that there may be potential for increased broadcasting of participatory music. The success of the Estover Project is a case in point. It would be to the mutual benefit of all concerned – broadcasters, musicians, Arts Councils, RABs, local authorities and broadcasting licensing authorities – if they could seek practical ways of encouraging this.

There is insufficient cheap access, especially for young people, to studios, recording equipment and other facilities and, where appropriate, rehearsal and performing spaces. This is a particular issue in the rock and pop sector and for young black musicians. The gap could be filled by the music resource centres I was proposing earlier at arts centres or community schools. But, as ever, money will be needed for equipment purchase, maintenance and, over the passage of time, re-equipment.

The Arts Councils should improve their own knowledge of the field. One way of doing so would be to recruit expert advisers who would enable them to monitor and disseminate up-to-date information on technological opportunities for the arts in general, and participatory music in particular, and who would advise on investment policies.

Government policy places a welcome emphasis on the participatory arts. As the case of music demonstrates, the promotion of creative practice is of concern to a wide range of social and voluntary services. Interdepartmental co-ordination should be encouraged especially in Health, Social Services and Education and Employment both at national and local government levels.

It is increasingly evident that music-making, and indeed the arts in general, are becoming a regular feature of the policies and programmes of charities, trusts and voluntary agencies with social remits. The surveys currently being conducted by Age Concern and the Youth Arts Network will form a useful basis for future policy development. The long-standing and distinguished record of arts in healthcare has charted ways in which music can enhance the quality of life of people working or undergoing treatment in hospitals. Likewise, as I have shown, there are many examples of good practice so far as music in prisons is concerned.

As the Department of National Heritage develops an ever more inclusive and holistic approach to arts policy, it should consider ways not only of supporting groups and individuals whose prime concern is artistic production, but the complete spectrum of agencies in community education, the social services, youth umbrella organisations and charities to initiate or (as appropriate) further develop musical and artistic activity among their 'constituencies'. Local authority arts strategies should also take an interdepartmental view (as many already do) and encompass a similar scope of activity.

The Arts Councils in England, Northern Ireland, Scotland and Wales should finance participatory music in a coherent manner. This will entail a revision of the rules of National Lottery distribution.

It is difficult to see how those working in the field and in the arts funding system will be able to address the issues I have outlined unless a strategic approach is agreed and implemented. The availability of National Lottery money for the amateur and community arts makes such an approach all the more necessary if these new resources are to be well spent.

When it established the National Lottery, the Government of the day eschewed a policy-led approach to the distribution of Lottery proceeds to good causes, believing that funds should be available to all on an equal basis. This openness and simplicity of process, with access for everyone at its heart, is both welcome and unprecedented. However, it is difficult to see for how long the Arts Councils can stand back from taking any strategic measures and perhaps it is time for the government to relax its rules. The regional audits I have recommended are likely to reveal areas of activity that call for special attention. The first step might simply be to fill the gaps identified. It would be sensible if the Arts Councils were allowed to take the necessary action – perhaps (following the example of the National Lottery Charities Board) by announcing favoured priorities with special reference to access and participation. In this way, it would be possible to address the needs of participatory music in an orderly rather than a piecemeal fashion. Priorities could be established after consultation with the local organisations concerned, local authorities, RABs and other relevant constituencies (for example, the education sector). In order to maintain the principle of open application, each priority would be time-limited and not consume more than a predetermined proportion of overall expenditure.

These are practical measures. A larger issue of principle also has to be faced. The Arts Councils and many local authorities have spent much of the last 50 years promoting excellence in the professional arts and, by most disinterested accounts, they have done a good job. They acted on the basis of assessed need: where they saw a gap they devised a policy to fill it. A classic example has been the establishment across the country of regional theatre companies in custom-designed buildings. Another has been balanced support for symphony orchestras to ensure that most people were within striking distance of live, high quality, classical music. The underlying assumption was that even if the professional arts were a minority interest of the well-off and the well-educated, they should nevertheless be made genuinely available to every citizen.

This is a worthy aim. But what it left out of account was that in music, for example, a very large number of citizens had their own cultures with which they were well satisfied – but in which the funding system showed little or no interest. Now that the situation is changing and all music is falling within the state's purview, the old habits of intervention are not so appropriate as they were. To use a military metaphor, the question is no longer how to raise, equip and train a small but effective professional army, but how to satisfy the requirements of a *levée en masse* or a nation of home militias.

The old watchword, 'We know what you need; here it is and we hope you like it' will have to yield to another more permissive one, 'We know what you like; so how can we help you do it as well as possible?' This suggests that when the funding bureaucracy finds itself responding to the creativity of citizens rather than focusing exclusively on the needs of a creative elite, it will be well-advised to adopt a humbler, more responsive attitude. The light regulatory touch I was recommending earlier in the context of evaluation has a wider relevance.

This does not mean that I am advocating an abdication from rigour and excellence, but it does call for an insight into the many varieties of excellence and a recognition that judgment can no longer be the monopoly of a class of highly trained experts applying a hierarchy of values. It will be a more complicated working environment for the politicians and the bureaucrats involved and they will face the hard task of erasing the old ingrained culture of well-intentioned paternalism. It will be a revolutionary change of heart and mind. But success will bring great prizes in its train.

A holistic arts policy, in which culture is broadly defined, will be likely to attract warm public support, if we can go by the example of countries like The Netherlands and Sweden. More to the point, it will be possible to foster a reintegration of the British artistic scene, divided as it still is into the mutually distrustful camps of the high arts, the amateur arts and mass popular culture. It is seldom that an alteration in administrative procedures can contribute to an artistic renaissance, but this may well be one such occasion.

photo: Frank Rodgers

ACTION POINTS

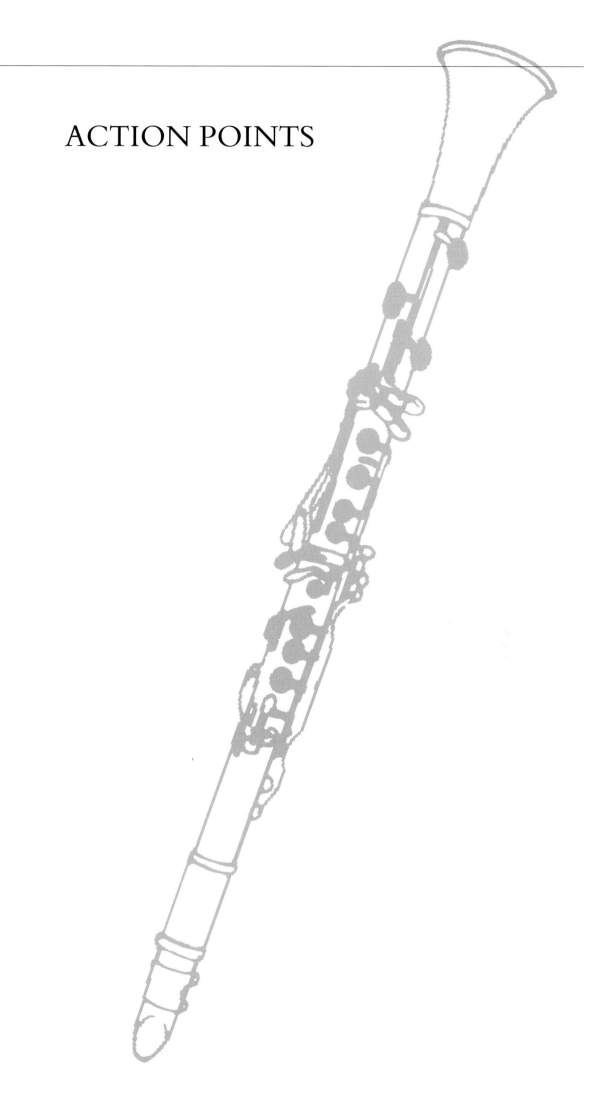

A *The first, and most fundamental, recommendation is the provision of easy access to music-making within striking distance of everyone in the country. The aim is to help individuals or groups to pursue their own ideas and practice.*

1 The establishment of 'one-stop shops' for music-makers – through the public library system or another appropriate set of agencies in association with music umbrella bodies providing a national music information network. The Department of National Heritage, the Libraries Association and local authorities should discuss ways and means.

2 The creation of a music Internet Website, so creating a national information database.

B *Music resource centres should be established across the country which can be a focus for music-making of every kind and can offer performance and rehearsal spaces, equipment, access to tuition and the opportunity to meet other people with similar interests.*

1 Selected existing arts organisations – arts centres, community projects and music development agencies, not necessarily those with buildings – to act as 'open' permanent resource centres for rehearsal, performance, training, cheap access to instruments and the exchange of ideas. In areas where there is no suitable existing body, one should be created.

2 Music resource centres to compile databases of all music activities in their locality; to be in touch with local musicians, music teachers, music groups and promoters who are in a position to introduce newcomers to the music scene; and to liaise with the non-cultural voluntary sector where it promotes musical activity.

3 Some community schools and community colleges also to be encouraged to be music resource centres, with National Lottery investment paying for music facilities (studios, rehearsal and performance spaces, new technology and instrument banks). They would serve the dual function of assisting the delivery of the music curriculum and being a resource for participatory musicians, as well as facilitating greater interaction between them and teachers.

4 The Department for Education and Employment and local authorities to consider ways of reducing hire fees for school halls and similar venues, the rising cost of which amateur music societies are finding it increasingly difficult to afford.

5 Proposals by music umbrella bodies and national music service agencies for the establishment of joint headquarters to be supported.

C *As policy-makers enter the field of participatory music, they will find themselves hampered by inadequate information. They should commission surveys measuring the extent of musical activity in all sections of society and in all parts of the country.*

1 The Arts Councils to consider commissioning a quantitative survey of participatory musics in the United Kingdom to assist them in policy development, perhaps through analysis of the proposed national information database.

2 As an aid to advocacy, the arts funding system to keep itself informed of the latest state of scientific research into the neurology and psychology of music and establish ongoing liaison with the scientific community.

D *It is essential that the music curriculum is made to work effectively. This means ensuring that music is a part of children's lives from playgroup through to nursery, primary and secondary school.*

1   The Schools Curriculum and Assessment Authority, in association with the Arts Councils of England, Scotland, Wales and Northern Ireland, to consider setting up a short-term working party drawn from teachers, music educationists, local authority representatives and practising musicians (both amateur and professional). Its task would be to find practical ways of helping to deliver the music curriculum; and also of supporting the development of music-in-education schemes and community schools.

2   Music to be compulsory in early years education.

3   More time to be made available for music in primary schools, with classroom choral singing and music at school assemblies. Music should play a larger part in primary teacher training, and, in the long term there should be a music specialist in every school.

4   Music is already compulsory for all up to and including Key Stage 3 and should be easily available for everyone throughout the school. Music GCSE should also be available at every school and more encouragement should be given to non-curricular musical activity.

5   In-service teacher training to be enhanced for music specialists, generalist primary teachers and visiting instrumental teachers.

6   Co-operation between schools and local musicians to be actively encouraged, enabling staff and pupils to gain access to a wide range of skills and talent.

E *Participatory music will thrive only if all those involved are given the opportunity to improve their skills. This will mean access to a wide range of training opportunities. Everyone working in music should have the chance to attend regular courses or summer schools so that they can improve their skills and exchange good practice.*

1   Music umbrella bodies to improve standards of performance by identifying and publicising training opportunities. They should also share and debate different training methodologies with all those involved – teachers, music project leaders, music therapists, peripatetic instrumentalists and private tutors.

2   Arts funding bodies to consider giving practical support to professional participatory music organisations which equip local musicians and community groups with the skills to establish independent music projects of their own.

3   Conservatoires to ensure that all music students are given direct experience of working on educational, community-based or outreach projects.

4   Music umbrella bodies to be given additional financial support from arts funding agencies to help amateur societies and ensembles in their membership to develop educational, community-based and outreach skills and to improve their marketing and administrative competence.

F *A catholic approach to music, which takes in every kind of musical activity, will entail a review of what is meant by artistic standards. The music world and the arts funding system should agree new, more flexible criteria of evaluation.*

1   Musicians, arts managements, arts funding bodies and business sponsors to move towards flexible criteria for the assessment of creative standards in participatory music. Funding bodies and managements should apply a light regulatory touch.

2   Music umbrella bodies to encourage debate on creative standards through magazines, conferences and summer schools.

3   Arts funding agencies, local authority arts and leisure departments and local education authorities to exchange ideas and examples of good practice, especially as regards policy development and evaluation, both at national and regional levels.

4 Arts funding agencies to consider appointing more amateur and participatory musicians onto their funding panels or advisory structures.

G *The arts funding system should systematically monitor the development of new technologies and their impact on musical practice.*

1 More resources to be invested in the development of hardware and software for music composition and employment.

2 Establishment of a national agency for electronic music. It would monitor and test developments as they occur, offering support and guidance for schools and music groups in every musical genre from rock to classical; its task would be to identify the best methods of exploiting new technology, to liaise with the commercial sector and to provide general information and advice.

3 Broadcasters, musicians, arts funding bodies, local authorities and broadcasting licensing authorities to consider practical ways of encouraging the broadcasting of participatory musics.

4 Music resource centres (see recommendation B 1 and 2) to help to ensure cheap access, especially for young people, to music studios, recording equipment and other facilities, with particular reference to rock, pop and black music.

5 The Arts Councils of England, Scotland, Wales and Northern Ireland to consider establishing a standing UK committee, or national committees, to monitor and disseminate information on opportunities for the arts in general, and participatory music in particular, in the new technologies.

H *Government policy places a welcome emphasis on the participatory arts. As the case of music demonstrates, the promotion of creative practice is of concern to a wide range of social and voluntary services. Interdepartmental co-ordination should be encouraged especially in Health, Social Services and Education and Employment.*

1 The Department of National Heritage should consider ways not only of supporting groups and individuals whose prime concern is artistic production, but the complete spectrum of agencies in community education, the social services, youth umbrella organisations and charities to initiate or (as appropriate) further develop musical and artistic activity among their 'constituencies'.

2 Local authority arts strategies should also take an interdepartmental view of cultural policy (as many already do) and encompass a range of activity similar to that recommended for national government.

I *Finally, the Arts Councils in England, Northern Ireland, Scotland and Wales should finance participatory music in a coherent manner. This will entail a revision of the rules of National Lottery distribution.*

1 The government should consider allowing the Arts Councils to distribute National Lotteries more strategically; for example, by selecting themes with special reference to access and participation, which would run for period of years and not consume more than a predetermined proportion of overall expenditure. This would enable them to address the needs of the participatory arts in general, and participatory music in particular, in the most efficient way possible.

APPENDICES

APPENDIX ONE

Some useful addresses for music participants

Adult Learning Project
184 Dalry Road
Edinburgh EH11 2EP
Scotland
Tel 0131 337 5442
Fax 0131 337 9316

Association of Irish Music Societies
24 Glenbourne Green
Leopardstown Valley
Dublin 18
Republic of Ireland
Tel +353 1 294 0775

Bharatiya Vidya Bhavan Centre
4a Castletown Road
London W14 9HQ
Tel 0171 381 3086/4608
Fax 0171 381 8758

British Association of Symphonic Bands and Wind Ensembles
3 Northbrook Road
Solihull
West Midlands B90 3NT
Tel/fax 0121 743 2483/0121 744 1529

British Federation of Brass Bands
3 Grendon Street
Coombe Vale Road
Teignmouth
Devon TQ14 9EW
Tel 01626 770362

British Federation of Festivals
Festivals House
198 Park Lane
Macclesfield
Cheshire SK11 6UD
Tel 01625 428297
Fax 01625 503229

British Federation of Youth Choirs
37 Frederick Street
Loughborough
Leics LE11 3BH
Tel 01509 211664
Fax 01509 233749

British Music Information Centre
10 Stratford Place
London W1N 9AE
Tel 0171 499 8567
Fax 0171 499 4795

Contemporary Music-making for Amateurs (COMA)
13 Wellington Way
London E3 4NE
Tel 0181 980 1527

English Folk Dance and Song Society
2 Regents Park Road
London NW1 7AY
Tel 0171 485 2206

Federation of Music Collectives
MusicBase
Temple Bar Music Centre
Curved Street
Temple Bar
Dublin 2
Republic of Ireland
Tel +353 1 679 0533
Fax +353 1 679 0535

Federation of Music Services
12 Lucas Road
High Wycombe
Bucks HP13 6QE
Tel/fax 01494 439572

Fèisean nan Gàidheal
Quay Brae
Portree
Isle of Skye IV51 9DB
Scotland
Tel 01478 612990
Fax 01478 613263

Folkworks
69 Westgate Road
Newcastle-upon-Tyne NE1 1SG
Tel 0191 222 1717
Fax 0191 230 2484

Jazz Services Ltd
5 Dryden Street
London WC2E 9NW
Tel 0171 829 8352/3/4
Fax 0171 829 8355/0171 240 5600

Music Association
71 Margaret Road
New Barnet
Herts EN4 9ND
Tel 0181 440 6919

Music for Youth
4 Blade Mews
London SW15 2NN
Tel 0181 870 9624
Fax 0181 870 9935
www.pjbpubs.co.uk/mfy

National Association of Choirs
21 Charmouth Road
Lower Weston
Bath BA1 3LJ
Tel 01225 426713

National Association of Music Educators and Schools Music Association
52 Hall Orchard Lane
Frisby-on-the-Wreake
Melton Mowbray
Leicestershire LE14 2NH
Tel 01664 434379
Fax 01664 434137

National Association of Youth Orchestras
Ainslie House
11 St Colme Street
Edinburgh EH3 6AG
Scotland
Tel 0131 225 4606
Fax 0131 225 3568

National Federation of Music Societies
Francis House
Francis Street
London SW1P 1DE
Tel 0171 828 7320
Fax 0171 828 5504

National Music and Disability Information Service
Sound Sense
Riverside House
Rattlesden
Bury St Edmunds IP30 0SF
Tel 01449 736287
Fax 01449 737649
E-mail 100256.30@compuserve.com

National Operatic and Dramatic Association
NODA House
1 Crestfield Street
London WC1H 8AU
Tel 0171 837 5655
Fax 0171 833 0609

Northern Ireland Bands Association
28 Knockfergus Park
Greenisland
Carrickfergus BT38 8SN
Northern Ireland
Tel 01232 866179

Royal Scottish Pipe Band Association
45 Washington Street
Glasgow G3 8AZ
Scotland
Tel 0141 221 5414
Fax 0141 221 1561

SAMPAD
mac
Cannon Hill Park
Birmingham B12 9QH
Tel 0121 440 4221 ext 206
Tel/fax 0121 440 8667

Society for the Promotion of New Music
Francis House
Francis Street
London SW1P 1DE
Tel 0171 828 9696
Fax 0171 931 9928

Sonic Arts Network
Francis House
Francis Street
London SW1P 1DE
Tel 0171 828 9796
Fax 0171 233 5159
E-mail jonathan@sonicart.demon.co.uk

Sound Sense
Riverside House, Rattlesden
Bury St Edmunds IP30 0SF
Tel 01449 736287
Fax 01449 737649
E-mail 100256.30@compuserve.com

Traditional Music and Song Association of Scotland
Level 3
Greenside House
25 Greenside Place
Edinburgh EH1 3AA
Scotland
Tel 0131 557 8484

Welsh Amateur Music Federation
9 Museum Place
Cardiff CF1 3NX
Wales
Tel 01222 394711

Arts Councils and English Regional Arts Boards

Arts Council of England
14 Great Peter Street
London SW1P 3NQ
Tel 0171 333 0100
Fax 0171 973 6590
E-mail info.music.ace@artsf6.org.uk

Arts Council of Northern Ireland
181a Stranmillis Road
Belfast BT9 5DU
Northern Ireland
Tel 01232 381591
Fax 01232 661715

**Arts Council of Wales/Cyngor
  Celfyddydau Cymru**
Museum Place
Cardiff CF1 3NX
Wales
Tel 01222 394711
Fax 01222 221447

Scottish Arts Council
12 Manor Place
Edinburgh EH3 7DD
Scotland
Tel 0131 226 6051
Fax 0131 225 9833
E-mail music.sac@artsf6.org.uk

East Midlands Arts Board
Mountfields House
Forest Road
Loughborough
Leics LE11 3HU
Tel 01509 218292
Fax 01509 26221
E-mail firstname.surname.ema@artsf6.org.uk

Eastern Arts Board
Cherry Hinton Hall
Cherry Hinton Road
Cambridge CB1 4DW
Tel 01223 215355
Fax 01223 248075
E-mail firstname.surname/department@
    eastern-arts.co.uk

London Arts Board
133 Long Acre
Covent Garden
London WC2E 9AF
Tel 0171 240 1313
Fax 0171 240 4580
E-mail lab@lonab.demon.co.uk

North West Arts Board
Manchester House
22 Bridge Street
Manchester M3 3AB
Tel 0161 834 6644
Fax 0161 834 6969
E-mail nwarts-info@mcr1.poptel.org.uk

Northern Arts Board
9-10 Jesmond Terrace
Jesmond
Newcastle-upon-Tyne
NE2 1NZ
Tel 0191 281 6334
Fax 0191 281 3276
E-mail nab@norab.demon.co.uk

South East Arts Board
10 Mount Ephraim
Tunbridge Wells
Kent TN4 8AS
Tel 01892 515210
Fax 01892 549383
E-mail firstname.surname.sea@artsf6.org.uk

South West Arts Board
Bradninch Place
Gandy Street
Exeter EX4 3LS
Tel 01392 218188
Fax 01392 413554
E-mail firstname.surname.swa@artsf6.org.uk

Southern Arts Board
  13 St Clement Street
Winchester SO23 9DQ
Tel 01962 855099
Fax 01962 861186
E-mail firstname.surname.southarts@
    artsf6.org.uk

West Midlands Arts Board
82 Granville Street
Birmingham B1 2LH
Tel 0121 631 3121
Fax 0121 643 7239
E-mail firstname.surname.wma@artsf6.org.uk

Yorkshire and Humberside Arts
21 Bond Street
Dewsbury
West Yorkshire WF13 1AX
Tel 01924 455555
Fax 01924 466522
E-mail firstname.surname.yha@artsf6.org.uk

APPENDIX TWO
Steering Group and list of those consulted

The names of those whom I consulted during the process of writing this report follow. Most of them I have spoken with personally, but others gave me texts they had written or publications by the organisations for which they work (these are marked by ★).

Pride of place goes to the Steering Group with whom I worked under the guidance of Siân Ede, Assistant Director (Arts), Gulbenkian Foundation, UK branch.

Jo Shapcott, *(Chair of the Steering Group)* poet and Education Consultant to the Association of British Orchestras

Keith Griffin, Director, Welsh Amateur Music Federation

Ben Higham, Director, Community Music East

Anne Hunt, Director, World Circuit Arts

Russell Jones, Chief Executive, National Federation of Music Societies

Kathryn McDowell, *(Observer)* Music Director, Arts Council of England

Joanna MacGregor, musician

Dermot McLaughlin, Music Officer, Arts Council of Ireland

Gillian Moore, Head of Education, South Bank Centre

Andrew Peggie, community musician

Peter Renshaw, Professor of Community Music, Guildhall School of Music and Drama

Errollyn Wallen, composer, pianist, singer songwriter

Mat Anderson, composer and performer
Judy Arnold, Manager, Sir Peter Maxwell Davies

Richard Bamford, community musician and composer
Ed Bicknell, popular music promoter, Manager of Damage
Roy Bohana, Music Director, Arts Council of Wales/Cyngor Celfyddydau Cymru
Professor Eric Bolton, former Senior Chief Inspector, HMI
Helena Braithwaite, Education Officer, BBC Wales (Music)
★Andrew Burn, Education and Community Director, Bournemouth Sinfonietta

George Caird, Principal, Birmingham Conservatoire
★Michael Calder, Head of Orchestral Studies, Royal Scottish Academy of Music and Drama
Ciaran Carson, Traditional Arts Officer, Arts Council of Northen Ireland
Duncan Chapman, community musician
★Ian Clarke, Arts Development Officer, Borough of Blackburn
Judith Clarke, formerly of South East Arts Board
Keith Clarke, Editor, *Classical Music*
Penny Collier, Sound It Out
Geraldine Connor, musician
★Arthur Cormack, Fèisean Nan Gaedheal
Alastair Creamer, Director, London College of Music
Pauline Crossley, Expressive Arts Officer, Welsh Joint Education Committee

Jane Dancer, Northern Sinfonia
Dr Jane Davidson, Department of Music, University of Sheffield
Kathryn Deane, Administrator, Sound Sense
Gordon Dougall, Director, Sounds of Progress

Adèle Drake, Project Director, Drake Music Project
Gail Dudson, consultant
Alice Dumas, Campaigns Officer, Latymer School, Enfield
★Jan Dungey, Arts Development Officer, Great Yarmouth Borough Council
★Roger Durston, Music Education Council

Jennifer Edwards, Director, National Campaign for the Arts
Jean Escott, Wrekin Council (Chairperson, National District Arts Officers Society)

Andrew Fairbairn, former Director of Education, Leicestershire County Council
Steve Fletcher, South Wales Intercultural Community Arts
Roger Fox, Director, Voluntary Arts Network
Simon Foxley, COMA
Fi Frances, Researcher for Age Concern

Sarah Gibbons, Education Officer, Society for the Promotion of New Music
Christopher Gordon, English Regional Arts Boards
Kathy Graham, Society for the Promotion of New Music

Sarah Harman, Community Music Wales
Bill Harpe, The Blackie, Liverpool
Wendy Harpe, freelance arts worker
Keith Harris, Glenys Hughes, Artistic Director, St Magnus Festival
Tony Haynes, Grand Union Music Theatre
★Steve Heap, Festival Director, Mrs Casey Music
Jane Hellings, consultant, The Arts Business
Gavin Henderson, Principal, Trinity College of Music
Michael Henry, composer
Clare Higney, community artist
Graham Hitchen, Director of Corporate Policy, Arts Council of England
★David Hoult, Principal, City of Leeds College of Music
Glenys Hughes, Artistic Director, St Magnus Festival

Emyr Jenkins, Chief Executive, Arts Council of Wales/Cyngor Celfyddydau Cymru
Marcel Jenkins, Arts Assistant, East Midlands Arts
Heather Johnson, Chairman, Scottish Committee, National Federation of Music Societies
Joint Officers Group (a standing committee of Arts Council of England and Regional Arts
    Board officers)

Naseem Khan, writer

★Heather Laing, formerly Music Officer, Eastern Arts Board
Terence Lloyd, Chairman, Music Committee, National Eisteddfod of Wales

Irene McDonald, music consultant
Andrew McKenzie, Principal Music Officer, London Arts Board
Ed McKeon, National Federation of Music Societies
Libby MacNamara, Association of British Orchestras
Richard McNicol, Apollo Trust
Michael Marx, formerly Music Officer, Southern Arts Board
Sir Peter Maxwell Davies
Mark Monument, Northern Arts
Nigel Morgan, composer and Research Fellow; University of Liverpool
John Muir, music consultant

Dr M N Nandakamura, Bhavan Centre, London
Roy Nevitt, Theatre Director, Stantonbury Campus, Milton Keynes

Jean Nicholson, Director, Opera and Music Theatre Forum
*Keith Nimmo, South West Arts

Professor George Odam, Bath College of Higher Education
David O'Donnell, Project Director, Community Music London

Andrew Pinnock, Music Officer, Arts Council of England
Jan Ponsford, musician
Curtis Price, Principal, Royal Academy of Music

Nick Randall, Director, Youth Arts Network
Piali Ray, Director, SAMPAD
Stan Reeves, Adult Learning Project, Edinburgh
Ros Rigby, Co-Director, Folkworks
Ian Ritchie, music consultant
Elfed Roberts, Director, Royal National Eisteddfod
Clare Robertson, North Area Cultural Development Officer, City of Glasgow
Sue Robertson, Director, London Arts Board
Judith Robinson, Education Officer, Philharmonia
Mathew Rooke, Music Director, Scottish Arts Council
Alison Rushby, music teacher and member of National Association of Music Educators

Sara Scott, Combined Arts Officer, Arts Council of England
Samantha Seabourne, Administrator, Sonic Arts Network
Maggie Semple, Education and Training Director, Arts Council of England
Peter Senior, Director, Arts For Health
Geoff Sims, Director, Midlands Arts Centre
Antony Smith, ActivAge Development Officer, Eurolink Age
Pamela Smith, Music Officer, Arts Council of Northern Ireland
Phil Spurr, Estover Community College
Glyn Stackhouse, formerly Director of Music, British Council
David Sulkin, music consultant
John Summers, Chief Executive, Northern Sinfonia

Roger Taylor, President, UK Branch, International Association of Music Libraries,
    Archives and Documentation Centres
Katie Tearle, Head of Education, Glyndebourne Opera Company
Chris Thomas, Secretary, Luton Music Club
Alison Tickell, Community Music London
Mary Turner, Artistic Director, Action Space Mobile
Richard Turner, Arts Council of Wales/Cyngor Celfyddydau Cymru

James Walker, Welsh College of Music and Dance
David Walters, Director, Music Research Institute
Judith Webster, Head of Education, Royal Philharmonic Orchestra
David Whelton, Managing Director, Philharmonia
James Whitbourn, Producer, *Choral Evensong*, Radio 3
Susan White, Director, Impact Arts Management
Jac Wilkinson, East Midlands Arts
Lesley Willis, Overtones
Dorothy Wilson, Programme Director, Midlands Arts Centre
Trevor Wishart, composer
Paul Wright, Education Officer, Sonic Arts Network

Linda Young, Project Co-ordinator, Strathaven Choral Society

APPENDIX THREE

Useful books, reports and other documents

This is by no means a comprehensive list of books and other documents on the subject of participation and music. They are simply the most useful ones I encountered during the process of my researches. Many are unpublished texts from the files of music organisations.

Access to Jazz, A series of workshops communicating through Jazz, Jazz Services Ltd, 1994.

Amateur Arts in the UK, by Robert Hutchison and Andrew Feist, Policy Studies Institute, London, 1991.

Apollo Trust annual reports, 1977-8 to 1981-2.

The Arts in a Time of Change, pamphlet by Emyr Jenkins, National Eisteddfod of Wales, Neath and District, 1994.

Association of British Orchestras, Response to the Arts Council of England Consultative Document on New Lottery Directions, ABO, 1996.

Association of British Orchestras, Response to the Arts Council of England Green Paper on Publicly Funded Music in England, *Striking a Note*, ABO, 1996.

Attitudes to Participation in the Arts: Heritage, Broadcasting and Sport: a Review of Recent Research, by John Harland, Kay Kinder, Kate Hartley and Anne Wilkin. A report for the Department of National Heritage from the National Foundation for Educational Research.

Bhavan Institute of Indian Culture, UK Centre 1972-92 (a brief history of the Bhavan Centre), London, 1992.

Blowing (and Striking) a New Note, a submission by the British Federation of Brass Bands and the Brass Band Heritage Trust in response to the consultative Green Paper on publicly funded music in England, May 1996.

British Federation of Brass Bands – New Lottery Programmes: the brass band response, June 1996.

The Cambridgeshire Report on the Teaching of Music, Cambridgeshire Council of Musical Education. Cambridge University Press, 1933.

The Changing Nature of the Music Profession, article by Ian Ritchie, based on his speech at the Annual Seminar of the Specialist Music Schools and Colleges, Edinburgh, September 1994.

Changing Times, Conference Report of the Association of British Orchestras' Eleventh National Conference, 1996.

Children and Music: a new approach (a project proposal), Richard McNicol, 1977.

The Children's Music Book, by Saville Kushner, Calouste Gulbenkian Foundation, London, 1991.

Civil Society and its Future, by Salvador Giner, Keynote address, European Round Table of the CIRCLE Network, Budapest, March 1994, International Arts Bureau, London, 1997.

Community Education and the Arts: the Estover Experience, by Phil Stevens, Phil Spurr, Nina Simpson and Donna-Lee Iffla. The Devon Papers, Devon County Council, 1995.

Community Music Wales, annual report 1994-5.

Concerts for Children, report of a conference in Stavanger, May 1996, Stavanger Symfoniorkester.

Consultative Green Paper for Education and Training in the English Arts Funding System, Arts Council of England, June 1996.

Contemporary Society and the Growth of Leisure, by Kenneth Roberts, Longman, London, 1978.

Creating New Notes, A policy for the support of new music in England, Arts Council of England, London, 1996.

A Creative Future: The way forward for the arts, crafts and media in England, Arts Council of Great Britain, London, 1991.

The Dance and the Drum, by John and Elizabeth Paynter, Universal, 1974.

Debussy: His Life and Mind, by Edward Lockspeiser, Cassell, London, 1962.

Did We Do That? An evaluation of the Calouste Gulbenkian Foundation's Rural Arts Agency Scheme. by Tess Hurson, Calouste Gulbenkian Foundation, London, 1996.

Digital Creativity, by Owen Kelly, Calouste Gulbenkian Foundation, London, 1996.

Dolphin Report, Artistic and Educational Aspects (evaluation of *Arion and the Dolphin*, a Baylis Programme at the English National community opera project), by Rebecca Meitlis, 1994.

Education and Training for the 21st Century, Department of Education and Science White Paper, HMSO, London, 1991.

Elements of Aycliffe, Evaluation of work undertaken by the full Orchestra ... 7-10 March 1995, in Newton Aycliffe, Co. Durham, Northern Sinfonia, 1995. Also other evaluation documentation.

Evaluation of Artists-in-Schools Development Projects in Gwynedd and Clwyd: a report by Sue Clive and Chris Burton for the Arts Council of Wales/Cyngor Celfyddydau Cymru.

Firebird Trust, Three Year Plan: 1996-9.

Future Support for the Arts in England and Wales, by Lord Redcliffe-Maud, Calouste Gulbenkian Foundation, London, 1976.

The Globe Music Exchange, May/June 1995, report of a World Circuit Arts project.

The Glory of the Garden, The Development of the Arts in England, Arts Council of Great Britain, London, 1984.

Gorleston-on-Sea-Change (proposal for an outdoor arts event) by Jan Dungey, Great Yarmouth Borough Council, December 1995.

Helping to Heal, The Arts in Health Care, by Peter Senior and Jonathan Croall, Calouste Gulbenkian Foundation, London, 1993.

The Hidden Musicians, Music-making in an English Town, by Ruth Finnegan, Cambridge University Press, 1989.

How musical is man? by John Blacking, Faber and Faber, London, 1976.

In from the Margins, A contribution to the debate on Culture and Development in Europe, Council of Europe, Strasbourg, 1996.

In Search of Angels, Glyndebourne Education, the *Peterborough Review* 6, 1995. Also video, *In Search of Angels,* Peterborough Community Opera.

In Tune with Heaven, The Report of the Archbishops' Commission on Church Music, Church House Publishing and Hodder and Stoughton, London, 1992.

Instrumental Teaching and Learning in Context, Sharing a Curriculum for Music Education, Music Advisers' National Association (now the National Association of Music Educators), Melton Mowbray, 1995.

Investing in Culture, Netherlands Policy Document on Culture 1993-6, Ministry of Welfare, Health and Cultural Affairs, The Hague, The Netherlands.

Jazz Services Ltd, Action Programme and Financial Budgets 1996-7.

Jazz Services' Response to the Arts Council of England's Consultative Document, *New Lottery Programmes,* Jazz Services Ltd, 1996.

Jazz Services' Response to the Arts Council of England's Consultative Green Paper on Education and Training in the English Arts Funding System, Jazz Services Ltd, 1996.

Jazz – the Case for Better Investment, Jazz Services' Submission to the Arts Council of Great Britain's National Review of Jazz, Jazz Services Ltd, 1993.

Learning Improved by Arts Training, by Martin F Gardiner, Alan Fox, Faith Knowles and Donna Jeffrey, *Nature,* vol. 381, 23 May 1996.

Lewisham Academy of Music annual report 1995.

Live Music-making in Rural Areas – a Dying or a Flourishing Tradition? a comparative study of amateur music in Sweden and the United Kingdom, a Major Project submitted as part of an MA in European Cultural Policy and Administrations, University of Warwick, by Margaret Jill Shuker, September 1995.

London Arts Board Corporate Plan 1996-7.

London Sinfonietta Education Project in Finland, Second Phase, Spring-Autumn 1995, report by Tuula Yrjö-Koskinen-Smith, London Sinfonietta Education.

London Symphony Orchestra, Discovery Department Policy Statement.

Looking Forward to the Year 2000, speech by Ian Ritchie to the Association of Canadian Orchestras, Winnipeg, May 1992.

Making Music in Schools – the Musical Imperative, by Andrew Peggie (an unpublished draft of a contextual report on the London Arts Board/Yamaha-Kemble Ltd project, Partnerships in the Classroom.

Mapping the Field: A research project on the education work of British orchestras, by Phyllida Shaw, Association of British Orchestras, London, 1996.

More than the Sum of its Parts: Cultural Policy and Planning in Birmingham, by Anthony Sargent, Cultural Policy, Harwood Academic Publishers, vol. 2, no. 2, The Netherlands, 1996.

Moving Culture, an enquiry into the cultural activities of young people, by Paul Willis, Calouste Gulbenkian Foundation, London, 1990.

Music and the Community, (undated pamphlet), Royal Academy of Music.

The Music of the Environment, no. 1 of an occasional journal devoted to Soundscape Studies, edited by R Murray Schafer, Universal Edition, Vienna, 1973.

Music Explorer, Video featuring the London Symphony Orchestra with Guidebook by Richard McNichol, London Symphony Orchestra, 1995.

Music Explorer Project Book, by Richard McNicol, Apollo Trust in association with Oxford University Press, 1995.

Music in the Five Towns 1840-1940, a Study of the Social Influence of Music in an Industrial District, by R Nettel, Oxford University Press, 1944.

Music Improvisation in Primary Schools, Access to Music, 1995.

Music and the Mind, by Paul Robertson, Channel 4 Television, London, 1996.

Music and the Mind, by Anthony Storr, HarperCollins, London, 1992.

Music, Mind and Education, by Keith Swanwick, Routledge, London and New York, 1988.

Music for Pleasure, by Simon Frith, Polity Press, Cambridge, 1988.

Music-Society-Education, by Christopher Small, John Calder, London, 1977.

Musical Education in Hungary, by Sándor Frigyes, Corvina Press, Budapest, 1966.

The Musical Temperament, by Anthony E Kemp, Oxford University Press, 1996.

National District Arts Officers Survey, A Survey of Arts Development in Local Authorities, August 1995.

National Federation Of Music Societies Five Year Development Plan, 1996-2000.

National Federation Of Music Societies New Lottery Programmes, a Response from the NFMS, 1996.

National Federation Of Music Societies Scotland, Four Year Plan, 1997-8 to 2001-01.

The National Lottery – Whatever Next? National Campaign for the Arts and National Music Council, 1996.

New Approaches to New Music, a report on the Contemporary Music Network educational activities 1980-1, by Andrew Peggie, Arts Council of Great Britain, 1981.

New Lottery Programmes, Consultative Document, Arts Council of England, June 1996.

New Technology in the Classroom, by Paul Wright, *Musical Times,* August 1992.

Northern Lights: The Social Impact of the Fèisean (Gaelic Festivals), The Social Impact of the Arts, Working Paper 6, by François Matarasso, Comedia, Stroud, 1996.

Now's the Time, Community Music East 1989-93, four year report.

On Tour – a week of communication Sunderland November 1-5 1994, report by Kathryn Deane of an Opera North community project.

Orchestral Development in the UK: a Case of Accelerated Evolution, a speech by Libby MacNamara at the European Orchestral Convention, Rome, 1995.

Our Creative Diversity, Report of the World Commission on Culture and Development, World Commission on Culture and Development, Paris, 1996.

Out and About, by Stewart, Andrew, *Music Teacher,* February 1995.

Overtones, annual report 1994-5.

Paynter, John and Aston, Peter, *Sound and Silence, Classroom Projects in Creative Music,* Cambridge University Press, 1970.

Paper by Ben Higham, submitted to ISME CMA Seminar and the 22nd ISME World Conference, July 1996.

People Taking Part (a study on access to the arts) Department of National Heritage, 1996.

Perception of Music by Infants, by Marcel R Zentner and Jerome Kagan, *Nature,* vol. 383, 5 September 1996.

Performing Right Yearbook 1996-7, Performing Right Society Ltd, London, 1996.

A Policy for the Arts: the first steps, Her Majesty's Stationery Office, London, 1968.

Pop 2000, European Cultural Centre, London, 1995.

The Power of Music, by Richard McNicol, Channel 4 Television, 1993.

Prospectus, Welsh College of Music and Drama, 1996.

Prospectus 1996-7, London College of Music at Thames Valley University.

Radical Perspectives in the Arts, Penguin Books, Harmondsworth, 1972.

The Review of Music in the Northern Arts Region, Northern Arts, October 1995.

Extract from the Seminar Report: The Role of Community Music in a Changing World, by Tim Joss, International Society for Music Education/Commission for Community Music Activity, 1994.

Royal Philharmonic Orchestra, Community and Education Programme Nottinghamshire, 1994-5 Report, 1995.

Royal Philharmonic Orchestra, Community and Education Programme Policy (undated).

Royal Philharmonic Orchestra Education Programme, Project Report (final draft), 1996.

Royal Philharmonic Orchestra, *Halifax Orchestra Now* Report, 1996.

RSGB Omnibus Arts Survey: Report on a Survey on Arts and Cultural Activities in GB, Research Surveys of Great Britain Ltd, Arts Council of Great Britain, London, 1991.

Search and Reflect, by John Stevens, Community Music London, 1985.

Singing in Schools Survey – Findings, British Federation of Youth Choirs, Loughborough, 1991.

The Song Sampler, (with cassette tape) by Sandra Kerr, Folkworks, 1994.

Sound and Silence, Classroom Projects in Creative Music, by John Paynter and Peter Aston, Cambridge University Press, 1970.

The Sounding Symbol, by George Odam, Stanley Thornes (Publishers) Ltd, Cheltenham, 1995.

Southern Arts Corporate Plan 1996-7.

The State We're In, by Will Hutton, Vintage, London, 1996.

Street Rhythms 94, report of the Estover Street Rhythms Festival, October 1994, by R W Mountjoy, Estover Community College, Plymouth.

Striking a New Note, Jazz Services' Response to the Arts Council of England's Green Paper, *Striking a New Note.*

Taking Part, Department of National Heritage, London, 1996.

Traditional Arts Projects, annual report 1994-5.

Traditional Arts Projects Development Plan 1995-8.

Turn of the Tide – Report, (report of the ABO's national education project April 1992-June 1993) by Phyllida Shaw, Association of British Orchestras.

The Value of Music, National Music Council Report into the Value of the UK Music Industry prepared by the University of Westminster, London, 1996.

The Voice in Community Music Seminar, University of East Anglia, 30 August-2 September 1994, a report, Community Music East, 1995.

Voluntary Arts Network Directory 1996, Voluntary Arts Network, Cardiff.

Welsh Music Live, Autumn 94 (music resource pack), BBC National Orchestra of Wales.

What is Music Anyway? by Paul Wright, Education Officer, Sonic Arts Network.

Young People and their Approach to Musical Participation, a report by Adrian Kirkwood for the Danesborough Chorus and the National Federation of Music Societies, June 1996.

Among the magazines I found useful were:

ABO News, monthly newsletter produced for Association of British Orchestras member orchestras.

Classical Music, fortnightly magazine, Rhinegold Publishing Ltd, London.

COMA Newsletter, quarterly magazine, COMA, London.

Diffusion, quarterly members' magazine, Sonic Arts Network.

Folkwords, bi-monthly magazine, Folkworks, Newcastle-upon-Tyne.

Journal of Electroacoustic Music, Sonic Arts Network.

LCM Magazine (twice yearly), London College of Music.

The Living Tradition, (six times a year), Kilmarnock, Ayrshire.

NCA News, quarterly magazine of the National Campaign for the Arts, London.

New Notes, published monthly by the Society for the Promotion of New Music, Francis House, Francis Street, London SW1P 1DE.

Sounding Board, the quarterly magazine of Sound Sense, the National Community Music Association, Sound Sense, Rattlesden, Bury St Edmunds.

Soundings, music in Britain today, quarterly magazine, the British Council.

photo: Marcus Tate

INDEX